# THE DEVIL'S PLAYGROUND

## The Story of Two Charlie and the Arghandab River Valley

*Written by*
ANDREW BRAGG
AS TOLD BY THE MEN OF TWO CHARLIE

*Pennsylvania & Yorkshire*

Published in the United States of America and Great Britain in 2024 by
CASEMATE PUBLISHERS
1950 Lawrence Road, Havertown, PA 19083
and
47 Church Street, Barnsley, S70 2AS, UK



Hardback Edition: ISBN 978-1-63624-471-6
Digital Edition: ISBN 978-1-63624-472-3

A CIP record for this book is available from the British Library



Printed and bound in the United Kingdom by CPI Group (UK) Ltd, Croydon, CR0 4YY

Typeset in India by Lapiz Digital Services, Chennai.

For a complete list of Casemate titles, please contact:

CASEMATE PUBLISHERS (US)
Telephone (610) 853-9131
Fax (610) 853-9146
Email: casemate@casematepublishers.com
www.casematepublishers.com

CASEMATE PUBLISHERS (UK)
Telephone (0)1226 734350
Email: casemate@casemateuk.com
www.casemateuk.com

*Front cover image:* Ethan McDaniel

The views expressed in this publication are those of the author and do not necessarily reflect the official policy or position of the Department of Defense or the U.S. government. The public release clearance of this publication by the Department of Defense does not imply Department of Defense endorsement or factual accuracy of the material.

To the men of Two Charlie. I hope I told our story well.

# Contents

# Foreword

The Arghandab Valley will go down in history as a years' long campaign. For the men and women of the 2nd Battalion, 508th Parachute Infantry Regiment, it was life altering.

In the years since my retirement, there hasn't been a day that I haven't thought of the Arghandab River Valley. The paratroopers who marched into that valley were given a mission that the Russians couldn't accomplish over thirty years before: Secure the Valley, thus securing the flank of Kandahar. When the Russians and the communist Afghan army attempted it in the 1980s, they failed miserably, sacrificing a motorized rifle regiment in the exchange. The 82nd was asked to do it with one battalion. And they did it.

This is an example of soldiering at the base level. In one of the most inhospitable locations on the planet. A story where heroism was defined by lacing up your boots and walking one more patrol. Hopefully you would still have two boots at the end of the day.

2 Fury showed the world what an airborne battalion can do in the worst possible conditions. I am proud to have been part of them. I am proud to call them my sons and daughters.

CSM Bert Puckett (retired)
AATW!
FFTS!
RLTW!

# Special Thanks

Thank you to the men of Two Charlie and their families for letting me into their homes and sharing with me our story. I know it wasn't easy, and I thank you for helping me with that journey. Thank you, Dale Knollinger, for making this all possible. If it wasn't for you and your hard work and dedication to us, we could never have gotten the band back together. Thank you to the Fabian family for supporting me during the writing of this book. It really means a lot to me and I couldn't have done it without your support. Thank you to my friends Josh and Kamryn Berry, Becca and Jason Dan, and Seth Dobson for always checking in on me on this journey. Your support got me through the hard times, and I am unworthy of your friendship. I'd like to thank the random libraries that allowed me to use their facilities to write this book, mainly the Idaho Falls Public Library. Last but not least, I'd like to thank my family for putting up with my bullshit before and after the military. I love you all.

Thank you.

CHAPTER I

# 22 Nov 2009

"Pack it up," Sergeant First Class (SFC) Santos said into his headset in his stereotypical calm demeanor, "let's go home."

Hearing those words come over the Humvee truck radios resulted in the men of each truck jolting to life from their mindless stare into the desert. "Let's go home" were the words they had been waiting to hear for a while, and when they were finally spoken not a second went by before the four truck engines were fired up. It was as if the drivers of each truck were waiting with their fingers on the ignition.

They had been out the last couple days tasked to assist a Canadian-led clearance operation outside of Panjwai District in Afghanistan. The men had done a whole lot of nothing the entire time. Maybe conducted a dismounted patrol for the Canadians here, set up a Traffic Control Point (TCP) there, but nothing substantial and no fights with the enemy had resulted. It was an uneventful operation. They were beginning to wonder if the Canadian forces had even remembered that they were there.

The men of 2nd Platoon, Two Charlie, hated being tasked out as a support element, especially to the Canadians troops back at Forward Operating Base (FOB) Masum Ghar. They had called these Canadian forces their FOB mates since arriving in Afghanistan. Since their battalion didn't really have an Area of Operation (AO) of their own, the boys of 2nd Platoon, Charlie Company, 2nd Battalion of the 508th Parachute Infantry Regiment, 4th Brigade Combat Team of the 82nd Airborne Division didn't really have a choice. The entire battalion was scattered across the southern region of the country, each with some miscellaneous counterinsurgency (COIN) operation task, and Two Charlie was to operate out of Masum Ghar in the Panjwai District and assist the Canadian forces who occupied it as necessary. Not what paratroopers of the 82nd Airborne are used to, and not what they train for.

Before deployment the men trained for endless months. They learned how to kick in doors, how to maneuver on the enemy, and how to fight effectively as a team. They spent every waking minute of countless days perfecting these lethal skills, in hopes of bringing a violent end of existence to their enemies. An end in which the poor bastards had never seen or could fathom, an unimaginable fury. It was the battalion's freaking motto for fuck sake—"Fury from the Sky." What they were not ready for was to freeze their asses off at night in the cool Afghan November desert and be the Canadians' bitches.

The men didn't have a completely lackadaisical couple of months in the Panjwai District, however. When they were out on their own patrolling the area, they had gotten into many fights with the enemy. There was a large hill that harbored the remains of three old Russian tanks from the invasion in the eighties that the men had cleverly named Three Tank Hill. The fighters in the area liked to attack any Coalition forces that occupied this hill, launching offensives on the cell phone tower that also occupied it, and they often did it right at dusk or the early hours of the night. It was easy for them to lob Rocket Propelled Grenades (RPGs) at the hill and attack it with machine-gun fire until the men would call in Close Combat Attack (CCA) helicopters, "Birds," to assist and either do gun runs to kill the enemies or make them retreat, tails tucked into the darkness of the night. The men of Two Charlie had spent many nights fighting on this hill. It had been the spot that had "popped the cherries" for a lot of the new soldiers in the platoon; the "Joes," the privates that had yet to deploy. Three Tank Hill was where the Joes experienced what naive young men would consider the thrill of being shot at.

Choa Ghar was another village that was a notorious place in the AO for these fights, and the men of Two Charlie would always lay down the scunion on the enemy when patrolling that area, leaving them completely devastated. The Two Charlie men had been pretty lucky. Most of these fights were initially intense but had all ended being fairly one sided and the men hadn't received any casualties.

"Truck One, we're up." Sergeant (SGT) Nolen said over the convoy radio.

"Truck Two, we're good." Staff Sergeant (SSG) DeMeo followed.

"Truck Three, up." Truck Three said over the radio.

"Truck Four, up. Let's roll." SFC Santos said and switched his radio from the platoon channel to the company channel, "Charlie Six, this is Charlie Two Five, SP to FOB Walton time now." The trucks began to all fall out of their security positions and fall in on the Afghan dirt road in the middle of the dry desert. The convoy would begin their journey to FOB Walton.

However, the entire platoon was not out on this operation. The platoon consisted of three line squads and one weapons squad. Each squad consisted of a squad leader and two teams, Alpha and Bravo. Weapons squad's two teams were gun teams, each team operating an M240 machine gun. The line teams consisted of a team leader, a M249 squad automatic weapon (SAW) light machine gunner, a M203 grenadier, and an extra rifleman. The main leaders of the platoon were made up of the platoon sergeant and the platoon leader (PL), or lieutenant (Lt.). The men of Two Charlie mostly operated in squad-sized elements, mainly because they only had four Humvees to carry troops in. However, if the operation was a dismounted patrol, the platoon would move as a larger-sized element.

Second Squad, led by SSG DeMeo, with weapons squad guys in the turrets and a few extra guys from First Squad to fill in as dismounts and drivers, were among the trucks for this operation. The main leader overseeing SSG DeMeo and the whole patrol was SFC Santos, the platoon's platoon sergeant. AKA "Dad." A select few of the guys from the platoon had been sent to FOB Walton to go through some training for the new radios the battalion was being issued. The convoy would pick them up before heading back to Masum Ghar, back home.

The rest of the platoon had stayed back at Masum Ghar with the platoon leader, Lt. Scrivner, since there was no room for them in the four trucks the platoon had to conduct mounted patrols and operations in. If SFC Santos was Dad, then one could say Lt. Scrivner was "Mom." However, the men hardly treated him as a leader, let alone a parental figure. They always gave him a hard time, calling him "Squeak" instead of "Sir." It just seemed right. You had to earn your spot in the hierarchy of Two Charlie and, well, he hadn't done that in the eyes of the men. The men at Masum Ghar would monitor the battalion, company, and platoon nets on the radios and that was about it. Masum Ghar wasn't an American base; it was owned and operated by the Canadian forces. So, the men of Two Charlie didn't have to worry about force protection and pulling guard duty in guard towers, as the Canadians took this responsibility. The guys of Two Charlie, when not on a mission, or got to stay back from a mission, really had it made. They could go work out at the Canadian gym, catch up with friends and family back home on the internet, or steal some Häagen-Dazs ice cream from the Canadians' chow hall. The struggle of being on a combat deployment to Afghanistan was real.

"Hey, Truck One, Charlie Two Two, make sure you dismount for all culverts and check your fives and twenty-fives," SSG DeMeo said over the radio, reiterating what one of his team leaders, SGT Nolen in Truck One, already knew. Everyone in the convoy had rolled their eyes at this comment, as everyone knew to dismount and check culverts before crossing them. It was what they had been doing ever since they had gotten to Afghanistan. That was the easiest place for the enemy to hide an Improvised Explosive Device (IED). The enemy liked blowing up the Coalition Forces' armored vehicles. IEDs were their way of leveling the playing field.

SSG DeMeo just liked to hear himself talk. He was kind of a narcissist, and the platoon wasn't fond of him. SSG DeMeo was a very toxic leader and would abuse his rank to harass his men. He would make them stand at positions of attention or parade rest, then shoot rocks at their nuts with a slingshot. If they were to move, he would punish them. He even went as far as breaking a private's nose by throwing a grenade at his face while doing this. He would have the gunners standing in the turrets of his truck turn their turrets from the direction they were pulling security to face the front of the vehicle, just so that he could hit them in the nuts. He even jokingly shot at another squad leader in the platoon. The platoon had finally had enough and tried to get rid of him in the past for this unnecessary harsh treatment, writing sworn statements against him and using the open-door policy of the company commander to try and get him fired and kicked out of the platoon. SFC Santos even wrote a statement against the man. Ultimately, nothing really came of it, the platoon was shuffled around a little so the guys directly affected by SSG DeMeo's actions were no longer in his squad and under his command, but SSG DeMeo still remained in the platoon and Second Squad's squad leader. It left an everlasting bad taste and hate for the man within the rest of the platoon.

"Roger that, Two Two," SGT Nolen replied respectfully. You couldn't tell by the tone of his voice that he was frustrated, but everyone knew. SGT Nolen was a quiet professional type, the exact opposite of SSG DeMeo, but it was hard not to get frustrated when SSG DeMeo opened his mouth and you had to do what he said.

The convoy came to their first culvert and a short halt as the men in the first truck got out to check it and the surrounding area for bombs. Some of the dismounted men would pull security along with the vehicles' turret gunners, looking for anyone watching the convoy or setting up an ambush on them while two men from the lead truck would make their way on each side of the culvert to check for anything that might be hidden underneath. It was typical troop Tactics, Techniques, and Procedures (TTPs).

The dismounted men from Truck One all got back into the truck after they were satisfied they were not going to blow up at this culvert and began to continue the patrol's movement.

"Truck One, Charlie Mike," SGT Nolen said over the convoy radio frequency, letting the other trucks know the culvert was clear and they were mounted back up and continuing on.

The sun was low on the horizon, and the cool Afghan November air blew over the men in the turrets of the vehicles. It wasn't quite freezing, but it was just the right temperature to cool off the gunners in all their armor. They could rest their plate carriers on the sides of the turret, which took the weight off their shoulders and created a small gap between the carriers and their bodies. This allowed for air to circulate and cool them. The few trees that grew along the culverts had already been stripped of their leaves in the early fall and stood like skeletons in the open desert.

The convoy came around a bend in the road and then to a large straightaway all the way to Highway One, a paved section of road that pretty much led all the way back to Masum Ghar. The men always felt a little bit safer once on paved roads, as it was a lot harder to dig an IED under asphalt than it was dirt or gravel. Just a little more than a kilometer before the pucker factor could subside.

"Hey, Tynes, you okay down there, bud?" Davis, Truck One's gunner, asked over his headset, probably setting himself up for a joke. Davis was a weapons squad team leader and one of the platoon's comedic reliefs. He was always cracking jokes, not always at the most appropriate of times, but he was always cracking them.

"Oh yea, Specialist, I'm good," Tynes, Truck One's driver, replied.

"Good, cuz I was gonna …"

BOOM.

A dust cloud erupted from the ground like a geyser, throwing dirt and debris in all directions, instantly replacing the lead Humvee's existence. The concussive force and loud thunderous roar from the blast shortly followed and shook the chests of the remaining men in the other trucks in the convoy. They stared in horror and disbelief as the cloud rose higher and higher into the sky. Amongst the debris was Davis, flying through the air with a dust trail tailing him through the sky. The M240 machine gun from his turret was still in his hand. The debris and Davis had reached their peak heights and started to make their way back down to the ground about thirty meters from where the main mushroom cloud of dirt remained sprouted from the earth. It all seemed to happen both in an instant and in slow motion.

"Oh my God," SFC Santos said under his breath as he leaned forward to see higher into the sky through his Humvee's narrow front three-inch-thick bulletproof windshield.

"IED, IED, IED!" SSG DeMeo yelled over the radio, then opened his door to dismount and prepare for what he was about to encounter. He ran into the cloud of dust as it began to dissipate and reveal what was left of the truck. SGT Cornelius and Leonard got out of their truck and followed him.

The 12,000-pound truck was flipped upside down and laid canted on the armor surrounding the turret, the rear tires reaching into the air like the legs of an overturned tortoise. The blast had thrown the vehicle a few meters back from the crater that stretched the width of the road. The front half of the vehicle was completely gone; all that remained was twisted and shredded metal revealing the back two passenger seats. The engine block rested in the road about ten meters away from the truck. The truck's trunk was open, and all its contents spilled out onto the gravel road. Everything was covered in gasoline and a layer of dust that had settled from the blast.

Tynes was the first one SSG DeMeo reached. He was lying across what was now the top of the vehicle, the steering wheel still in his hands. SSG DeMeo grabbed him, yanked him off the truck and laid him down on the ground by the wreckage. He checked Tynes for a pulse—nothing. He removed Tynes's body armor and helmet and began to do CPR as he started yelling for a medic.

"Doc" Taylor, the platoon's medic, was tending to Davis with Johnny Nguyen and Ryan in the field 30 meters away from the wreckage. Nguyen and Ryan had gone through EMT training and certification before deploying to have more individuals in the platoon with medical knowledge. They were no medic like Doc Taylor, but they were a step above the rest of the guys who just received the basic Combat Lifesaver course the unit put everyone through, so Doc felt comfortable leaving Davis with them. His injuries seemed less life-threatening after his initial trauma swoop—just a couple of broken ankles, probably a severe back injury, and a tongue hanging on by a thread. Davis must have bitten it off in the blast. He needed to see the other casualties to see how severe they were, to assess where he was needed most.

"Splint his legs, control the bleeding, and don't move him till we get a stretcher," Doc yelled to the two as he sprinted toward SSG DeMeo to continue his triage.

As Doc Taylor approached, SSG DeMeo was continuing CPR on Tynes. He looked up at Doc from giving a rescue breath, there was blood around his mouth. Blood was running from Tynes's mouth and spurted all over his uniform with each compression SSG DeMeo gave.

Doc took over CPR from SSG DeMeo. When he went to give a rescue breath, blood filled his mouth, and he had to spit out blood and bits of Tynes's teeth, "Keep doing CPR." Doc shouted to SSG DeMeo. He needed to continue his triage. "Who all is here?!" He called out, looking for an answer in the chaos.

"Medic!" Leonard yelled out. He and SGT Cornelius had found SGT Nolen. He lay against a dirt wall that paralleled the road about twenty meters to its south. His face was covered in blood and unrecognizable. It looked like the blast used his face to bash open the 400-pound uparmored Humvee door and threw him like a projectile into the wall. The blood from his face had begun dripping all over his camouflaged gear. His arms had multiple fractures and moved erratically when he would try and use them to upright himself. Both legs had multiple compound fractures as well. He looked like he had gotten sucked up into a machine and spit out. Blood started collecting everywhere.

Doc Taylor ran over to the men. He did his initial assessment and began applying tourniquets to all SGT Nolen's limbs. He was afraid if he tried to splint anything he would just cause more bleeding; there was already too much blood loss to begin with. So, he did what he could to stop the bleeding.

SGT Nolen roared in pain with each turn of each tourniquet. The tourniquets were all ratcheted down until the bleeding slowed, then stopped.

"Don't let me die," SGT Nolen managed to groan out from under all the blood that was on his face. He tried to take off his fighting rig and bullet proof vest, "I can't breathe." Leonard, Doc, and SGT Cornelius all stopped him from removing his vest. "Sit me up," he said, "I can't breathe. Don't let me die. I have to go home."

Suddenly Doc Taylor heard a faint thud come from the wreckage of the truck, like something or someone had just hit the ground. He looked over and to his surprise saw Munoz stumble out of the truck wreckage. He was on all fours and crawling away from the heap of metal. As far as he could tell, all he had was a gash behind his ear where he could feel his skull and his bell had been rung pretty good but, miraculously, he was still alive. He had no idea what had just happened. He thought he was dreaming back at Masum Ghar until he felt the sharp pain behind his ear and the blood began to run down the side of his face.

"Don't move, Munoz!" Doc yelled over to him. "Who else was in the truck?" he thought to himself.

Young lay under the truck wreckage as well. He and Munoz had been the two back-seat passengers. SSG DeMeo reached under to pull him out as he slowly regained consciousness and laid him down next to Tynes. Young, to SSG DeMeo's surprise, opened his eyes. He had been peppered by shrapnel in his arms and legs and had a large cut to his nose. He took off his eye protection to get a better look of his surroundings, as it was cracked from a piece of metal lodged into it.

"Don't move, Young," SSG DeMeo yelled to him, "You were just in an IED."

Young looked over to see SSG DeMeo continuing CPR on Tynes. He could see the blood coming out of Tynes's mouth. Young reached over to grab his lifeless hand as Nguyen ran up to take over CPR from SSG DeMeo.

"Doc," SFC Santos said in his calm demeanor, though they could tell in his voice he was a little shaken from the chaos going on all around. He was doing his best to bring order to that chaos, "I've got the Nine Line started, what do we got?"

Lt. Scrivner, along with SSG Staley, SGT Farquhar, SGT Thomson, and SGT Knollinger all huddled around the radio back in the small little room that was the platoon's Tactical Operations Center (TOC) at Masum Ghar. They were just a few of the guys who were left back at Masum Ghar for that operation. The TOC was just a small room with a computer and a couple radios and was usually only occupied by one or two individuals, but since the call of the IED had come over the net all the leadership had crammed in there and had been glued to the radios. The TOC was kind of off limits for privates, so the lower enlisted guys waited anxiously outside to be filled in on the situation.

SFC Santos had started the first two lines of a Nine Line MedEvac request over the company radio frequency before initiating a break in the transmission. The first five are all that is necessary to get a MedEvac Bird in the air. The other four can be relayed to the MedEvac Bird while it's in flight. But the third line is where the ground troops give the report of the number of patients on the ground and by precedence. This was the one the men at Masum Ghar were waiting to hear.

It always felt shitty being back at the base when the guys outside the wire on a patrol had shit hit the fan, especially when it came to a MedEvac. How many guys were hurt? How bad are they? So many questions ran through all their heads, meanwhile feeling so helpless. They couldn't do anything to help. All they could do was wait in limbo.

"Line 3: two urgent surgical, three urgent."

SSG Staley left the TOC. He had so many things running through his head. He was First Squad's squad leader and had loaned Second Squad a few of his men for this operation. He was angry they were out there, and that he wasn't. He had no idea of their status, and the unknown ate at him. All he could do was wait. His heart sank to his stomach.

"Get some stretchers," SFC Santos said to Godard. Godard wasted no time and ran back to his truck, yelling to the other men to grab their stretchers off their trucks. The vehicles had been setting in a security perimeter in case of a follow-on ambush. If anyone were planning on shooting at the men treating casualties, they would have to answer to two .50-caliber machine guns and a MK 19 automatic grenade launcher. Godard climbed up onto the back hatch of his Humvee, where the men had tied down the folded collapsible litters. He struggled to free the thing from the netting and the five-fifty cord that had secured it to the hatch, cursing under his breath. SGT Bragg climbed out of the turret with a knife to help him free the stretcher and Godard was off, lugging the bundle of metal poles and cloth material back to the havoc.

The men worked to get the injured onto the stretchers as the low rumble of the MedEvac Birds could be heard approaching in the distance. Each injured man was moved to the ditch on the side of the road, a Casualty Collection Point (CCP), a place to provide cover and concealment from the enemy while continuing to provide medical care until the evac arrived.

"They're two minutes out," SFC Santos said to the guys working on the injured, referring to the MedEvac Birds. Doc Taylor ran between the patients, double and triple checking tourniquets and other things that needed to be monitored. The "whop whop whop" of the helicopter blades got louder and more distinct as the two small figures appeared in the sky on the horizon. The setting sun burned orange along the flat desert plain.

"Thirty seconds!" SFC Santos yelled over the roar as the Birds flew directly over them, circling and slowing for their landing. As the flying machines did their pass, the dust from the ground began to kick up all around the men. "Cover their eyes!" SFC Santos instructed, as he wrapped himself over SGT Nolen, trying to use his body to shield SGT Nolen's from the debris kicked up from the rotary-wing aircraft.

The men loaded up SGT Nolen and Tynes in the first Bird, then Davis, Young, and Munoz in the second. When the last man was finally loaded on the Bird, the men ran back to the ditch on the side of the road to take shelter from the dirt and debris as the two Birds took off and flew into the dusk sky. The remaining men sat and listened as the noise of the helicopters taking their wounded into the darkness got fainter and fainter, and the cold night air closed in around them.

CHAPTER 2

# A Time to Grieve

SGT Lachance, SGT Brown, Jackson, and McDaniel were the men that had been at FOB Walton. They had been learning the ins and outs of the new 117G radios over the last few days and were awaiting their ride back home, back to Masum Ghar. They were lounging in the white tarp tent they had been staying at on their green army cots, with their assault packs packed and ready to go, when a faint rumble could be heard in the distance. SGT Lachance, one of the platoon's Forward Observers (FOs) heard the rumble and knew that that was never a good sound. Somebody was having a bad day. He didn't think much of it and rolled over in his cot, trying to grab an hour of sleep before the Two Charlie convoy came to pick them up. Then, very abruptly, a soldier ran into the tent.

"SGT Lachance?" the soldier called out into the dark tent.

"What?" SGT Lachance said in a who-dare-wake-me-from-my-slumber kind of tone. There was no way the convoy had reached FOB Walton already, as they had just started their movement when he left the Battalion TOC.

"You're with Two Charlie, right?" the soldier asked. You could see SGT Brown's, McDaniel's, and Jackson's ears perk up upon that question.

"Yea, we all are. What's up? Are they here?" SGT Lachance inquired, shocked.

"Come with me," is all the unknown soldier replied.

SGT Lachance left the other men in the tent and followed the soldier back to the Battalion TOC. The soldier turned to him as he opened the TOC door for SGT Lachance. "Two Charlie just hit an IED."

SGT Lachance stood in the room and listened to all the radio chatter. It took a minute to figure out the details of the situation, but what he could gather from the Nine Line was there were two men in dire condition. From the battle roster numbers sent up he figured out it was Tynes and SGT Nolen, and there were three others injured. He didn't know the details of their injuries. All he could gather was there was one expected, then two expected. As more time went by, and the MedEvacs had made their way back to Kandahar Airfield (KAF) with the wounded, it had come over the radios those two men had been pronounced dead on arrival.

The news was overwhelming and SGT Lachance's stomach hit the ground. He knew SGT Brown was close with SGT Nolen. The three of them had all come to Two Charlie from 3rd Platoon, Three Charlie, before the unit deployed. And McDaniel and Tynes were inseparable from each other. Always joking and roasting each other. The two of them could put a smile on any of the guys' faces and make light of any situation. And now, SGT Lachance had to walk out of the TOC and inform those men their friends had been killed.

It was one of the hardest things he had ever done. SGT Lachance was a very physically strong man the men looked up to not only because of his rank, but because of his natural skills as an FO. An FO was definitely an important position in the platoon, as he was responsible for communicating and coordinating attacks with the close air support of the Kiowa helicopters and sometimes Apache helicopters. He would also call in indirect fire for the platoon, however the AO's rules of engagement didn't allow for it. He had proven time and time again to the men that they could rely on him in both training and combat. He was a natural warrior. But no amount of training or combat could ever get a man ready to inform a friend of another friend's passing. SGT Lachance would rather be thrown into a gunfight any day. That was easy compared to what he was about to do.

SGT Lachance opened the door to step out of the TOC. Right outside, SGT Brown, McDaniel, and Jackson were waiting for him in the darkness, waiting to be informed. He looked at them, sorrow on his face. He didn't know how to break it to them, what words to use to make it any easier, so he just cut it to them clean. "The guys hit an IED. Nolen and Tynes are dead."

The men on patrol sat in the stillness of the dusk sky. It was eerily quiet, and the only thing they could hear after the sound of the helicopters faded was the faint growl of the Canadian tanks and armored vehicles approaching them in the distance. The Canadians had been notified of Two Charlie's IED attack and were en route as a Quick Reaction Force (QRF) to assist and fight off any possible follow-on attacks from enemy in the area.

When the Canadian forces finally arrived, the men had already been gathering whatever pieces and parts of the wreckage they could find, piling it up, trying to organize and make sense of the disorder. SFC Santos and Godard were going through the pile of junk the men had created, searching for serialized and sensitive items, and putting them in a separate pile among the gear they had removed from the wounded. Night vision, mangled weapons, radios, and ammo were among the items the men were seeking accountability for. They still couldn't find the Blue Force Tracker, a computer system hooked up in the truck to help with land navigation and monitoring mounted troops in the area. It was originally mounted in the front passenger's side of the truck, the Truck Commander's (TC's) side, but that part of the vehicle was completely gone, scattered across the barren dirt fields on each side of the road.

The Humvees were pulling security; when the Canadians arrived, they established an outer cordon. With all the white lights from the Canadian vehicles, it was silly for the men of Two Charlie to continue looking for gear under their Night Optic Devices (NODs), so Santos had the men grab their headlamps. One by one, each man would come out of the darkness carrying something back with him. They moved like zombies, and some of them looked like them too, with Tynes's and SGT Nolen's blood still splattered on their Army Combat Uniforms (ACUs). They were all covered in a thin layer of dust, both from the blast and having spent the last few days in the field. They were filthy, like antique furniture in an abandoned house. After recovering all they could find and photographing everything for a Battle Damage Assessment (BDA) report that command would most certainly ask of them, the men returned to their trucks to wait for further instructions on how they were to go about recovering the vehicle.

The men were all tired. The adrenaline from the intensity of the IED had worn off and each man was now feeling the full effect of everything they had just done. They all knew they were going to have to wait for a wrecker to recover the truck, and nobody knew how long that was going to actually take. It was going to be a long night.

The men had gathered their trucks in a small circle in one of the barren fields. They were pulling security, though they didn't really have to as the Canadian forces were all around them. It was mainly a distraction, it kept them from staring at what was left of the lead truck and realizing what had just occurred. However, nothing could keep their minds from wandering. Each man caught himself glancing over at the remains. It was like a ghostly figure in the darkness that one could feel constantly staring at them.

Finally, SFC Santos got a call over the battalion radio frequency. "Charlie Two Five, this is Two Fury Six Romeo."

"This is Charlie Two Five," SFC Santos replied softly. The rest of the men could hear the chirp of the radio when they called in and Santos's quick reply, but they were not close enough to hear what was being said. Any of the men could have turned their radios over to the battalion frequency, but none of them did. They were delaying what they already knew. SFC Santos held the handset close to his ear trying to trap every word that came over the radio.

"Roger Two Five, you need to Charlie Mike (Continue Mission) to FOB Walton. Canadian forces will secure the site and wait for HHC with the wrecker to recover the vehicle. How copy?"

"Roger, Charlie Mike to FOB Walton. Is battalion aware we will be running only three vehicles in the convoy?"

"Roger, they are tracking, the Canadians are going to use their mine rollers to clear the rest of the soft road till you get to hardpack, then it's less than a kilometer to Walton."

"Roger," SFC Santos said.

"Oh, and Two Five, an update on the casualties …"

SFC Santos smashed the handset to his ear as hard as he could and waited quietly.

"Battle roster numbers Bravo Yankee 5513, Romeo Delta 3219, and Kilo Mike 4552 are all at KAF in the ICU."

SFC Santos's ear was going numb. He spoke gently, "Roger, and the other two?"

"Mike Tango 5877 and Juliet November 8991 have been pronounced KIA."

SFC Santos eased the handset from his ear and stared at the ground and road ahead. "Copy," was all he was able to muster up for a reply.

"I'm sorry, Two Fury Six Romeo out."

He sat there in the darkness for what seemed like an eternity, silently gathering his thoughts. He could feel the other men in his truck looking at him, and the other men in the other trucks were all doing the same. They were waiting on him to give them command, to take the lead. He had been the man they all turned to, and he knew they needed him to be that man for them now.

"What's the word, sergeant?" Godard, SFC Santos's truck driver, finally broke the silence, looking at him from the driver's seat over the radios mounted between them. You could barely make out the outline of his face from the green glow of the lights from the radios. SGT Bragg leaned down from the turret to listen in and Doc Taylor listened anxiously in the back seat as well.

"How do you boys feel about being lead truck?" SFC Santos asked, staring at the road. There was a silence among the men in the truck. It was weird, because they knew they didn't really have a choice in the matter, but it was odd because SFC Santos was legitimately asking them. He didn't want to ask any of his men to have to be in that position directly after what had just happened, so he was going to take the lead, but in doing so he would need the men of his truck with him.

"Fuck it," Godard finally said, as he fired up the Humvee's engine.

"Somebody's gotta do it," SGT Bragg said as he stood back up in the turret, grabbed the .50-cal machine gun and rested his foot on the top of the radio mount.

SFC Santos cracked his stereotypical smirk of a smile. He grabbed the platoon radio handset in his truck to let the other trucks know. "All trucks, this is Charlie Two Five. We are going to take the lead and head to Walton. Fall in behind us. Canadians will clear the rest of the route and recover the vehicle. How copy?"

"Truck Two, good copy, and we are up," SSG DeMeo replied over the radio.

"Truck Three, roger, we're up."

"Roger. FOB Walton, this is Charlie Two Five, SP to FOB Walton, time now."

SGT Brown, SGT Lachance, Jackson, and McDaniel all waited anxiously as the Two Charlie vehicles pulled through FOB Walton's Entrance Control Point (ECP). The entrance was a maze of dirt-filled Hesco walls, forcing the entering vehicles to slalom back and forth. The idea was to prevent a direct line of entry into the FOB and slow any possible vehicle-borne IEDs that might make it through the front-gate security. It definitely did its job slowing the men of Two Charlie, as it seemed forever until the trucks rolled up to the white tent where the four men had been staying.

The men all got out of their Humvees and stripped their armor, piling it in the seats or in the turrets of their vehicles. They all gathered around SFC Santos for instructions. He stood there, still kitted up in his armor and ammo rig.

"Stand by," was all he said as he walked into the company TOC, leaving the men in the darkness. The men sat quietly in the pitch-black night sky, not a word was spoke from any of them. It was another one of those moments that seemed like an eternity before the plywood door swung back open and the light from the TOC pierced out of the room, momentarily blinding them as SFC Santos emerged.

He paused a second, looking at the men all waiting for his words. It was the first time he had seen them in the light since the blast. He examined each one of them closely. Each one of them had looked to him for guidance, for his leadership, and he had delivered every time. He especially needed to be that leader for these men at this moment. He took one last look at them all before closing the door so that the men would be back in the dark when he spoke—so that only his words could be heard.

"Davis, Munoz, and Young are in intensive care. They are going to be alright." SFC Santos paused. "Tynes and Nolen didn't make it." He didn't need to see their faces to know the expressions on them. None of the men did. Their shoulders sank as their heads lowered to the ground. They all knew deep down that Tynes and Nolen were gone, but there had been an uncertainty up until SFC Santos spoke those words, the words they all knew deep down inside. Those words made it a reality. It was like the men had a blanket of defeat pulled over them at that moment.

"Leave one guy per truck to watch our shit and the rest of you go to the chow hall and see if there is anything left to eat. We will be staying here tonight," SFC Santos instructed. The men executed and walked off into the darkness. McDaniel, Jackson, SGT Brown, and SGT Lachance all volunteered to watch the gear and the trucks and let the other men go eat. Doc Taylor stayed behind; he wasn't hungry.

SSG DeMeo found McDaniel by one of the trucks smoking a cigarette in the dark by himself. He approached him and very gently placed both his hands on McDaniel's shoulders to console him. McDaniel could smell the gasoline aroma coming off SSG DeMeo's uniform and could see the dark patches of blood all over him even in the darkness. SSG DeMeo leaned in and said "I'm really sorry about Tynes. We did everything we could. I'm sorry." McDaniel took another drag from his cigarette and began to cry.

Doc sat in the back seat of his truck; SGT Lachance and SFC Santos quietly joined him. Leaning against the outside of the vehicle, SFC Santos lit up a cigarette. The three men just sat in the darkness. Doc Taylor could see the cherry of the cigarette glow as SFC Santos took a puff and then dim as he exhaled. Not a word was spoken.

Doc Taylor couldn't help but focus his thoughts on something he had been taught when he had gone through medic school. He kept playing over and over in his head the three types of casualties. The first type of casualty: no matter what you do, they are going to survive. Davis, Munoz, and Young fell into this category. The second type of casualty: No matter what you do, they are going to die. Tynes fell under this type in Doc's mind for sure. He loved Tynes just as every other man did in the platoon, but there was nothing Doc could have done for him, and it absolutely sucked. And then there is the third type of casualty: every single thing you do for this casualty determines if they will live or die. He was struggling with this one, as SGT Nolen fell into this category in his mind. Did he not do enough? Should he have done something differently? The "what ifs" and "should haves, could haves" kept playing back in his head, like examining game footage after a high school football game. It was the worst feeling in the world and it was eating him alive.

Doc looked out of the open vehicle door at the silhouettes of SGT Lachance and SFC Santos. He knew both had been hardened on combat deployments before, and SGT Lachance had lost a good friend on a previous deployment. "Does it ever go away?" he asked, looking at the ground.

The two men sat there in silence, unsure of how to answer him. SGT Lachance thought back to his loss from his first deployment for a moment and tried to scramble up a reasonable answer for Taylor. "No, it doesn't go away, but it gets easier." He wished he hadn't said that. It didn't seem right, but it was all that he could think of at the moment to offer his fellow soldier. He left it at that and didn't say more.

SFC Santos took another puff of his cigarette and exhaled, "You can't save us all, Doc." He paused to let Taylor take the reality of those words in, "But you are going to do what you can." He took one more drag from his cigarette, flicked the butt into the gravel, and walked back into the TOC.

The word about Tynes and SGT Nolen was being broken to the rest of the platoon at Masum Ghar, and they had taken it much like the other men had, but with more disbelief.

Nichols could not believe the words spoken to him when he was told about Tynes. He had just been talking with him the other day before they rolled out on the patrol. Tynes had volunteered to drive the lead truck, to overcome his fear from the last patrol he was on. Literally the day before that, Tynes was on a patrol where his truck hit a smaller, "toe popper" IED in the road. It blew off his Humvee's tire, but that was about it. Luckily, nobody got hurt. Tynes was pretty shaken by the blast, trying to nervously laugh it off. Nichols remembered talking with him that night after they had gotten back. Nichols reassured him nothing was going to happen, that they had been there for months and there was nothing for him to worry about. Nichols was surprised to see Tynes the next morning doing the pre-patrol Preventative Maintenance Checks and Services (PMCS) on the lead truck vehicle. Nichols had sworn he was assigned to drive Truck Three or Four, so he asked Tynes what happened? Why was he moved? Was he good being lead truck? Tynes reassured Nichols he would be alright, that he had asked to be lead truck driver. Tynes then asked him to help with the PMCS. Nichols obliged and when the trucks rolled out, he never thought that would be the last time he would ever see his friend.

Nichols couldn't help but feel guilty for Tynes. If he hadn't talked with Tynes the night before they set out on the operation, then maybe he wouldn't have tried to conquer his fear. Maybe he would still be with them.

SGT Farquhar couldn't believe Tynes was gone either. He was his team leader and had volunteered Tynes for this patrol when he was asked to give Second Squad a guy. Tynes was one of his best soldiers, the one he was going to build up with all his knowledge and experience. The one he would one day hope to see become a team leader himself. He saw all the potential Tynes had to be a great leader because he was a great soldier. And now he was gone.

The men at Masum Ghar didn't know what to do. They knew their brothers were dead, some wounded, but the rest was all unknown. How were the rest of the guys? All they could do was sit and wait for the rest of the men to return home, to get more information, more details. All they could do was wait.

The men at Walton came up to the chow hall tent. The doors to the entrance were locked. It wasn't uncommon for some chow halls to remain open throughout the day and night, maybe not offering up a full meal but at the minimum a snack bar that had junk food like muffins, granola bars, trail mix, cereal, maybe some cheap beef jerky packets. They knew from prior visits this chow hall had just that, however it apparently wasn't open. They were too late. It was approaching midnight and, according to the hours of operation sign on the front doors of the tent, it had been closed for some time now.

Leonard let out a sigh after shaking the locked doors. His stomach let out one too. "Of course," he said, turning to walk back to the vehicles.

"Just a second, Drama," SGT Culver said, holding his hand out to stop Leonard in his tracks. He and SGT Bragg walked around the corner of the tent and found one of the seams. The two of them knew some tents were held together with Velcro at points; luckily, this had been one of those points. They unvelcroed the seam and held it open for the other men to sneak in.

The men entered the chow hall tent and began filling their cargo pockets with the junk food laid out in the assorted baskets. Muffins, chewy bars, Gatorades, whatever they could get their hands on and could fit in their pockets. The light was still on in the back where the cooks prepared the food, so Leonard went to see if there was anything left. He was greeted by a couple of cooks that had been finishing up the last bit of dishes.

"Y'all can't be in here," the first cook said, as he followed Leonard back into the main room where the rest of the guys were. The men's pockets bulged like chipmunks' cheeks with all the food they had stuffed in them. "Uh uh, no, you can't have that," he said.

The men just froze, staring at the three cooks. Some even had food in their mouths they had stopped chewing, as though if they remained still they wouldn't be heard or seen. They looked at the cooks wide-eyed like deer in headlights. The senior of the cooks walked over to Leonard to take away some of the food he had stuffed in his pockets when he caught a whiff of gasoline. The smell was all over the men and overtook the room. He took a step back and glared at the men in disgust, then he noticed the splotches of dried blood all over the guys' uniforms. He paused his advance for a moment, then noticed the 82nd Airborne patches on the men's uniform sleeves. "Y'all with Two Charlie?"

"Yes, Sergeant," Rostran said as he slid one last muffin into his back pocket.

The cook looked the men over, then went into the back room. He reentered with a collapsible cardboard box in his hand. He threw it to the men. "Take what you want, lock the door on your way out."

The word must have gotten out about Tynes and Nolen. They were the first combat KIA in the battalion. The men emptied the contents of their pockets into the box and then returned to the white tent where they would be staying, unknown to them, for the next two days.

They stayed in that tent, sulking in their loss. It hit them all hard, and no one could get to sleep. Every man broke down that night at one point or another, crying at the thought of never seeing Tynes or SGT Nolen again, or constantly thinking of the last moments they did see them.

SGT Brown couldn't help but think of his friend Nolen. They had been through a lot together with a prior deployment together and being in the same platoon before being assigned to Two Charlie. SGT Brown couldn't help but think about Nolen's family, his wife, and his stepson. You couldn't even tell the boy wasn't his son; that man treated him and cared for him like his own and he even looked like Nolen. Nolen's wife got word right before they deployed that she was pregnant; SGT Nolen found out during a call on the platoon's satellite phone they could use to call home every now and again that it was going to be a girl. He was going to have a baby girl. It was all he would talk about. SGT Brown broke down thinking of the little girl who would never get to meet her father. A lot of guys broke down with that thought.

The men went through a lot of different emotions, from sorrow to anger. Anger towards the enemy, but also anger towards the higher command. They were the ones that ultimately made the decision for them to go out to assist the Canadians in the clearance operation they obviously weren't needed for. They had already returned once from the operation, as the Canadian forces said they were not needed and could return, but Two Charlie's higher command wanted them back out there.

The men remained in the white tent all the next day, sitting in their blood- and gasoline-soaked uniforms, just waiting to be allowed to go back to Masum Ghar, to be back with the rest of their platoon, the rest of their family. But they weren't allowed to leave.

The senior guys with prior combat experience tried to console the Joes, but they too were suffering on the inside. Very few of them had experienced what it was like to lose a brother, and it isn't like that would have made it easier anyway. The fight Two Charlie had been in up to this point was very one sided. They had witnessed the enemy get hurt or killed, they had even seen the Afghan National Police (ANP) officers they had been working with get maimed or killed. But, up until the 22nd of November, it had all been a fun game. The 22nd of November was the day they all realized this was not a game, that they too were just pawns on the chess board. They had been hit in the gut hard with this realization, and now, more than ever, the men understood they were not invincible.

The men finally got the go ahead to head back to Masum Ghar. They were given a MAXPRO uparmored vehicle to replace the Humvee that had been destroyed. Finally, the men could head back home to be whole with the rest of their platoon, with the rest of their brothers.

The men arrived at Masum Ghar and were greeted by the ones that had been left behind. They were all anxiously waiting as the vehicles rolled up to the section of the Combat Outpost (COP) the Canadians designated Two Charlie's home. They stared as one by one each vehicle was backed into its staging spot and the engines killed. The men slowly emerged from the vehicles.

It felt good to have them home, as good as it could feel considering the circumstances and what they all had just been through. It was easy to see a piece missing from each man, they were not the same.

As days went by, and the sting of their loss numbed, it was clear something had drastically changed among the men. They had become a new platoon, a stronger one. They realized this was not a game or some training exercise they would run back at Fort Bragg over and over until perfection. They realized they were not invincible, that there were no do overs, no mulligans, no resets. They needed to be at the top of their game all the time for every task outside the wire really could be a life-or-death situation. The lines between Joe and leadership blurred a little throughout those days, as each private started to begin to understand why the leadership had been harping on them about what they seemed to think were the little things. The leadership noticed it too in their men. They had to harp on them a lot less. Guys were more likely to check up on each other, help one another out if they had fallen before making fun of them. The making fun part would never subside, but they became a closer family.

The platoon was shy five guys now, so the battalion ended up sending some guys from Bravo and Delta Company, some of Charlie Company's sister companies. SGT McPherson was sent to replace SGT Nolen as one of Second Squad's team leaders. He knew it was going to be some hard boots to fill, but he was a good leader in Bravo, and one of the more mature ones. He was in his mid-twenties, as he had gone to college prior to enlisting. He was mad he was leaving the guys of Bravo Company, the guys he trained up with before deployment, but he understood why it was necessary. He had a job to do, and he was the best man to do it in the Army's eyes. He was just thankful SGT Flannery was in Two Charlie.

SGT Flannery and he had gotten to the unit together and were both college grads. Flannery had been sent to Alpha Company originally before being moved to Charlie Company and being assigned to Two Charlie right before deployment. At least SGT McPherson would have a familiar face to talk to and hang out with.

Along with SGT McPherson, Bravo Company sent Winston, and Delta sent Thompson. The two were younger but fit in with the rest of the platoon just fine. The new men could tell the Two Charlie guys were a tight-knit group, one that had just taken a tremendous loss. The tension lingered in the air, as they had not quite gotten back into the swing of things. Not until the Turkey Bowl.

On Thanksgiving, the boys had to go back to Walton to grab their Thanksgiving dinner. It was a pointless patrol, only meant to boost morale. The men loved nothing more than to risk their lives for some lukewarm turkey and instant mashed potatoes provided by the Army in an attempt to raise morale. They did that plenty when they would do convoys to KAF to retrieve their own mail.

They were all waiting around the trucks for the mermites of food they would take back to Masum Ghar. Some laid out on top of the trucks, some inside them, all just waiting. They had all gotten used to the hurry-up-and-wait mentality of the Army and had become masters at their craft of time-wasting. SFC Santos, determined to use the football he had somehow acquired from who knows where, stared out at the small gravel clearing. "Come on, let's go," he said to the men, calling them to gather around him.

The men weren't exactly thrilled with this, as the losses of Tynes and Nolen were still pretty fresh on their minds and the last thing they wanted to do was play a game. They didn't even want to be there in the first place. They just wanted to grab the food, do the whole dog and pony show, and be on their way back to Masum Ghar.

"I don't want to play football," SGT Bragg said. He was one of the shorter slender guys and knew from Physical Training sessions back at Fort Bragg before deployment that playing "football" was just code for the bigger guys getting to clobber the smaller ones, AKA him.

"You're playing football, Bragg," SFC Santos said as he threw the ball to him.

SGT Bragg caught the ball and threw it right back. "I'm not playing football," he protested.

SFC Santos caught the ball and threw it right back at SGT Bragg, this time harder so it made a thud when he caught it. "You're playing fucking football, Bragg," he said with a glare in his eye.

SGT Bragg looked at him, unsure if he was just messing with him or if he was actually mad. Santos was really good at messing with the guys in that way.

508

Bragg didn't dare to find out. He sighed, "Rostran, Ryan, McDaniel, we're playing football." The rest of the weapons squad guys climbed down from their turrets to join him. SFC Santos's grin was from ear to ear. The rest of the guys emerged from the trucks, some eager to play, others just following suit.

Just like SGT Bragg expected, it was a slugfest of a football game. The smaller of the men were at the mercy of the bigger guys like SGT Knollinger and SGT Thomson, who were only maddened more when they were outrun by them. A clothesline would happen here, a fist was thrown there, and by the end of the "game" guys were limping and bleeding back to their trucks. But among the bruises and blood, there were also smiles. Every man had a smile leaving that day, especially SFC Santos.

"I told you it would be fun, Bragg." He smirked as SGT Bragg gimped back into the truck turret. SGT Bragg had no reply.

It wasn't long before the battalion would hold the boots and rifle ceremony for both Tynes and SGT Nolen. The men of Two Charlie would travel back to FOB Walton, this time they would be joined by Three Charlie as well. 1st Platoon, One Charlie, had already pushed into the Arghandab River Valley and would not be attending the ceremony. That was the supposed next play for the battalion. The men of Two Charlie had gotten word the battalion was moving into their own AO. The battalion commander and sergeant major had come to visit the platoon after the loss of Tynes and Nolen. He had pitched the idea to the men, told them they were about to get into the fight, that they were going to finally be able to do their jobs as paratroopers. The men were confused. What did they think they were doing at Masum Ghar? If they wanted to get into a fight, they could get them into one tomorrow.

They all stood in the gravel clearing of the compound, catching up with their Three Charlie buddies. They told stories of things that had happened on patrols and firefights they had gotten into. No one was a cherry anymore—not in Charlie Company—and they were all proud of it.

The laughter of the men was constantly interrupted when they would glance across the gravel clearing at the two helmets resting on rifles standing straight up between two pairs of boots on a podium. Each rifle had a set of dog tags dangling from its handle. At the base of each pair of boots a photo stared at them, one of Tynes and one of SGT Nolen, both in their military dress uniforms.

The company First Sergeant made his way to the front of the displays. "Fall in!" he shouted, ordering the company to form up in front of him. The men got up off the dirt on which they had been lounging on and ran to form up into their two platoons. Each platoon made different ranks of men, each rank designated for a certain squad. It was kind of strange, the men hadn't had to form up in formation like this for some time now as it was really a garrison practice and not something you do in a combat theater. Almost as soon as the First Sergeant had barked the order, the men had formed two boxes in front of him, one for each platoon present. They all stood straight as an arrow, at Attention, in the dry heat of the breezeless Afghanistan sun.

The First Sergeant paused for a moment to inspect his men. "At Ease!" he shouted, ordering the men to change their position of stance. They went from Attention, hands fisted straight at their sides and feet together, to At Ease, a more relaxed position in which the hands were placed in the small of the back and the feet are moved shoulder-width apart. They executed and snapped into this position.

The chaplain made his way to the podium behind the First Sergeant, who did an about face and saluted the chaplain, then fell into the back of the formation of men.

The chaplain began his speech, reading scripture from the bible and talking about two men he hadn't even known. It felt like the typical cookie-cutter speech a pastor or priest would give at a typical funeral. Cut and dry, but a good sentiment.

The men listened in formation until the chaplain was complete. He fell back into his spot in the formation of speakers behind the podium. McDaniel then fell out and took the podium. He read a speech, one he and SSG Staley had written. It was a much more personal speech than that given by the chaplain, one that told what kind of a man Tynes really was, what kind of a friend Tynes was, and it gave McDaniel a chance to say one last goodbye to his friend. In classic McDaniel style, his speech ended with an inside joke only the guys of Two Charlie would get, and they all shared a good laugh followed by a tearful goodbye. McDaniel stepped down from the podium and back into the formation. SSG DeMeo then took the podium, doing the same for Nolen. The men had mixed emotions about SSG DeMeo's speech. It made them angry to watch SSG DeMeo stand up there and speak as though SGT Nolen and he were good friends, when they knew they were not. However, the sadness of Nolen's loss overcame the anger.

After SSG DeMeo fell back in, the First Sergeant retook his position at the front of the formation. It was time for the roll call.

"Company, Attention!" The men all snapped to attention, awaiting their name to be called. The First Sergeant paused for a second before finally shouting across the ranks, "Sergeant First Class Santos!"

"Here, First Sergeant!" SFC Santos replied acknowledging his presence in the formation.

"Sergeant Brown!" the First Sergeant shouted again.

"Here, First Sergeant!" SGT Brown called out.

"Private Rostran!" the First Sergeant continued.

"Here, First Sergeant," a very tearful Rostran replied.

"Sergeant Nolen!" the First Sergeant said. There was a pause, a silence among the ranks as the men waited for a reply that would not come. "Sergeant Nolen!" the First Sergeant shouted once more, still to have no reply. "Sergeant James Nolen!" the First Sergeant shouted for a final time.

He continued the roll call. "Private First Class Tynes!"

"Private First Class Tynes!"

"Private First Class Marcus Tynes!"

The First Sergeant paused, looking across a very tearful group of men, then ordered them to render their salute. "Present arms!"

They all slowly began to render their salutes. The 21-gun salute began as the seven men with rifles fired three shots each into the air at the command of "Ready, aim, fire!" Immediately following the gun salute, Taps was played. That was when a lot of the men lost their composure and finally let it out. Men cried, some wept. It was good to let it out.

The ceremony concluded and the men were ordered to fall out of formation, one squad at a time, and file through to the boots and rifle displays. There, they could leave things among the display that reminded them of the fallen, things that would go to their families. They could hold the dog tags dangling from the rifles; could put their hand on their helmets one more time; could say their goodbyes.

They finished this spectacle and then made their way back to the trucks to head back to Masum Ghar. Before they even donned their armor the company's commander, Captain (CPT) Razuri, made his way to the men. He wanted to speak to them before they headed out.

"Hey, guys, form up again for me real quick," he shouted so they could all hear him.

The men all obliged, forming their squad ranks in front of the captain. He had them all at Attention, and he had their attention. "What was this going to be about?" was the question on each of their minds.

"You see this, men?" CPT Razuri asked, holding up a fist with one hand while running his index finger from the other along his knuckles. "This is a ridgeline."

The men knew what he was referring to, but were extremely confused where he was going with it. In land navigation, they often taught terrain features to the privates using a closed fist. A single knuckle represented a hill, all your knuckles in a line represented a ridgeline. In between the knuckles were saddles, the fingers were spurs, and in between them were draws. The men, still locked at Attention, couldn't move their heads but looked at each other out of the corner of their eyes to confirm they were not the only one confused. CPT Razuri was an amazing company commander and if his actions could be conveyed into words, he would have been a fantastic leader, but a motivational speaker he was not.

CPT Razuri continued. He put his fist down and then pointed to the small mountain range behind him, just on the horizon. "Do you see that, men? That is also a ridgeline. And just on the other side of that ridgeline is the Arghandab River

Valley. Now I know Lieutenant Colonel Jenio had already spoken to you about that place, and now it's official. We are moving into the valley, replacing the Stryker brigade that is currently there. They have taken many casualties in that AO, a lot of men have died. Our One Charlie brothers are already there, and they too have taken their first casualties." He paused, remembering seeing Duke in the hospital in KAF after his IED blast injury. He had lost both his legs the same evening of Tynes's and Nolen's death. CPT Razuri had visited many of his men in the hospital at KAF that night. He reflected on telling the news of Tynes and Nolen to Young and Munoz and helping them to see off the caskets of their friends. That night was a big hit for the entire company, and he didn't know how to put what he was about to say next to the men. "Now, I would have taken any of those guys' spots," he said, pointing to the boots and rifle displays, "but we can't dwell on that. Men, we have to keep bounding forward. We have to face the fact that there is probably going to be more casualties, more deaths. Now, I need you to get ready for that fight, men." He paused, looking them over. "I need you to buckle up."

CHAPTER 3

# Welcome to the Dab

The men of Two Charlie returned to Masum Ghar and prepared themselves for the move into the Arghandab River Valley (ARV). Little did they know they would be abandoning their Canadian paradise and heading into a much different way of living, and a much different way of fighting.

Curious, the men of Two Charlie began to look for more information on the area they were about to occupy. They had only heard words of the Stryker brigade they were replacing, the casualties they had taken. Men found articles online about the ARV. The valley was vastly different looking than the desert of the Panjwai district they had been in the last few months. Tucked over a mountain ridge just north of Kandahar city, the ARV was a jungle made up of pomegranate orchards and grape vineyards. It was extremely agricultural and very green, making it a night and day difference from the city just around the mountains. There was so much vegetation in the pictures the guys joked that it looked like Vietnam. They started referring to it as "The Dab" as Vietnam veterans referred to Vietnam as "Nam." The thing was the Arghandab had a history of fighting, not so different from Vietnam. The Russians struggled with this area in the '80s. Some articles wrote that the guerrillas in the valley had "fortifications and thousands of mines" and would let the Soviet troops get within ten meters before opening fire on them. They wanted to make sure they killed them on the first shot, and they didn't want to allow for their escape. There were severe casualties among the Russian ranks. This caused them to employ the tactics they are most known for, massive artillery bombings and helicopter attacks. The Soviets don't search and destroy, they destroy then search. Despite this brutal tactic, the Soviet forces were still unable to take this valley from the fighters.

The Coalition forces that were currently fighting in the ARV had been experiencing a much similar type of fight. The Brits had fought in the valley. Then the Canadians took over. And now it was an American Stryker unit, and soon to be the battlefield for a bunch of American paratroopers. The Coalition forces fell under a different Rule of Engagement (ROE) than the Russians in the '80s and were not allowed to be as brutal. They weren't there to win a war, they were there to win the hearts and minds of the Afghani people, and to establish a government that could govern the country. The COIN operation had become heavily weighted on training the Afghan National Army (ANA) and Afghan National Police (ANP) forces. The ANA usually received most of the funding and mentoring from the Coalition forces, leaving the scraps to the ANP. This resulted in the ANP organization being riddled with corruption.

Two Charlie had been working with the ANP at Masum Ghar for the last couple months. The police station was located just outside the Canadian base and SFC Santos and Lt. Scrivner would regularly meet up with the police chief to plan patrols and training with the station's police force. The men taught the police officers how to patrol their district, how to fight against the enemy, even how to carry themselves in a manner the locals could deem respectable. There was a lot of progress with this station's police force, and the men of Two Charlie had formed a trust with them. It was kind of sad they would be leaving those men now, along with the many other things they grew accustomed to at Masum Ghar.

SFC Santos was informed by command to pack up as much as they could, as there wasn't much of anything out there for them in the valley. The men tried to enjoy the last remaining days they had of their home away from home. No longer would they have the comforts of Masum Ghar. No more concrete bunker with air conditioning to sleep in. No more internet in their rooms. No more Canadian gym. No more Canadian chow hall with Häagen-Dazs ice cream. No more gawking at the only two Canadian female soldiers on the base after long missions out in the desert of Panjwai. No more.

Before the big move, SFC Santos wanted to get something done he had been thinking about since the day of 22 November. SGT Lachance had ordered a tattoo gun online and had it mailed to himself. Ever since he finally received it in the mail, he had been working on his tattooing skills. He started practicing on his own thighs. As his skills improved, he began to show some of the guys his work, and they absolutely wanted in on it. There wasn't anything cooler than a tattoo received from a good friend while in one of the dirtiest and dustiest countries they knew of. What could go wrong?

The guys would discreetly come to Lachance with pictures or some sort of design, asking him if he could do it. Lachance would always just reply with a simple shrug of the shoulder and a joking, "I don't know, let's try." Many nights were spent with the dull electrical buzz of the gun coming from Lachance's hooch. Everyone that received a tattoo from him would walk out with the biggest shit-eating grin and a different part of their body wrapped up in saran wrap. It was their own underground tattoo parlor, and how no one got infected is still a mystery to this day.

SFC Santos made his way to Lachance's room, a poncho draped across the doorway like a makeshift privacy curtain. He knocked on the plywood wall to warn him he was about to enter. SFC Santos had a way of just barging into guys' rooms to mess with them. This time was no different, however he didn't want to walk in on the man if he was jerking off or something, so he gave a fair warning.

"Yo," SGT Lachance said, as SFC Santos peeked his head in through the poncho.

"What's going on in here?" SFC Santos said with his characteristic mischievous smile.

"Nothing, just going through some stuff that came in the mail. What's up?" SGT Lachance said as he dropped whatever was in his hand back in the United States Postal box and pushed it away from the foot of his bed to make room for Santos to enter the room.

"I was thinking about another tattoo," SFC Santos said as he stepped into the room.

"What do you got?" SGT Lachance asked as he reached for the paper in SFC Santos's hands. Santos handed it to him. It read, "The only thing necessary for the triumph of evil is for good men to do nothing. 22 Nov 09."

SFC Santos's mischievous smile had vanished, and a somber look had replaced it. "You think you can do that in that font?"

Lachance stared at the piece of paper in his hand, focusing on the date. He paused a moment then looked back up at Santos, "Yea," he said, handing him back the piece of paper, "I can do that."

The men gutted everything they could from Masum Ghar. They stripped mattresses from the beds, ripped lighting out from the walls, tore down the plywood walls, and collected all the internet cords. Anything they thought they might be able to use in the future was packed away. If they could have taken the Jersey barriers that made up the bunker, they would have. It was all loaded into Conex boxes that would be transported to the outpost later. They took everything except the mice that inhabited the bunker with them.

The trip out to the new outpost was quite a process, and not a very direct one. The platoon only had three Humvees and a MAXPRO, so they had to execute a shuttle service to get the whole platoon into the valley. Initially, the men would stage at a barren outpost north of their new AO. It was occupied by an engineering company and was used for refueling vehicles in the area. It was only a few kilometers north of the luscious greenery of the Arghandab River Valley, but it might as well have been on the surface of the moon. Nothing but desert lay to the north. They would spend the next few days there, making trips to grab some of the supplies they packed and transfer it to the temporary outpost.

"You guys still have Humvees?" one of the engineer soldiers at the temporary outposts asked SFC Santos.

"Yea," SFC Santos replied, confused as to why the man seemed so shocked and upset about their situation.

"It's come down from higher that nobody is supposed to be driving those anymore. All Coalition forces are to be equipped with MRAPs or MAXPROs. How long have you had these?"

Santos looked at Lt. Scrivner. "The whole time we've been here."

"That's a big no no and going to change. Who are you with? We will get with your S4 and get you some new shit," the soldier said. SFC Santos and Lt. Scrivner replied, and the soldier walked off. Lt. Scrivner looked at SFC Santos, who just shrugged.

Along with the hopes and dreams of MRAPs and MAXPROs, the Two Charlie guys were also issued new combat uniforms at the temporary outpost. The Army Combat Uniforms (ACUs) were digital-camouflage pattern uniforms the Army had chosen to replace the old Battle Dress Uniform (BDUs) sometime mid-way through the Global War on Terror (GWOT). The Army had handpicked the different colors of the uniform to specifically camouflage with absolutely nothing. The blocky pattern was hated by every soldier in the military, and millions of dollars were probably spent on them. Either the ACU contract was coming to an end, or the Army realized the ACUs absolutely sucked and were planning on contracting a new pattern, one of which the 2nd Battalion of the 508th Parachute Infantry Regiment got to trial run. The men of Two Charlie got introduced to the ACU-Deltas. Now, one would think the Army would try to go as far away from the digital pattern as they could; one would be wrong. They decided that all the ACU pattern was missing was a shit-brown color, so they incorporated the new color among the old ones and the ACU-Deltas were born. After the initial cool-guy feeling of having a different camouflage uniform than literally everyone else in the Army wore off, the men of Two Charlie ended up just referring to their new uniforms as the "Shit-stained ACUs."

The next couple of days the men tried not to freeze as they waited for word on when they were to go into the outpost to replace the Stryker guys. It was early December, and the men only had their poncho liners to sleep with, everything else was packed up. They had regretted packing their sleeping bags, though they only ever used their poncho liners to sleep in at Masum Ghar. They were beginning to get a feel for what life was going to be like in the valley. Miserable.

They began to learn about their new home via maps. The Arghandab River ran from the northeast to the southwest, with many canals through the orchards and vineyards. The main road that paralleled the river a few kilometers north was known as Route Red Dog. Though it was a main road, it was not a paved one, more like hard-packed dirt. It had two smaller roads that branched perpendicularly off it—Route Phillies and Route Highlife.

There were three outposts, the first was what Charlie Company would refer to as Terra Nova. It was where the company headquarters element would be located and operate out of. The company commander (CO) and the First Sergeant would be there, so it was the last place the men of Two Charlie wanted to be. It was along Route Red Dog directly west of the large village of Jelawur.

The second outpost was referred to as COP Nolen. This was where One Charlie had already been conducting operations in the valley, and Three Charlie was getting ready to join them. It was south of Terra Nova and among the pomegranate orchards and vineyards. Route Phillies ran right up to it off Red Dog and was historically heavily IEDed.

The third and final outpost was where Two Charlie would call home. It would be called COP Tynes. It was east of Terra Nova and Jelawur and located at the intersection of Route Red Dog and Route Highlife. It was the furthest east outpost in the company AO and they would be responsible for covering three quarters of it. All the terrain south to the Arghandab River and east to the villages of the Shuyens was Two Charlie's new AO. It consisted of the villages of Jelawur, Druia, Babur, the Shuyens, the Khosrows, and Tarok Kolache. The Shuyens consisted of three sub-villages—Shuyen Olya, Shuyen Mian, and Shuyen Sofla—and likewise the Khosrows did as well (Khosrow Olya, Khosrow Mian, and Khosrow Sofla). The men of Two Charlie would have their hands full for sure with this new area.

In the Army, there is a process called Left Seat Right Seat that is conducted when being relieved or relieving another unit. Initially, the old unit that has been in the area will be in the Left Seat, the metaphorical driver seat. There, they are the ones that oversee the patrols with the new unit coming in to replace them. They take out an entire squad or platoon—whichever they have been operating within the area or feel necessary to accomplish this task—to escort, educate, and mentor the new unit's leadership about the area. The new unit's leadership's responsibility is hardly to sit back and enjoy the ride. They are to be like a sponge and learn as much as they can from both the leadership and the Joes of the unit that is "driving" them. After a few patrols like this, the roles switch, and the new unit takes out its men and a few of the leadership from the old unit. The old leadership is there just to make sure the new unit doesn't do anything stupid. They are not supposed to oversee the patrol, just ensure the new unit is following their guidelines. Once this process is completed, the old unit leaves and the AO is entirely in the hands of the new unit.

After much reluctance, the 2nd Infantry Division (ID) Stryker guys coordinated with Two Charlie to conduct their first Left Seat Right Seat patrol out of COP Tynes. Based on the conversation Lt. Scrivener and SFC Santos had with them, it didn't seem like the Stryker guys wanted to leave the safety of the outpost at all. They were adamant about just getting relieved after showing the Two Charlie guys around the outpost. But, in the end, it was decided Two Charlie would drive down to COP Tynes with their trucks where they would leave their vehicles and Joes and the leadership would go on a dismounted patrol of the area with them.

They were going to get to see the valley with their own eyes and not just stare at a map. Their drive down to COP Tynes was filled with both excitement and anticipation. They were finally going to see firsthand if all they had heard about the valley was what it was cracked up to be.

The men drove south, kicking up a plume of dust with their vehicles. As they turned on Route Red Dog, they gained a good first look of what lay ahead of them to the south. A forest of trees stared at them from over the mud walls. The branches tangled together as they reached into the air. It was a sea of brown twigs and looked nothing of what they had imagined.

"It's not green at all," McDaniel shouted down with a smart-aleck smirk on his face from the turret.

"It's December," SFC Santos said as he stared out the window of the MAXPRO.

The convoy arrived at COP Tynes. A 2nd ID guy popped out of a plywood guard tower on the south side of the road to remove the concertina wire fence that stretched across it. He leisurely dragged the wire through the dirt to clear a path for the convoy to drive through. There was a Stryker parked along the compound's southernmost dirt wall, blocking a large frail-looking metal Afghan gate. The Stryker's engine fired up and the driver moved the vehicle out of the way while another soldier fought to open the old gate. When he finally got the damn thing opened, he waved the convoy to enter.

"That's a hell of a front gate," Lt. Scrivner said satirically over the truck radios as the convoy pulled through and entered the outpost.

"What do they keep in there, a shitty King Kong?" McDaniel said as the whole thing reminded him of a very low-budget rusted *Jurassic Park* gate. He watched as the soldier struggled to close the gate behind them and they repositioned the Stryker to block the entrance.

The men parked their vehicles and got out to look around. Inside there was a lot of nothing. A large clearing about a hundred feet by a hundred feet surrounded by ten-foot-tall mud walls was literally all the men could see protecting them from the outside world. In the middle of the clearing stood a makeshift volleyball net in the mud. The 2nd ID guys had made it out of radio antennas and parachute cord.

The southeast corner of the compound had what looked like a well spicket and a few buckets where the 2nd ID guys had been doing their laundry. One of the soldiers was standing there shirtless, pumping the well handle to fill up his bucket. An interior mud wall jutted out of the perimeter wall to separate the well from what looked to be the outpost burn pit. The pile of unburnt trash resting on the pile of burnt trash in the corner and smoked charred mud walls was the dead giveaway. They hadn't even dug a pit for the trash, it was literally just piled in the corner. To the left of the burn pit, a single piss tube stuck out of the ground, and a 55-gallon drum was cut in half to use as a shitter. A metal safety fencepost leaned against the wall. It had been used as a stir stick to stir the shit while it was burning.

Along the west wall there was an old mosque building made of archways and a missing roof. Sandbags stacked under the arches sealed the building to make a room, one in which the 2nd ID guys had been sleeping. A blue tarp was laid over the top of what remained of one section of the roof, sandbags piled randomly on top to secure it from the wind. The southwest corner's mud wall was gone, so a wall of four-foot Hescos stacked on top of eight-foot Hescos was used to fill the gap.

The north wall consisted of what used to be a very primitive school. Rows of Quonset hut-shaped mud structures lined the wall, and they all shared a common external arched vestibule. Each arch led to a small room.

At the northwest corner, a group of ANP were cooking something. Above them on the roof of the Quonset mud huts was a very depressing-looking structure. It was a small tower, made of a row of poorly stacked tan and green sandbags. An olive-drab green parachute was draped over what looked like a bed frame to give the structure a "roof" and shelter its occupants from the sun. The ANP had a PKM machine gun sticking out of the tower and were pulling security. Well, they had a few policemen standing on the roof in the vicinity of the tower; that was probably as good as it was going to get when it came to ANP pulling security.

Just as SFC Santos was about to say something, question how the 2nd ID guys could let the poor bastards fight from a position like that, his eye caught another tower built identical to the one along the east wall, only the 2nd ID guys were pulling security from it. A bed frame was leaned against the mud wall to be able to climb to the roof to reach the tower.

The hatch of the Stryker blocking the front gate opened, breaking the silence, and narrowing the attention of the Two Charlie men. A soldier climbed out and jumped to the ground, making his way through the nearly closed gate, and made his way towards the men. He had a bandana wrapped around his head and was literally wearing a belt of 7.62-mm machine-gun ammo draped over his shoulders and wrapped around his body armor. His pants appeared to be bloused in his boots at first glance, but upon a closer examination the men realized they had just been cut off at boot level. The man had made ACU-capris out of his uniform.

"Is this guy fucking serious?" Bowman said quiet enough so "Rambo" couldn't hear him, but the rest of the Two Charlie guys sitting on the trucks could.

"These guys are well past their expiration date, man," Jackson replied, as he examined the other men that had begun to emerge from what seemed like every corner of the outpost. They all had a similar appearance. Some had rolled sleeves, some had them completely cut off. Some wrote things on their helmets. It was wild. Two Charlie had been known to get in trouble for rolling a sleeve or two or unblousing their boots on patrols, but nothing like this. They couldn't even fathom getting away with the lack of discipline they were seeing. They would expect this from a National Guard unit, but not an Active Duty one. If their appearance didn't say it, then the 2nd ID guy's eyes and demeanor did. These men were done and had checked out some time ago.

"Staff Sergeant Blake," Rambo said, holding his hand out to shake SFC Santos's, who didn't know what to do. He reached out to shake the man's hand while looking at Lt. Scrivner. Both of their jaws were dropped. "Shall we?" SSG Blake said as he walked away from the men toward the mud huts on the north side of the compound. Lt. Scrivner just looked at SFC Santos; they both mouthed "What the fuck?" to each other and followed the man.

He led them to a small room where there was a map hanging from the wall and a radio in the corner. A 2nd ID Joe was petting a German shepherd-looking dog and manning the radio when they all walked in. It must have been the room they were using for their TOC. SSG Blake looked at the map, and pointed to the intersection in which the outpost was located. "We are here. We are going to take you south, just past the second canal north of Khosrow Olya and show you the orchards in that area." His finger moved along the map, pointing to the area they were about to patrol. "We don't really go down there, it's damn impossible to get our Strykers down there so we haven't been there in a while."

"They get stuck in the mud?" Lt. Scrivner asked.

"No, the paths aren't meant for large vehicles like ours. Hell, I'd be surprised if you could get one of your Humvees back there. Speaking of which, what are you doing with Humvees?"

"Working on getting MRAPs," SFC Santos replied.

"Right. Regardless, you won't be able to get them down there," SSG Blake said.

"Are there any roads you do bring the Strykers on? Route Red Dog seems pretty wide and open, not in the thick of the fields," Lt. Scrivner asked.

"We don't drive on Red Dog east of the outpost," SSG Blake spoke hastily.

"Why not?" Lt. Scrivner pushed.

"We've lost too many men on that damn road. The IEDs they use on that road are big enough to crack our Strykers in half. If you know what's good for you, sir, I'd suggest that you keep your trucks off that road," SSG Blake replied with anger. You could tell he did not want to talk about the subject.

"Roger, understood," Lt. Scrivner replied, partially embarrassed for being yelled at by the man, and partially angry from it. "So, we will dismount."

The SSG smiled. "You won't get far."

"What do you mean?" Lt. Scrivner asked.

SSG Blake didn't reply. You could tell from the look on his face that he regretted saying it, like it was one of those moments one can see the words leaving your mouth and you try to catch them in midair before they reach the ears of who they were initially intended for. He looked at Lt. Scrivner and SFC Santos, both eager for a reply. "Look, we just haven't patrolled that area in a while."

"Noted," Lt. Scrivner replied with his stereotypical smug officer style. "What areas have you been patrolling?"

Again, SSG Blake did not reply. He dropped his finger from the map and began walking out of the mud room. "Who all is coming on this patrol?" was all he said.

"Myself and eight others," Lt. Scrivner answered.

"Grab them and meet us outside the front gate. We'll show you your best chance of surviving the valley."

Lt. Scrivner, SFC Santos, SGT Knollinger, SGT Farquhar, SGT Maher, SGT Lachance, SGT Flannery, SGT McPherson, and SSG DeMeo all geared up and met the 2nd ID guys outside the front gate. The 2nd ID guys were not thrilled by the fact they were going out on a patrol.

"I thought we were done with this?" one of the Joes whined. His leadership quickly hushed him and had him get on his equipment. The German shepherd-like dog came out from the schoolhouse, yelping with excitement. He acted like he knew what the men were about to do and was adamant about joining in.

"That your dog?" SFC Santos asked.

"That's Nepal. Technically he's the ANP's dog, but he don't like Afghans very much so he stays with us." One of the 2nd ID soldiers responded as he grabbed Nepal to give him pets. Nepal wagged his tail and headed toward the break in the concertina wire. He sat there, eagerly waiting for the men.

"So, he's not a bomb dog?" Lt. Scrivner asked.

"Nope, he's not trained at all. Just an Afghan mutt that hates these savages as much as we do," the soldier replied and went to join the dog.

"Could have fooled me," Lt. Scrivner said. The dog looked like a full-bred German shepherd that had been trained by the military.

SSG Blake moved to the front of the gaggle of soldiers for his patrol brief. "Alright, today we are going to show these guys what it's like south of the second canal. We are going to cross the canal, push into the orchards, then head back to the outpost. Any questions?"

The Two Charlie guys just looked at each other. Yeah, there were plenty of questions. What was the plan for MedEvac? Were there any planned Helicopter Landing Zones (HLZs)? What was the status for Close Air Support (CAS)? Did they not go over react-to-contact in their patrol briefs? The briefing was very half-assed it seemed.

"Alright, let's roll out," SSG Blake said.

A soldier held the concertina wire open as Nepal and the 2nd ID and Two Charlie men filed through. The Two Charlie men immediately wedged out in a wedge formation, making a kind of "V" shape like geese do when they fly. It is how infantrymen train to maneuver while on patrol, to have fields of fire for each man that cover the most ground. However, the 2nd ID guys did not wedge out. They remained in the same file they squeezed through the wire in. It was odd watching the line of men, one by one, like ants following a chemical trail. Each soldier was evenly spaced, about ten meters from each other, and watching the soldier in front of them to see where they stepped.

"What the hell are they doing?" SSG DeMeo asked.

"It's called a file," SSG Blake replied.

"Well, yeah, no shit. But you guys don't wedge?" SSG DeMeo asked, irritated from the smart-ass remark.

"South of the first canal, there are grape vineyards, which consist of rows upon rows of mud walls. Then south of the second canal, you get the added bonus of pomegranate orchards mixed in with grape vineyards. Plenty of hiding places for IEDs, and the place is littered with them. A file ensures that we travel on the same path, to avoid stepping on any pressure plates." SSG Blake explained. "We try to stay in the tracks of the man in front of us."

The men came to the first canal. It was a small canal, no more than knee-deep water and maybe about five feet wide. It looked like it wasn't quite full, as the water didn't quite reach all the way to the muddy banks. The Two Charlie guys watched as one by one, the 2nd ID guys waded through the cold water, each man pulling security for the man in front of him as he crossed the canal. The Two Charlie guys watched and then noticed just 20 meters down the canal there was a man-made bridge constructed out of sticks and mud.

"Why aren't we using that? Why are we wading into this shit water?" SSG DeMeo intervened again with his know-it-all ego as he started walking towards the bridge. It was unclear if the 2nd ID guys were irritated with him yet, but it was clear the Two Charlie guys were.

"I wouldn't do that if I were you," SSG Blake shouted at SSG DeMeo. "They put bombs on those too. Safest place to be is in the water."

The patrol continued south. The men climbed over an eight-foot mud wall that led them to the first vineyard. It had row after row of muddy furrows and three-foot mud walls that had brown leafless vines growing up them. The wall they had climbed was part of a perimeter wall that enclosed the vineyard field like a fence. When the men were on top of this wall, they could see that much of the land south of the canal consisted of a labyrinth of these vineyards. There wasn't a farmer or anyone tending the fields in sight.

SGT Knollinger watched as Nepal came up to the wall, following the 2nd ID guys. "There is no way he is going to make it up that wall," he said, judging the size of the dog compared to the large wall. The dog must have heard him because he sized up the wall, took a few steps back, and did a bounding leap to the top, dropping to join the soldiers on the other side. SGT Knollinger looked at SFC Santos. "Damn."

"These fields are good cover and concealment to fight out of when it picks up," SSG Blake said to Lt. Scrivner, "but they like to put their bombs in these fields too, so tread softly."

"Is there anywhere they don't have bombs?" Lt. Scrivner asked.

"Nope." One of the 2nd ID Joes said, overhearing their conversation. He hadn't looked toward them, instead his eyes were fixed in the distance, scanning. "They're everywhere."

SSG Blake looked at Lt. Scrivner and shrugged, then nodded. "Your best chance is being unpredictable. Never take the same path twice. Don't develop patterns. Never come home the same way you left. You know, common sense."

"Where is everyone?" Lt. Scrivner asked, scanning the fields in the distance, expecting to see farmers tending to their fields.

"It's December," SFC Santos replied and then made his way into the vineyard.

The movement was slow, climbing over perimeter walls, wading through the sea of vines, and crossing random open fields where the locals had planted their winter wheat. In one of these clearings, the men got a clear look at the second canal; it was a little wider than the first, and a little deeper in areas. The men approached it much like they did the first, with a bounding overwatch, pulling security for the man crossing and moving through the water one at a time. The water was waist deep in this area, which made the crossing a little slower than the first. The men followed a path along the canal until they hopped over another wall. This time they did not jump into the maze of the vineyards; they plopped into a pomegranate orchard.

The orchard was dark, as the mass of twisted branches of the pomegranate trees provided a canopy over the men that blocked out the sun. The branches were eerie and reminded them of a Tim Burton film. It definitely gave off *Sleepy Hollow* vibes as the leafless branches remained still in the sky above them. They had to squat to see under the mess of entangled branches, to see rows upon rows of trunks spurting from the ground. SGT Farquhar felt comfortable in this environment. He had grown up in California and been in orchards before. The mud walls were a little different, but he knew this dirt and it kind of reminded him of home. The other men, not so much.

SFC Santos took a knee in the mud. He scanned the orchard and took a deep breath. It was kind of a peaceful place, if it wasn't in the middle of a warzone. This was going to be his men's new home for the next 10 months, their new playground.

The patrol continued, pushing through orchards and vineyards, climbing over mud wall after mud wall, and crossing little streams and small canals. They even walked along a wall and climbed a tree at one point. The mud walls were all similar in construction, just varying in height. All of them were just over a foot thick and were constructed by packing a mixture of wet Afghan dirt and hay around skinny sticks that provided the structure, much like rebar does in concrete. It was a very primitive style of building, but these walls had lasted centuries and were surprisingly solid, providing good cover in a fight and surprisingly being able to stop large rounds from penetrating even their surface.

"Are these guys fucking with us?" SGT Lachance questioned the 2nd ID guys' tactics out loud to SFC Santos as he hopped down from one of the walls.

SFC Santos shrugged. "Maybe a little," he said as he prepared to climb over another wall. He threw his leg over and hopped with the other to straddle the wall. "Maybe not."

The Two Charlie guys were wondering where the heck they were and if the 2nd ID pointman even knew where he was going, as the mud on their uniform and boots began to build up and weigh them down, making each wall climb harder than the next one. Then, suddenly, the men climbed one more wall and found themselves in a massive clearing, not a tree in sight. They had made their way back north of the first canal, back to the village of Druia, back to COP Tynes.

One by one, they all filed through the concertina wire, and through the gate. Wet and muddy, the men stayed in their gear and waited by the vehicles for further instructions from SFC Santos.

"So?" Jackson asked SGT Knollinger as he attempted to use the side of the Humvee's tire to scrape the mud off the bottom of his boots, "How was it?"

Knollinger looked at him, a little irritated by the question. "How do you think it was?" He placed his freshly scraped boot in the mud to try to scrape off the globs of mud on the other. "Muddy."

They watched from the trucks as SFC Santos and Lt. Scrivner talked with the 2nd ID leadership. Santos and Scrivner both nodded, then began walking through the vast nothingness that was COP Tynes, their heads didn't leave the ground until they got to the trucks.

"Mount up, we are going back to the checkpoint. Then in the morning, we will load up our vehicles and the Strykers and take over COP Tynes."

Early the next morning, as the light of the sun began to luminate the valley, the dust trail from the Strykers grew in the horizon as they approached the checkpoint. The men of Two Charlie watched as they neared, packing up the last of their things into rucks and assault packs. The large vehicles snaked through the ECP and the loud engines roared to a halt. The men loaded up into the back of the Strykers and their Humvees and started the trek to COP Tynes.

It was their first time in a vehicle like a Stryker. Paratroopers don't usually conduct mounted operations in heavily uparmored machines. It was dark, as there were only a few peep holes letting in light from the outside, but it was also warm. The men packed in like sardines, with all their bags and gear acting like insulation inside the vehicle. That and the walls of uparmor around them sheltered them from the elements outside. Despite this comfort, the men were very uneasy, as they had no idea what was going on outside the vehicle. They knew they were moving; that was apparent from the constant back and forth jarring they felt each time the vehicle sped up or slowed down or hit a bump. But there was nothing they could do. Nothing but wait in the dark.

Finally, the vehicle came to a stop. The back hatch dropped and light pierced the darkness, momentarily blinding them. They all started piling out and unloading their gear inside. For the soldiers that hadn't been a part of the first trip to COP Tynes, you could see the disappointment in their eyes. There was literally nothing.

The 2nd ID guys ensured there was no more of Two Charlie's stuff in their vehicles and then began loading up their men. There was no equipment for them to sign over, so as soon as the guys in the guard towers were replaced, they got a head count of all their men and just left. They had to tie Nepal to a post to keep him from following them. He barked as the Stryker engines fired up and the men began to drive away. The Two Charlie Joes quickly untied him and reassured him it would be alright, he was part of Two Charlie now.

The Joes of Two Charlie, now seeing their new home for the first time, were in disbelief. They watched as the Strykers drove down Route Red Dog and the growls of the engines faded; the sound of the parachutes flapping on the bedframes of each tower took over the silence. They had grown too accustomed to the life Masum Ghar had provided. That was their only deployment experience and they had come to expect that. The guys who had deployed before knew otherwise. This was the type of deployment they had all been on, and unfortunately were going to be on again.

"We can't live here. They can't be serious?" Nichols said in disbelief.

SFC Santos smiled his stereotypical smirk as he walked over to the young soldier. "Eh, it'll be alright."

As soon as SFC Santos spoke the words it began to rain, and his smirk grew a little wider that day.

First things first, the men had to establish better security positions for their new home and fix the fact they literally had a road going through the middle of their outpost. SGT Maher took point on this task. He had done a 15-month deployment with the 173rd Airborne Brigade a year ago before he got reassigned to the 82nd. The entire deployment consisted of building COPs out in the mountains of Paktika province of Afghanistan so the enemy had something to shoot at other than the FOBs. COP fortification and defense building had become a strength of his, and he was no stranger to filling sandbags and Hescos.

"We use the southwest corner Hescos and build a tower there to replace the plywood one across the road. That tower will have good eyes down Route Phillies to the south and Route Red Dog to the west. We can build another tower in the corner next to the metal gate. That one can watch east down Red Dog and to the south, interlocking with the southeast tower's sector of fire." SGT Maher lowered his rough topo sketch of the outpost and surrounding area so SFC Santos, Lt. Scrivner, SGT Thomson, and SGT Knollinger could see. He had drawn plans for three towers, all to be made by stacking Hescos and had sketched a crude range card for each to show their coverage. "We can get rid of the ANP tower and replace it so that we have something overwatching the north, though that is pretty open up that direction."

"Sounds good. What do you want to do about that gate?" SFC Santos asked, looking across the clearing at the rusted hunk of metal barely holding on to the mud wall. "That's got to go."

"We get rid of it when we get more Hescos, replace it with an ECP," SGT Maher suggested.

SFC Santos nodded. "When we get the Hescos we can extend the wall to the north, maybe stage the vehicles up there. Move the burn pit back there. Make some more piss tubes, maybe an outhouse for the shit cans, give us a little privacy." He looked around; you could see the wheels turning in his head. "See if we can get some wood with the FOO money once you get it, Rosa, build a TOC and wood structure coming out of the schoolhouse." SSG Rosa had been deemed the FOO (Field Ordering Officer) guy for Two Charlie since he was the second most senior non-commissioned officer (NCO) in the platoon. These individuals went through training and were responsible for handling the purchase of things to upgrade military units or could be used to buy supplies or hire local workers. Basically, try to boost the local economy while developing relations with the local people. SSG Rosa had gone through the training and was just waiting to receive the money.

SFC Santos walked over to the corner to see how big an area they had to work with. He disappeared in a little corner, then reemerged with a smile on his face as he started to pull a full olive-drab parachute out with him. "Look at this!" he said, still pulling hand over hand. SGT Knollinger, SGT Lachance, SGT Maher, and SGT Thomson all watched as he continued to unveil the chute. His reaction on his face was like a kid in a candy store. "This is so cool."

The four men just looked at him. "Oh, come on, you don't think this is cool? Get some of the Joes, hang this shit up." He called for the men that had been moving green army cots into the four rooms of the schoolhouse to climb on the roof and hang up the apex of the parachute. They did and the remaining two spread the chute open and staked it down at two ends, creating a canopy over the opening of the vestibule. They positioned some steel pipe that was lying in the corner to help prop the chute up and create another peak. The whole thing looked like a green circus tent.

"Look at that," SFC Santos said with a smile.

The other men didn't know what to do. Nobody shared his enthusiasm for the parachute. "I guess it will keep us somewhat sheltered from the elements," Bowman said and went back to work moving cots into the school.

The school rooms were not the biggest. They probably were only eight feet wide by fifteen feet long, of mud walls with a small hole in the ceiling for circulation. Six guys on cots could fit in there but they would be pretty much living on top of each other with all their gear. So, some of the men moved their shit into the blown-up mosque, and some of them in the vestibule and under the newly hung parachute canopy.

The men continued to unload and make do with what they had as the sun began to set in the valley. It was a pretty sunset, a bright orange that faded to a dark purple and then to a black star-filled sky. The men gathered around the fire pit and watched the light of the flames dance around the outer mud walls of the outpost.

"Get some rest, boys," SFC Santos said, staring into the flame. "Tomorrow, we go to work."

CHAPTER 4

# A Home Away From Home

The next day, the men woke up and grabbed whatever MRE they could find for breakfast. They made a quick run to Terra Nova to load up the trucks with supplies to begin fortifying COP Tynes. They loaded up sandbags, Hescos, and concertina wire and headed back. The men unloaded the supplies at the southwest corner and started working on the tower to replace the plywood one across the street. This would be called Tower One; it would overlook the first and second canal. They had no excavator, no backhoe, no equipment at all. All they had was their E-tools, small collapsible shovels the Army had issued them.

An assembly line was formed. Some men used their E-tools to fill sandbags with dirt. A line of men passed those bags from the filling area to the Hesco wall, where they were passed up to guys who had set up the next level of Hescos on top of the already existing ones. The sandbags were then dumped in the Hescos and thrown down to be refilled and the process started all over again.

Dirt and dust filled the air as the men worked throughout the day. It covered them and the colors of their new uniforms began to fade to a solid dirt brown. The only break they had was when they were assigned a guard shift in the existing 2nd ID towers. The men would go from working to tower guard, back to working, and back to tower guard. Team leaders would pull Sergeant of the Guard (SOG) duties, which consisted of mainly monitoring the radio chatter on company and battalion net and monitoring the radio of the guys in the towers, bringing them anything they may need or responding to anything they may have seen from their tower.

The men did try to sneak a little fun into their labor. A sandbag was accidentally tipped and dumped on Thompson while handing it up, covering him in the loose dirt. SGT Flannery laughed at the scene of him trying to shake the dirt off like a dog. Thompson wasn't very fond of his laughter and grabbed some dirt and threw it at him. A dirt fight commenced and grew as more and more men fell victim to the dirt clods flying through the air. It was all fun and games until Lt. Scrivner made the mistake of throwing some dirt SGT Lachance's way, which happened to contain a few rocks in the mix.

The dirt and rocks collided against his chest. SGT Lachance looked up with fire in his eyes as he grabbed the lieutenant by the shirt. He was one of the guys in the platoon that was built like a brick house, and you didn't want to mess with him when he was in a bad mood. He must have been in one, as he glared at Lt. Scrivner, who now realized the mistake he had made.

"It's just a game," Lt. Scrivner said shakily in his defense, trying not to further anger the bear standing in front of him.

"I don't play games," SGT Lachance growled. The whole lot of men had gone quiet and were watching, wondering what he was going to do. The tension in the air could have settled all the dust. SGT Lachance, realizing it was probably not the best idea to physically alter the platoon leader's face, let him go and turned to walk away to let his anger off on something other than a commissioned officer.

Lt. Scrivner gave SFC Santos a worried look. SFC Santos just shrugged and had his normal smirk on his face. "Eh, he'll be alright," was all he said as he handed up another sandbag.

The men worked throughout the day until the sun reached the horizon and slowly fell out of sight. Only a few eight-foot Hescos were filled, but they were getting the process down. They laid a few pieces of plywood for a more level and sturdier base for the next layer of Hescos to be placed upon. Exhausted, they retired back under the parachute and into the mud classrooms of the school.

Along with the building of the towers, the men started to patrol the area they would now be calling home. The initial plan was to spend the winter months getting to know the area and documenting the locals, creating a type of census. They wanted to know who was who and where people were supposed to be; that way, if in the future they came across anyone they didn't know, or someone they did know far away from their field or village, they could question it.

To do this, the men used another expensive piece of equipment the Army had purchased—the Handheld Interagency Identity Detection Equipment (HIIDE). It was an extension of the Biometrics Automated Toolset System (BATS) the Army was attempting to employ. Basically, the men would go around and gather information from each individual—their name, age, where they lived, who their family was, fingerprints, iris scan, picture of their face, etc. This information would be entered into a database. The database contained information on known Taliban and Al Qaeda leaders and members so, if the men came across someone who was a High Value Target (HVT), they would know it.

The system was also supposed to recognize individuals who had already been entered into the system. So, if a fighting-age male who was already in the system from Paktika province wound up in the Arghandab River Valley, the men would be informed of this, and they could question what the individual was doing there, and possibly have the ANP detain them.

This seemed really cool and high tech but, like most of the expensive things the military spends their money on, it rarely ever worked. The HIIDE was like a big plastic camera with a touch screen on the back and a fingerprint reader on the top. The men had to go up to locals one by one and through their interpreter ask to take their information, a picture, an iris scan, and fingerprints. The locals didn't mind giving their name and information, but there was definitely some confusion when the men asked to take their fingerprints and iris scans. It was almost impossible to get a fingerprint off a farmer's hands. The dirt that had engrained itself in their skin from a lifetime of farming by hand did not cooperate with the fingerprint reader. The manual instructed them to use rubbing alcohol on the pad to help, but that never did the trick. The men would end up sitting there trying to get a dude's thumb to read until either they or the farmer would say "fuck it." The same thing would happen with the iris scan. The camera wasn't the greatest, especially after crossing a canal. To have a local sit there and stare into a lens that was being held in front of their face must have made them a little uneasy. The men mainly stuck to the bio section and the face photo before moving on.

The men also grew quite fond of their furry companion, Nepal. The dog would accompany them on their dismounted patrols through the valley and hang out with the men back at COP Tynes. It was nice having a pet, as it was a little reminder of home for a lot of the guys. Nepal would run up and down the fields, flushing out any villagers or farmers the men hadn't seen. They all thought it was hilarious, as the locals would come running for their lives as the mutt chased them, biting them on the ass if he ever were to catch them. The locals didn't appreciate it much, and Nepal did kind of give away their position, so the men ended up tying him up back home at Tynes when they went out. It was hard to get information and win the hearts and minds of the people when your dog was constantly attacking them, but it was funny to watch the children scatter upon the mention of Nepal. They came to know him by name.

Along with gathering information, the company commander, CPT Razuri, wanted to saturate the AO. Always having someone out somewhere between his three platoons of men would hinder the enemy's freedom of movement in the area. For Two Charlie, this would mean patrolling their AO at least three times a day. Two of these patrols would be during the day, to talk with locals and gather information, and one at night. The night patrol was mainly just setting up a Listening Post/Observation Post (LP/OP) where the men would hunker down in an orchard or an abandoned compound and listen and wait for any possible enemy night movement.

CPT Razuri referred to these patrols as "Hunter Killer" patrols, though the men never came across the enemy during them. The villagers for the most part went to sleep at night.

The men didn't always come up empty handed, however. On a few patrols they discovered older IEDs buried along the canals, to which they would have Explosive Ordnance Disposal (EOD) called out to blow the explosives in place. There weren't a lot of them out there, not nearly as many as the 2nd ID guys had implied, but just enough that the men decided to continue to climb walls and avoid paths, doors, and bridges as much as possible. What was weird was they all seemed to be deactivated, like they left the bomb in the ground but took the initiation device out. During a patrol to Lower Babur, the men came across stashes of weapons and ammo wrapped in trash bags and buried along a canal. They found some grenades, old Russian mortar rounds, etc. They would bring all they found back to COP Tynes and either blow it up or give it to the ANP if they could use it. The next couple of nights they would set up their Hunter Killer patrol LP/OPs in the area they found the stuff in hopes of coming across anyone who might come back for it or bury more. No one ever did. The fighters weren't in the valley, not yet at least.

As the men started to learn the area like the back of their hands, little details started popping out to them. Some perimeter walls contained rows of small holes in them, no more than a foot in diameter. These rows of holes were below knee-level along the paths on the outside of the walls, but when on the orchard side they were right about shoulder height and had a good field of view.

"What do you think these are?" SGT Brown asked, puzzled by the strange array. Each hole lined up with a row of grapes or pomegranate.

"Maybe they run irrigation hoses through them instead of pumping the water up and over the walls from the canals." Lt. Scrivner suggested.

"I don't know, you got a pretty good view outside the field through these," SGT Brown said while resting his rifle through the hole.

"Keep an eye out for them and try to avoid them." SGT Thomson told him.

SGT Brown scanned the other walls of the orchard. They each had a couple of holes in them. "Alright," SGT Brown said and continued. That would be a lot easier said than done.

It turned out the soldier that told the Two Charlie men they weren't supposed to be using Humvees anymore was indeed correct, and he had done what he said he was going to do and talked with the Battalion S4, who pushed it up the line.

Apparently, word got around about the loss the men had taken on 22 November and, long story short, they were assigned to get new vehicles. Young and Munoz, after they had been cleared from their recovery of their injuries from that day, were assigned to go through driver training for the brand-new military armored vehicle, the Military All-Terrain Vehicles (MATVs). These things were cool. They weren't slow, clunky, and top-heavy like the MRAPs or MAXPROs the rest of the Army was using. No, these things were built like uparmored monster trucks. And they drove and looked like monster trucks too. They had a long smooth hood that extended the front of the vehicle. The tires were huge, lifting the V-shaped hull of the cab high above the ground. The four doors on each side opened suicide-style to reveal the cab. The seats were suspended from the ceiling of the cab and were larger than the Humvees by a long shot. The trucks had a very short bed over the rear tires, packed to the top with boxes. A rack system surrounded the bed and a large spare tire hung from it. The turrets all had uparmor to protect the gunners with windows and rear-view mirrors to see behind them.

The Two Charlie guys convoyed out of Tynes to KAF to pick up their recovered men and get their new vehicles. It was a good day all round. SGT Thomson was the one signing for the MATVs. He was going over the checklist with one of the civilian contractors who was showing him everything he was signing for and walking him through how to use it. He opened the driver's seat door and climbed in. Everything was brand new and clean. The plastic wrap was still on the seats. He smiled with the biggest shit-eating grin.

"What?" The man asked, noticing his smile.

"I have never been in a military vehicle that had a new-car smell." SGT Thomson continued to smile.

The men loaded the MATVs and convoyed back to Tynes. Along Route Red Dog, there was a compound that a group of Special Forces Operational Detachment Alphas (ODA) had been operating out of with the Afghan National Army spec-ops. The men saw the vehicles and came out of the compound to stop the convoy. The ODA guys walked around the vehicles, checking them out. The Two Charlie guys were all a little jubilant as they exited their vehicles with smiles on their faces. Usually, they were the ones gawking over the cool-guy stuff the spec-ops guys got, not the other way around. The men soaked it up while they could, then got back in their vehicles and continued to COP Tynes.

Now, getting new vehicles doesn't come without a price. Since the rest of Charlie Company didn't have vehicles, Two Charlie would often become the company's bitch. They would get tasked out to help with Forward Support Company (FSC) tasks. Basically, they would pick up and deliver supplies, ammo, and sometimes mail for the company. SFC Santos started referring to these convoys as "Thunder Runs," after an Army physical-training exercise, and the name stuck with the rest of the guys. A Thunder Run usually took all day; the men would leave early in the morning and get back to COP Tynes under night vision. They weren't all bad though, as they got to go to KAF each time; while they were there, it was a good excuse to take a shower. The men hadn't had a proper shower for weeks. Their pants stood on their own from having so much dirt and sweat caked in them. All they could do was either use baby wipes to wipe off or have a buddy poke a hole in a water bottle cap and squeeze it over them while they lathered and rinsed. They were disgusting, so when they finally did get a chance to shower at KAF, they took full advantage. They disregarded the "5-minute shower" signs and took as long as they wanted, enjoying the hot water.

They also used this opportunity to enjoy what KAF had to offer. The boardwalk had a bunch of shops and places to eat, and it was always nice to stop by and get a fresh baguette from the French PX. Hell, the boardwalk even had a TGI Fridays on it. To them, it was Disneyworld, and whoever spent an entire deployment stationed there couldn't rightfully say they had been deployed to a combat theater. Not like they could.

Because the men had so little, and everyone on KAF had so much, they also took the opportunity to take things while there. Now, in the Army, there is no such thing as stealing, only "tactically acquiring." If it wasn't secured or being watched, then it wasn't important enough to whoever it belonged to. The men would sneak behind the big dining facilities and find pallets of goodies. Snacks, Gatorades, milk, candy—anything left unattended was fair game. SGT Knollinger even had the guys acquire weights and workout equipment one night for the gym they wanted to construct back at COP Tynes.

"Just go in there and everyone grab a weight. Make sure that someone gets a bench bar." He instructed. The men all snuck into the tent gym and saturated themselves among the other soldiers and airmen working out. One by one, each man snuck his way past the front desk out into the darkness with dumbbells, plates, workout bars, you name it. That gym was a little more empty the next morning.

When the men arrived back at COP Tynes, the other soldiers were excited to see the new vehicles and even more so to see their wounded buddies. They welcomed Young and Munoz back and showed them around the new home. The new vehicles came with a bunch of accessories, all of which were in the cardboard boxes stacked in the short beds of the vehicles. The Joes started removing these boxes and opening them, pulling out plastic-wrapped aid bags, mounting brackets, jacks, you name it, for the trucks. The dirt clearing in COP Tynes was littered with boxes and plastic bags. It was like an early Christmas for the men. SFC Santos smiled at the sight and realized Christmas was just around the corner.

The outpost continued to improve, as the men got more supplies from Terra Nova. They dug and filled more piss tubes and were even able to use the FOO money SSG Rosa had finally received to purchase plywood, two-by-fours, and nails from the locals to build with. Nobody knew where the heck in Afghanistan the locals got plywood, as there was no Home Depot down the road, but one day they showed up with a jingle truck full of the thinnest plywood the men had seen.

SGT Lachance looked at the material. The two-by-fours were very rough cut and the plywood looked like the wind could blow a hole through it but, hey, wood was wood. Beggars couldn't be choosers in Afghanistan. They unloaded it, paid the men, and began to get to work.

Doc Taylor, SGT Lachance, Rae, Ryan, and Young all had carpentry skills that came in handy. Doc Taylor designed an outhouse and a couple of the men threw it together. It turned out well and served its purpose, providing some privacy for the men relieving themselves. SGT Flannery had a go at constructing a second one, using any scrap wood he could find. He copied the one the other men had constructed exactly and was quite proud of how it turned out. The outhouses were a major upgrade for the men.

Knollinger got on with building his gym. They took the equipment they had acquired from KAF, and some of the scrap wood, and constructed a makeshift squat/bench rack in the blown-up mosque in the southwest corner of the outpost. It was a bit rickety—as it was just made from two by fours, nails, and duct tape—but it would do the trick and was better than nothing. The men now had a place to work out.

SGT Lachance and Ryan began designing a structure for the TOC and started planning on making rooms for the men. The intent was to use the arches of the vestibule to tie in the structure, having a hallway for each arch. This made three hallways where they could create bays on each side of the hallways.

SGT Lachance showed SFC Santos his initial plans. "Usually, each squad gets a room for their Joes and a room for the team leaders and squad leaders. At least that's how I've seen it everywhere else. I kind of want my own room, but I'm not the type of person who is just going to make a room for myself and then make everyone else share."

SFC Santos looked at the amateur sketch. "Can we just get everyone their own room?" he asked, looking at the pile of plywood and two-by-fours they had purchased.

"Yea, if that's what you want," SGT Lachance replied. "It will be more work, but it's not like we are going anywhere." He laughed and SFC Santos smiled. "We are going to need more nails though."

Christmas came early for Two Charlie this year. They were getting a new staff sergeant, SSG Loredo, to join the platoon. The platoon only had two E-6s as squad leaders, SSG Staley and SSG DeMeo. Third Squad's squad leader position was being held by one of the senior E-5s, SGT Thomson.

"You're losing your squad," SFC Santos said to SGT Thomson. "We are getting another E-6."

SGT Thomson didn't want to give up his squad but understood the politics of the military. He was an excellent soldier, very smart and knowledgeable in the skills necessary to be an effective infantryman. However, the First Sergeant always had it out for him, partly because he was part of Two Charlie, and the First Sergeant hated Two Charlie, but also because he wasn't much of a runner. He was a bigger man and running six miles every morning back at Fort Bragg at a sub-seven-minute pace was not something he was an expert on. To paratroopers, running was all they did. So, if you couldn't run, you were looked down upon. What SGT Thomson lacked in running, he made up for in rucking, as he was a rucking machine. SGT Thomson and the First Sergeant also got into it on a company patrol while they were at Masum Ghar. A small firefight broke out, and instead of the First Sergeant worrying about tactical advantage and maneuvering on the enemy, he questioned where SGT Thomson's eye protection was as he had removed it to see better. The ballistic eyeglasses would always fog up, and the men found themselves in a constant battle of deciding if they wanted to see, or if they wanted plastic glasses to maybe protect them. SGT Thomson hated being micromanaged and kind of told the First Sergeant he needed to just hang back in the rear of the formation and worry about not getting shot.

Regardless of all that, SSG Loredo outranked SGT Thomson. SSG Loredo had the rank, and he didn't. He would lose that battle every time. "Where am I going?" he asked SFC Santos.

"Well," SFC Santos said, thinking for a moment. The platoon leadership positions were all occupied at the time, making that question a difficult one to answer. SGT Thomson was a good leader worth holding on to. "What if we put you in charge of the ANP? You can oversee their training and monitor them on patrols. They will be your 'squad.'"

SGT Thomson thought about this for a moment. The ANP at the outpost had proven themselves to be quite undisciplined so far. The police chief, Bismullah, did not have a solid grip on his men. They came and went as they pleased, were hardly ever in their uniforms, and were constantly smoking hash while back at COP Tynes. They would regularly go out on patrol with bloodshot eyes, high as kites. There was a day-and-night difference between the COP Tynes ANP and the ANP force they had worked with at Masum Ghar. SGT Thomson knew it would be like herding cats, but what other option did he have.

The men prepped the trucks and made the short convoy over to Terra Nova to pick up their new squad leader on Christmas Eve. Terra Nova had had some improvements of its own since the men had been there last, as the Hesco wall perimeter had been expanded, allowing for a large HLZ to land helicopters, and there even was a couple fuel bladders for refueling vehicles. The headquarters element even got a few MAXPROs of their own; they weren't as impressive as the Two Charlie MATVs. They had more structures and tents set up, and it really seemed to be growing. A tall guide tower was erected and a camera with 360-degree rotation and zoom capability was installed at the top. It reminded the men of the tower from *The Lord of the Rings*, and they started to refer to it as the "eye in the sky."

"Johnny Nguyen, come here," SSG Rosa said. Nguyen had just pulled out a cigarette to light. He put it back in the pack and ran over. "Take a couple of the guys, see if you can find some nails and some other stuff we might need. Me and Knollinger are going to go see if we can get some more batteries." Nguyen nodded and started to scurry off when SSG Rosa caught him, "Hey, don't get caught," he added. The men had gotten quite good at acquiring things for their outpost and had been lucky so far.

McDaniel and SGT Cornelius made their way to the Conex boxes stacked along the Hesco wall. One of the containers wasn't locked, so they decided to see what was inside. They opened the large shipping container and walked in. It was full of random cardboard boxes full of cooking supplies and plasticware. A larger box was opened, so they decided to pry at its contents.

To both their surprise, the box contained what appeared to be a white plastic ice sculpture mold. It was about a meter wide and looked to be of an eagle with its wings spread wide.

"These motherfuckers have fucking ice sculptures over here?!" McDaniel said in disbelief. They didn't even have electricity at COP Tynes and these guys were making ice sculptures.

SGT Cornelius laughed. The sculpture was probably meant to represent the rank of lieutenant colonel, but he couldn't help but think the eagle reminded him of all the World War II Nazi Germany eagles on the Third Reich flags. He jokingly said, "Dude, they have an ice sculpture for the Führer." McDaniel laughed as he picked the mold up and went to load it into one of the trucks.

SGT Knollinger followed SSG Rosa into the TOC with a box of the platoon's used batteries. One of the headquarter NCOs, a TOC bitch, was monitoring the radios as the two men walked in. He had a nose that kind of reminded SGT Knollinger of a young Kevin Bacon.

"Where are your batteries?" SSG Rosa asked.

The soldier pointed over at the array of chargers on the table in the corner. SGT Knollinger went over and began taking the ones with green lights, indicating they were fully charged. He replaced the batteries he had taken off the chargers with the dead ones he had in his box. When he was done, there was nothing but red lights across the charging station.

"Why do you guys keep coming and taking all our batteries?" the TOC soldier asked, annoyed that he didn't have any charged batteries ready to go.

"You guys have two generators outside, we don't even have one. We don't have a way of charging these things," SGT Knollinger replied, irritated with the question as he took the box and left. SSG Rosa stayed as he had to do some paperwork for the FOO money the platoon had spent so far, and he was going to link up with the First Sergeant and CO and get introduced to SSG Loredo.

SGT Knollinger loaded up the box of charged batteries in his truck. He was just about to sit down when he noticed Nguyen and a few other soldiers, carrying boxes of nails and shrink-wrapped chocolate Gatorade drinks. SGT Knollinger smiled and got out of the truck. "Hurry up," he said, waving them onto the trucks. "Get that stuff loaded out of sight." He knew the men didn't have much time before the First Sergeant would come out with SSG Rosa and SSG Loredo.

They stowed the boxes and drinks under the seats and in every nook and cranny of the trucks. Just as they were putting the last case of drinks behind the ammo cans, SSG Rosa called out, "Hey, 2nd Platoon, hey, fall in!"

The men all piled out of the vehicles and gathered around in front of SSG Rosa. Beside him was the First Sergeant and SSG Loredo, a short, stocky man who carried himself quite professionally. His rig was tight and uniform, and he looked like he had been to combat before. He wore a 173rd patch on his right shoulder under his flag, as he had spent some time in the 173rd and deployed with them. He also did some time in a scout Long Range Surveillance (LRS) team as part of the 18th Airborne Corps. He was well acquainted as an infantryman and knew his stuff. He stood there next to the First Sergeant and SSG Rosa, not saying a word. He was quite intimidating despite how much shorter he was compared to the rest of the men.

"SSG Loredo, I believe that this is most, if not all, of Third Squad. Third Squad, SSG Loredo," the First Sergeant said, extending his hand out to present the new man. "I'll leave you to it." He walked away back into the TOC.

As soon as the First Sergeant was out of earshot, SSG Loredo asked the men, "He always like that?"

"Yeah, he isn't too fond of 2nd Platoon, sergeant," SGT Knollinger answered, extending a hand to shake SSG Loredo's. "I'm Knollinger, I'm your Bravo team leader." SSG Loredo examined SGT Knollinger up and down as he shook his hand.

SGT Brown and the rest of the men all introduced themselves, and SSG Loredo examined each one of them. He shot questions to all the Joes, like why they wore their equipment the way they did or what the rate of fire of their weapon system was. They all answered to his liking. He could tell they were a pretty tight-knit group of guys and were no longer Cherries at this point.

"Well," he said, "Let's get on to COP Tynes. I'd like to meet the rest of the platoon."

The men got back to their vehicles and loaded up. SSG Loredo climbed in the back seat of SGT Knollinger's truck. He had a couple boxes of nails on the floorboard blocking his feet. "What's with the nails?" he asked as he moved them out of the way. Nguyen hopped out of the driver's seat to help him.

"Those little guys? I wouldn't worry about those little guys. Just a little resupply for the outpost," SGT Knollinger said with a smile as they did their final radio checks in the trucks and started to roll out back to COP Tynes.

Now Christmas Day comes but once a year and, fortunately for the men of Two Charlie, they had Dad to thank for that. The platoon was all up early that day as they were assigned to do another Thunder Run for Battalion. SGT Knollinger had just begun to shave, using the side-view mirror of the old Humvee, when he heard his name being called. "What?" he shouted back.

"SFC Santos wants you." A soldier's voice faintly came from under the parachute.

"Tell him I'll be right there." SGT Knollinger made his final swipes with the razor and put it in the cup of water on the top of the door. He didn't even clean his face of the remaining shaving cream. He approached the parachute and heard laughter. He walked around the edge to see SFC Santos wearing a Santa hat, and a small Christmas tree set up on a table. He was sitting on a green army cot and had a box full of stockings, each one with a different name on it. He had in his hand one that said "Knollinger," and he was wearing his stereotypical smirk. He patted his thigh with his empty hand, "Come sit on Santa's lap and get your stocking, Knolly," he said, grinning ear to ear.

Knollinger looked at him, confused. It was never easy to tell if SFC Santos was serious or just messing with them. This was one of those times. He leaned in to grab the stocking. Santos moved it out of his reach.

"Come here," he said softly, waving closer.

Knollinger got closer until SFC Santos grabbed him and sat him on his lap. "Smile for the FRG," he said as he smiled for the camera SGT Maher was holding. The Family Readiness Group (FRG) must have organized the stockings. SFC Santos's wife was the head of the group for Charlie Company. She must have wanted pictures of the guys to share with the families back home. SGT Knollinger smiled awkwardly as they took a picture of him receiving his stocking. One by one, they called guys in until everyone got their stocking. SFC Santos definitely took the opportunity to mess with the guys during this whole time, and the guys really enjoyed it. Nguyen and Jackson posed for a picture with SFC Santos holding them in the air. Everyone knew SGT Maher hated hugs, so SFC Santos had First Squad hold him down to give him one.

"Come on, Maher Bear," he said as he slowly made his way to the pile of soldiers that were holding him down and gave him a hug. It put a smile on the guys' faces, maybe a black eye or two as well, and made Christmas morning a little less cold and muddy.

The men spent the rest of the day on another Thunder Run for the battalion. The Army likes to try to boost morale for the troops on holidays, especially Thanksgiving and Christmas. These are the ones where being away from family hits the hardest. So, what the Army does is try to give everyone a warm meal that day. Much like on Thanksgiving, mermites full of turkey, mashed potatoes, carrots, green beans, etc., are prepared for the troops. The only problem was getting it to them. Two Charlie, with their cool new MATVs, yet again got tasked out with a Thunder Run to pick up the food and deliver it to different COPs throughout the valley.

Along with the other logistic runs they were sent on, they were gone all day. SGT Knollinger looked over at his driver, Winston, in the truck. He was dozing off, sucking to stay awake. He and the other drivers had been driving for over twelve hours now. SGT Knollinger laughed. Winston heard him and was startled awake.

"Sorry, Sergeant," Winston said, sitting up straight in his seat.

"Dude," SGT Knollinger said, "I got you." He was bored himself and wanted to do something besides sit in the passenger seat. He got out of the truck and opened Winston's door. Winston climbed down and took SGT Knollinger's seat so he could drive the remainder of the trip.

"Thanks, Sergeant," Winston said as he sank into his new seat.

The guys on the convoy didn't get back to COP Tynes until late that night, or possibly into the early morning hours of the next day. They unloaded their mermites of food, sat them out under the parachute, and began to eat their cold Christmas meal by the fire.

The next morning, the men were woken up to the headquarters element at their front door. They weren't expecting them so it must have meant one of two things: they either needed something from them or that they were in trouble for something. SGT Brown and SGT Knollinger ran through the mud rooms where the guys were sleeping and woke them all up and ensured they all got in the proper uniform. "First Sergeant is here. Get up," they said as they kicked the cots of the guys who were still asleep.

The First Sergeant came storming into the compound. He walked right by all the men huddled around the fire under the parachute and didn't say a word to them.

He went straight into the TOC. They now knew which of the two reasons he was there for. They were in trouble. For what, they were about to find out.

McDaniel and SGT Cornelius looked at each other. "The Führer!" they both said. He must have somehow found out they had taken it. The two ran to their room where they had been keeping the mold. They grabbed it and snuck it out back past all the men to the nearest unfilled Hesco. The two men frantically began shoveling dirt into the Hesco with their small E-tools to hide the evidence of their theft.

The First Sergeant's face looked irate as he scanned the men in the TOC. "Where is Santos?" he asked sternly.

SGT Farquhar got out of his seat. "I'll go get him, First Sergeant," he said as he slid past to exit the room.

"Where is your cover?" the First Sergeant yelled at him, as SGT Farquhar didn't place his patrol cap (PC) on his head as he left the room. SGT Farquhar acted like he didn't hear him as he left to retrieve SFC Santos. His PC was most likely in his ruck by his cot. The men never wore them at COP Tynes, the only time they did was when they went to other outposts on Thunder Runs, or on the rare occasion higher leadership ever came out to COP Tynes. The First Sergeant had got the jump on them this morning.

SGT Farquhar returned to the TOC with SFC Santos and had swung by his cot to grab his PC. SFC Santos was unprepared for the First Sergeant's unannounced visit. He knew this wasn't going to be good; the last thing he wanted was to get chewed out first thing in the morning.

"Get your men outside, I want to talk with all of them," the First Sergeant scolded SFC Santos.

SFC Santos looked at SGT Farquhar to signal to do as instructed. He followed him out of the TOC. The men formed up in the clearing in front of SFC Santos and waited whatever lashing they were about to receive for whatever it was they had done this time. SGT Cornelius and McDaniel were the last to join the formation. They were covered in sweat. The rest of the men looked at them, confused, but locked up as they noticed the First Sergeant approaching the formation.

He walked up in front of the formation with a box of nails in his hands. Uh-oh. The men put two and two together. SGT Cornelius and McDaniel looked at each other and let out a sigh of relief, but the rest of the men dreaded the punishment they were about to receive. They had been lucky with their tactical acquiring up until this point. Looks like it was finally going to catch up to them. They had taken from the wrong person this time.

"SSG Rosa you aren't a part of this, you fall out of this formation. And SSG Loredo, you haven't been here long enough to be corrupted by these lowly men. You fall out too." The First Sergeant announced. SSG Rosa and SSG Loredo looked at each other, fell out and walked away. They remained in earshot, however, to hear what was to be said. "Just when I thought that you couldn't get any lower, you go and pull this." He held up the box of nails in his hand. "Stealing from your own company."

He looked the men up and down. They weren't ashamed of what they had done, just the fact they had gotten caught. Plus, they didn't take all the nails, they had left a few boxes. It looked like they were done with them at Terra Nova anyway.

"What a bunch of shitbags. I am disgusted to call you my own. If you would have asked, we would have given you some. Why you felt obligated to steal them is beyond me. It just goes to show how corrupt you have become. It's time to cut the head off the snake. Now I don't know which of you was behind all this, but I have my suspicions." He continued as he walked in front of SGT Knollinger. "Knollinger, pack up your shit, you're going to A Co."

SGT Knollinger's jaw dropped. He turned to look at SFC Santos, who had the same shocked expression on his face as well. This could not be happening.

"Don't look at him, I've already decided. Get your shit. You're coming with me."

The men tried to keep their minds off losing SGT Knollinger to the "nailgate" scandal by staying busy and beginning the construction of the great wood structure they would call home with the nails the First Sergeant didn't find and take back. SGT Lachance and Ryan got on to nailing the frame of the floor together and then stood up the wall frames. They had the other men do the grunt work of nailing on the paper-thin plywood after the framing was erected.

"Just put a couple nails through the plywood," SGT Lachance said, handing SGT Thomson a handful of nails and a hammer. SGT Thomson took the nail, sized it up with the hammer and swung. His first swing missed the nail and went through the plywood. "Jesus," SGT Lachance said as he took away the hammer from SGT Thomson. "Fucking Bamm-Bamm. Go do something else." He relieved him of his construction duties and forbade him from helping in the future. SGT Thomson went to help the other guys fill sandbags.

SSG Rosa shook his head and laughed. "That's Tommy for ya."

The first "wing" floor was laid down and the first few rooms constructed. The first room would be the new TOC, which they kind of built around the existing mud structure; right next to it would be the platoon leader's room. Now, SGT Lachance swears it was not done on purpose, but the cant of the roof of the TOC sort of drained right over the room adjacent to it. It was a little humorous that it was Lt. Scrivner's room, so he didn't put a lot of effort into fixing it.

Row by row, the men constructed the wood structure and, as each wing was completed, men would claim their rooms and move into them. It was super nice having their own little space; it was a huge morale boost for the men, even if it was just having privacy behind one-eighth-inch-thick plywood walls.

Plywood was nailed on top for a makeshift roof as they didn't have enough wood to complete a proper canted roof for the whole structure—that would come later. At least this would keep the sun off the men and give them shelter from the drizzle they had been experiencing. It was better than the parachute.

The men had worked hard on the wood structure and filling Hescos for a week now, and SFC Santos wanted to do something special for New Year's. They were tired of eating MREs so, while on patrol, SFC Santos flagged down a goat herder. He had the platoon's interpreter ask the man how much he would sell two goats for. The old man listed his price and SFC Santos had SSG Rosa give him the money. Lt. Scrivner and SSG Rosa both carried a goat over their shoulder back to COP Tynes that day.

The men were excited, not just that they were going to get a hot fresh meal, but that they would get to kill and butcher the animals. They argued over how to go about killing them.

"We can use the power tools," SGT Culver suggested vilely, "Cut its head off with the reciprocating saw."

"No, you're not ruining our saw," Doc Taylor replied.

"What about a grenade?" Nguyen continued.

"No! There wouldn't be anything left to eat," Doc protested again.

One of the platoon's interpreters saw the commotion the men were causing with their argument. He walked over to them and asked what was going on.

"We are trying to figure out a way to kill the goats to eat," Doc Taylor said.

"Oh, you must do it the Muslim way," the interpreter said. He put his hand on the goat's head and began to pray in Arabic. He then pulled out a knife from his pocket and slit the goat's throat. Bright red blood began to flow from the wound and pool on the ground as the goat struggled to get away. The interpreter held it until its struggling stopped.

This satisfied the men, and the arguing stopped. Doc Taylor, Lovelace, Thompson, and Ryan were the platoon rednecks who probably were the only ones with experience dressing an animal. They hung the goat up in the gym from one of the rafters and pulled their knives out to skin and quarter the animal. The other interpreters came out of their hooch and joined them. They suggested they cook dinner so the men could taste an authentic Afghan meal. To the men's surprise, it wasn't that bad. Things were getting better at COP Tynes.

The next day, the goat herder showed up at the front entrance of the outpost. Lt. Scrivner, along with an interpreter and a few of the ANP, went out to ask what he wanted. The man seemed to be yelling at the interpreter, however most Afghans kind of spoke in that manner, so it wasn't anything unusual—not until the interpreter told Lt. Scrivner what he was saying.

"Uh, he says he wants more money for his goats."

"What?" Lt. Scrivner said. "No, we asked him how much he wanted, and he named his price. We didn't even haggle him down from that. We gave him his asking price."

The interpreter relayed this message to the herder to which the man replied. "He says that he did not know we were going to kill the goats, uh, so he wants more money."

"What did he think, we were going to start our own herd? Tell him no," Lt. Scrivner said. The interpreter relayed the message once more and the old man looked up in arms. He yelled at Scrivner, whipped his shemagh over his shoulders, and turned and walked away.

Scrivner went back into the COP and into the TOC. "What was that about?" SFC Santos asked.

"The man wanted more money for the goats." Lt. Scrivner said.

"Did you give him any more?" SFC Santos inquired.

"No," Lt. Scrivner replied, laughing under his breath. Santos didn't reply. They just sat there in silence for a few moments. "Should I have?" Lt. Scrivner finally asked.

"Nah, it'll be fine," SFC Santos said with a big smile. The two of them went back to silence and worked on what they were working on. "That, or we just made ourselves a powerful enemy."

SGT Knollinger spent a week with the headquarters element at Terra Nova waiting to be shipped out to Alpha Company. The entire time he was at the mercy of the First Sergeant, who had him doing tasks for SGT Rod, a cocky NCO. He had never deployed before but, because he had his Ranger tab, he fell above a lot of the other lower NCOs in the hierarchy of things. It was kind of dumb really. SGT Rod had him filling sandbags and doing a lot of the grunt work for the headquarters element, all while treating him like shit. It was hell on earth. SGT Knollinger didn't mind filling Hescos at COP Tynes, but he hated doing it for these assholes. He just wanted them to send him away already so he could get away from them.

The worst part was that a couple of times he could see the Two Charlie guys roll up to Terra Nova in their vehicles to grab supplies. He was forbidden from talking with them, so all he could do was fill sandbags and watch them from afar. Never had he been angrier than he had been that last week.

He'd spent all New Year's Day filling sandbags and was exhausted. He walked into the tent they had him staying in and collapsed on his cot. The lights were off, as most of the soldiers in that tent pulled TOC duty during the night and were asleep. He laid there and tried to join them.

Just as he was about to fall asleep, the tent door opened. The outside light blinded SGT Knollinger, and he quickly closed his eyes again. He rolled over in his cot. If this was SGT Rod coming to get him to do more shit, he was going to lose it. He wouldn't be going to Alpha Company; he would be going to jail for beating a fellow NCO to a pulp.

"Knollinger," a familiar voice said from the piercing light. It wasn't SGT Rod. SGT Knollinger rolled back over and glared into the sunlight. He knew that silhouette anywhere. He had seen it on countless night patrols. He could pick that man out anywhere. It was SFC Santos. "Get your shit. You're coming home."

Nobody knew what SFC Santos had to do to convince the First Sergeant to get SGT Knollinger back, and no one really cared. The platoon was back to normal and January kicked off another month in the valley. One brisk morning, SGT Thomson sat down to take his morning dump in one of the outhouses. He was just thinking how great these things were when he heard a very loud crack come from underneath him and, to his surprise, the board on which he sat had just snapped in two, causing him to plunge down into the contents of the shit can below. He erupted from the outhouse, breaking the door off the hinges. He immediately began stripping his clothes from his body, because he thought that was the right thing to do and ran around the outpost pleading for help. The men watched as this helpless large naked man walked around the outpost with a massive shit streak on his ass and up his lower back. They exploded with laughter.

"Help me get it off," SGT Thomson pleaded as he chased them around with a pack of baby wipes in his hands. None of them responded, as they couldn't even stand, they were laughing so hard.

"Nobody is going to help a man covered in shit and cum!" McDaniel yelled over the laughter that grew louder with that comment. "Oh, yeah, no! It's just me beating off in there, ya lying filthy animals," he continued.

"There's no cum in here, it's purely shit. It's a fresh barrel," SGT Thomson yelled at the men. They continued to laugh and ignore his pleads for help. "Where's Doc Taylor?"

Doc Taylor came out from the schoolhouse and saw the men laughing hysterically, then realized what they were laughing so hard at. He smiled. "What the fuck did you do?"

"You need to clean me!" SGT Thomson told him.

"The fuck I do!" Doc Taylor replied. There was no way he was getting anywhere near him.

"This is a medical emergency, I could get infections," SGT Thomson protested.

Doc took a second to think that statement over. He wasn't wrong; if SGT Thomson did get infected from this, it would cause problems for him later. He sighed, unable to come up with a good excuse to get out of helping the poor bastard. "God damn it," he said, taking the packet of baby wipes from him. Yeah, everything was back to normal.

CHAPTER 5

# The Drug Deal Trade

January came to the valley, ushering in signs of new life. The men started noticing the small leaf buds more and more as they continued to patrol the AO. More and more farmers started returning to their fields, prepping for the spring season. The signs of a new Arghandab were all showing their early stages of emergence. Spring would arrive in another month or two. Change was in the air.

Nepal had proven time and time again that he hated the locals. He needed to be held back if villagers came to the outpost and would even go after the ANP if they turned their backs. It was like he was protecting the Two Charlie men. He made it evident he did not trust the Afghan people, and his people were the American soldiers. Who could blame him? The Two Charlie men fed him, pet him, even let him sleep in their rooms at night. The Afghans threw rocks at him and probably beat him. He was probably suffering from a little PTSD of his own, which is probably why he fit in with the men so well. But as much as the Two Charlie men loved him, it was hard to deny he was becoming quite problematic if unattended.

Initially, the ANP's response to Nepal was to get a bigger dog on their side of the outpost to protect them. They brought in what the men referred to as a "bear dog", a huge Russian Caucasian shepherd-looking dog. This dog was pretty lazy and ended up liking the Two Charlie men and Nepal anyway since they would come over and feed him, though it was kind of terrifying to go take a piss at night and turn around to literally be face-to-face with a monster. It was like *The Sandlot* movie, but in real life.

The bear dog didn't stay around for long, and the ANP went back to just hating Nepal. It wasn't until Nepal bit Bismullah that they finally acted. The ANP chief tied him up and threw him in the back of one of their pickups. He flew out of the outpost with the rest of his men as the Two Charlie men watched from the guard towers.

"What are they doing with Nepal?" Young asked the SOG over the radio.

"Beats me," SGT Maher replied.

An hour or so later, the ANP returned. Nepal was not in the bed of the truck. Bismullah told the men he drove him down to another ANP station a few miles away and left him there. The Two Charlie men were pissed. They demanded he bring him back. Bismullah refused and walked back into the ANP section of the outpost.

The men got over the loss of their dog, as there wasn't anything they could really do about it. They hoped he was happy where he was, chasing Afghans and biting the shit out of them. To the men's surprise, about three days later, Nepal found his way home. The men were happy to have their companion back and filled his stomach with some warm food. Bismullah was less than thrilled with this and decided to get rid of Nepal for good this time. That afternoon he threw down a large piece of meat for Nepal to find, meat he had filled with ground-up glass. Nepal never said no to a hot meal, so he gobbled it down.

The following days, Nepal was not himself. He walked hunched over, like his stomach was killing him. He got more and more lethargic and wound up not wanting to move on the second day. The men didn't know what to do. They asked Doc Taylor to help him, but he was a medic, not a veterinarian. There was nothing he could do. Instead of watching their friend suffer, they finally decided to put him down on the third day of him being sick.

COP Tynes continued to improve, as the men received a generator to power the TOC. This also meant they would have to do additional runs to Terra Nova for fuel, but it was worth it. Rae, being the oldest man in the platoon with the most life experience and kind of an ultimate handyman, helped wire it up. Initially, he ran wires so the radios and computers of the TOC could have constant power and they wouldn't need to continue to swap out their batteries.

"Hey, Rae," SFC Santos said, "if we get you outlets and more wire, could you run them and install one in each of the rooms?"

"I don't see why not. I'll have to set up a breaker, but I think I can get it done," Rae replied.

"Get me a list of everything you need," SFC Santos replied. He was glad to have Rae as one of the guys. Rae was smart as hell and there wasn't anything he couldn't make happen.

They were able to get the wire and supplies Rae needed but fell short on the breaker box. That was no big deal, Rae was able to MacGyver one out of nuts and bolts and other scrap metal he found lying around and, much to the surprise of the other men, it worked. Rae and Young ran wires through the halls and installed an outlet in each man's room.

Santos looked over Rae's contraption. Not having a lot of electrical work knowledge, the appearance of the nuts and bolts soldered to make and break connections in an ammo box was a little terrifying to him. "You're not going to start a fire with this thing are you, Rae?" he asked wide eyed.

Rae smiled at him. "Nah, it should be okay," he said as he went on to explain the layout of what he had created, pointing things out to Santos.

Santos had a very unsure look on his face, but he trusted Rae knew what he was doing. He hadn't failed them yet. "Nobody touches this thing but you, Rae. I don't want anybody getting electrocuted."

Now they had power, they could dust off the computers they hadn't touched since Masum Ghar, and unpack the Playstation to play games during the night. SFC Santos would drag guys into SSG Rosa's room to play *Call of Duty* with him. He had to keep his skills up so he could play with his son when he went home on leave.

They could also finally keep and refrigerate food, which meant no more MREs. They hooked up the fridge and microwave they had taken from Masum Ghar in the common vestibule area of the school. This had been where guys would leave snacks and other things they had gotten in their mail or received in an FSC clip. The usual muffins, Gatorade, and beef jerky packets the Army provided were all in boxes for the men to pick through along with candy and other things the guys had got in the mail. SFC Santos was now able to order meat and freezer foods for the platoon, and eventually a freezer Conex was delivered to them on an FSC clip. The men could finally microwave a breakfast sandwich in the morning or make a cup of coffee. Things were looking up for Two Charlie.

SSG Loredo took it upon himself to organize the random assortment of foods in the common area so it wasn't just piled in boxes all over. They built tables to put the food on so the mice had a harder time getting to them. He made a sign that read "Loredo's Kitchen" and hung it above the door next to the fridge.

"Loredo's Kitchen, huh?" SGT Knollinger asked him, laughing.

"Yeah," SSG Loredo replied. "This is my kitchen!"

SSG Loredo made his place in 2nd Platoon and had come to be known as "The Task Master" among the men. If they weren't on patrol, SSG Loredo would have them working. From sunup to sundown, they were always doing some kind of work. He had them fill sandbags to fill a Hesco wall inside the COP to protect the wood structure from getting peppered by any enemy indirect fire. He made them dig out a new trash pit out back and extend the outer perimeter wall to the north. They moved the Conex from outside the outpost to inside the outpost so Doc Taylor could have an aid station to treat people in. He was always finding things to improve on, and he was one of the hardest-working men they knew. It was a little overwhelming sometimes.

"Hey, Bowman!" SSG Loredo yelled through the wood structure.

"Yeah?" Bowman hesitantly replied.

"Grab some guys, we need to move this tower," SSG Loredo explained.

"What?" Bowman said, not particularly to him just thinking out loud. He climbed out of his bed and left his room to see what he was talking about. He followed SSG Loredo to Tower Two and climbed up with him.

"See, look," SSG Loredo said manning the 240 machine gun in the tower like he was about to engage the enemy. He turned the weapon to the east down Route Red Dog. "That wall is in the way. I can't get a good field of fire down the road from here," he said pointing at the mud wall that stuck out from the khalat and ran parallel to the road. He climbed out of the front of the tower and onto the Hescos. "If we bring it out here then you have a perfect view down the road."

Bowman just looked at him. "You want us to move the tower three feet to the south?"

"Yeah," SSG Loredo replied. "Go get some guys."

For as much as SSG Loredo put men to work, and the men hated him for it, he at least was always out there working with them. They couldn't hold that against him. He was always out there filling sandbags with the guys, and usually filling two or three sandbags to their one. The Joes got breaks pulling tower guard, while he would be out there all day, working hard with the men to extend a wall, or to move a tower three feet to the south.

"COP Tynes, this is Charlie Six." A call came over the radio from Terra Nova in the TOC.

SGT Farquhar was on SOG duties and grabbed the hand mic to reply. "Charlie Six, this is COP Tynes, send it."

"Roger, are Two Six and Two Five available? I need to speak with them directly, an issue has come up," Charlie Six said.

"Stand by," SGT Farquhar replied. He walked out of the TOC to snag up Lt. Scrivner and SFC Santos; both had just gotten up and were conducting their usual morning rituals. Scrivner was sitting in his room, so he had heard the radio transmission come over and was on his way, passing SGT Farquhar in the hall. "Have you seen Sergeant Santos?" SGT Farquhar asked.

"Check the gym," Lt. Scrivner offered as he walked into the TOC.

SGT Farquhar made his way to the blown-up mosque, where he found SSG Rosa and SGT Knollinger getting some sets in before starting their tasks for the day. "You guys see Sergeant Santos?" he asked as SGT Knollinger grunted, pushing up his last set on the bench. SSG Rosa spotted him and guided the bar back on the wood rest, the whole rack shaking as it took on the weight.

"Right there," SSG Rosa said, pointing to the corner of the gym. SFC Santos had been doing dips on the dip bar.

He dismounted the shaky contraption made of wood and spare piping and walked over. "What's up, Farquhar?"

"Charlie Six wants you on the radio," SGT Farquhar replied.

"OK," he said, throwing his sweat towel over his shoulder and joined SGT Farquhar in walking to the TOC. "He say what it pertained to?"

"Nope, didn't say a thing," SGT Farquhar replied.

"Great," SFC Santos uttered. "What did we do now?" He joined Lt. Scrivner in the TOC.

"Charlie Six, this is Two Six, Two Five and myself are ready for your transmission. Go ahead and send it," Lt. Scrivner said over the hand mic.

"Roger Two Six, looks like we are going to have to rearrange the platoons a little bit. We had an incident happen with Three Charlie. We'll talk more when I see you, but until then we are to stand down operations until this gets dealt with. How copy?" CPT Razuri came sternly over the radio.

"Stand down, sir?" SFC Santos asked.

"Roger, stand down on patrols. A headquarters element and myself will be heading your way around noon. We will speak then. Charlie Six out." The radio went silent.

SFC Santos and Lt. Scrivner just looked at each other, puzzled. SFC Santos looked at SGT Farquhar. "Let the guys know Charlie Six is on his way. Have them clean up and look presentable. Tell SSG Staley that you guys won't be patrolling this morning."

"Roger," SGT Farquhar said as he left to relay the word to his squad leader and the rest of the guys.

Charlie Six came to COP Tynes that afternoon with an entourage of leadership from First Platoon. The situation was as follows: a Kiowa helicopter flying over COP Nolen noticed marijuana plants growing on the roof of the building. They called it up, thinking it was the ANP in the compound growing it and reported it to company to investigate it. Upon further investigation, the plants did not end up belonging to the ANP. Some Three Charlie men had planted them and had been growing and smoking them. After an investigation, it boiled down to three main perpetrators who were punished by being chaptered out of the Army. There were other culprits, however Charlie Company couldn't lose any more men. The others were to be separated and moved out of the platoon, and their places needed to be filled. Moving the Three Charlie men to One Charlie wouldn't suffice according to battalion command, as they were both at COP Nolen and nothing would really change. Instead, the Three Charlie guys would be sent to Two Charlie, and Two Charlie would send men to fill their places.

On top of this, the leadership from One Charlie along with the Headquarters element would be searching the rooms and belongings of the men of Two Charlie to ensure there was no contraband present there as well. They dumped bags out, went through equipment, checked out guard towers, the Full Monty until they were satisfied the men had nothing.

It was the first time a lot of One Charlie guys had seen COP Tynes, so they spent most of the time asking about the wood structure and complaining about how good they had it there compared to COP Nolen. The Two Charlie guys just nodded and waved, waiting for the manhunt to subside.

When they finally left, CPT Razuri gave Lt. Scrivner and SFC Santos this bit of information: the men of Two Charlie would receive four of the Three Charlie guys involved in the investigation. This didn't necessarily mean they were guilty of anything, just named in the investigation. In return, Two Charlie would send five of their own to Three Charlie. The specifics were a staff sergeant, two sergeants, and two Joes. The staff sergeant was already chosen for them. They wanted SSG Staley, as SSG Loredo had just gotten to the platoon, and no one really wanted SSG DeMeo. SSG Rosa had been grandfathered into Second Platoon, as he had been a part of it since what seemed the beginning of time. Plus, he was the platoon's FOO representative so moving him would implement even more logistical problems. The sergeants and Joes to be moved could be determined internally among the Two Charlie men and approved by Company. They had 24 hours to make their decisions, and for those chosen men to be packed and ready to make the move.

That evening was a somber one at COP Tynes as morale sank to an all-time low. This one was out of SFC Santos's hands; he couldn't keep guys from leaving this time. No one wanted to leave Two Charlie. It had become their home, their family. To some of the Joes, it had become the only family they had ever known. It was the same for some of the team leaders; it was almost the equivalent of a death sentence to the men.

Some of the discussion became heated as team leaders were fighting to keep their Joes.

"They aren't taking my SAW gunner," SGT Brown protested to SSG Loredo.

"They need a SAW gunner," SSG Loredo said.

"I don't care, they aren't taking mine," SGT Brown protested as he stormed off to his room. SGT Brown was one of the guys who was ineligible for the trade as well because he had been moved to Two Charlie right before the beginning of deployment from Three Charlie. It really sucked, and each team leader felt the same and fought for his men. You spend so much time together and training them up to be a good soldier and how you want them. The guys just worked well together as it was and getting someone else would be like adding another piece to a puzzle, one that may or may not fit.

Two men had decided to volunteer as tribute—SGT Culver and one of the other guys also named Young. SGT Culver had served with the 173rd in his prior deployment and had two good friends over at COP Nolen from that deployment. He would be leaving his friends in Two Charlie, but not for nothing. The other Young just wanted to get away from SSG DeMeo so, as soon as he found out SSG DeMeo wasn't going to be traded, he jumped on the opportunity to get out of his squad. The rest of the platoon decided they would send Howe over with them, as he hadn't proven to be the greatest fit for the platoon. It all boiled down to the second non-commissioned officer (NCO) that needed to be sent, the second sergeant.

The NCOs of Two Charlie had all become a close bunch, and they pretty much ran the platoon. None of the remaining sergeants would budge on the notion. This was their family. They weren't leaving.

"Bragg?" SFC Santos asked.

SGT Bragg had come with SGT Culver from the 173rd, however he was in a different platoon from Culver during that deployment, so wasn't close to the guys SGT Culver knew. "Nope," was all SGT Bragg replied. Two Charlie was all he knew in the 82nd.

"Maher?" SFC Santos turned his smile to SGT Maher.

SGT Maher had come from the 173rd as well but felt exactly how SGT Bragg did. His home was here with Two Charlie. He didn't even verbally reply, just shook his head.

"Farquhar?" SFC Santos continued.

"Ain't no fucking way," SGT Farquhar snapped.

"Knolly?" SFC Santos asked, knowing the answer. SGT Knollinger just looked at him. SFC Santos didn't know what to do. He didn't want to make any of them leave, as they had all had not only proven themselves to be good team leaders and valuable assets to the platoon but had also been a big part of the family. There was no easy way to do it. He glanced over at SGT Thomson; he was wearing a beanie hat. "Give me your hat," he said, reaching out his hand.

SGT Thomson obliged, removing his hat, and giving it to SFC Santos, who walked into the TOC with it. He ripped a piece of paper out of a Rite in the Rain notebook and started ripping it into smaller pieces. He began writing names down on each piece and putting it into the hat. "We draw," he said. "It's the only fair way I can think of."

SGT Farquhar laughed and headed to his room. "Let me know who you pick," he said as he closed the door behind him. He had lightened the mood and been the comic relief for the platoon alongside McDaniel, so he was convinced that because he could make Santos laugh that he didn't even put his name in the hat. There was no way SFC Santos was going to get rid of him.

The rest of the men waited as their future relied on a piece of paper in a hat. SFC Santos slowly put his hand in the hat, stirred it around, and pulled one of the pieces out. He cautiously unfolded it and showed it to the group. In very small print, the paper read, "Farquhar."

The men all let out a sigh of relief, but at the same time felt guilt in the pit of their stomachs. Not one of them wanted to leave, but they all didn't want to see a brother go either. SFC Santos took the piece of paper and sighed as he walked to knock on Farquhar's door.

"Yep," SGT Farquhar replied to the knock.

SFC Santos walked in with a serious look on his face. The guys never really got good at being able to tell if SFC Santos was being serious or just messing with them. This was one of those times for SGT Farquhar. "Pack your stuff, you're moving," was all SFC Santos said.

SGT Farquhar's stomach ached. There was no way. He sat up and looked at the piece of paper SFC Santos presented to him as reality sunk in. He was the last victim of the drug deal trade.

The drug deal trade had left a sour taste in the mouths of the guys of Two Charlie. They hadn't done anything wrong, and yet they had taken another loss. It was nowhere near the loss they had taken on 22 November, but similar in that they would no longer have a few good men around. The frustration was short lived, much like every other emotion in the valley.

With the loss of some, there was a gain of some too, and a restructuring of the platoon occurred yet again. Two Charlie hadn't just got the four guys from Three Charlie. They were expecting three more brand-new soldiers they would be picking up within the week, their new "Cherries."

A staff sergeant from Three Charlie, SSG Craumer, would take SSG Staley's place in First Squad as squad leader. SGT Bragg would move from Weapons Squad to First Squad Alpha team to take over SGT Farquhar's team (consisting now of Young, Neenan, and Nguyen). SGT Maher would be First Squad Bravo team leader with Rae, McCune, and one of the Cherries.

Two more guys from Three Charlie, Figueroa and Barthel, were sent to Second Squad. SSG DeMeo now had SGT Flannery as his Alpha team leader and SGT McPherson as his Bravo. Alpha consisted of Leonard, Figueroa, and another Cherry. Bravo consisted of Barthel, Munoz, and Thompson.

Not much changed in Third Squad. SSG Loredo was still their squad leader, with SGT Brown and SGT Knollinger as Alpha and Bravo team leaders. SGT Brown had Nichols, Lovelace, and Winston under him while SGT Knollinger had Dru, Jackson, and Ryan. Godard was moved from SAW gunner to RTO to replace Jackson.

Bowman and Danziger were moved into Weapons Squad to become gun team leaders with SSG Rosa still as the Weapons Squad's squad leader. McDaniel and Rostran remained in Weapons Squad, and the last guy from Three Charlie, Stegic, was put in with them. They would also get one of the new Cherries. SGT Thomson was still assigned to work with the ANP, and SGT Cornelius and SGT Lachance were still the platoon's FOs. Doc Taylor remained the platoon medic.

The Three Charlie guys settled in, and it became business as usual. Squads continued to patrol, and improvements continued to be made. Just when they thought they had seen the last of change, at least for a hot minute, they were taken back yet again. The universe told them to hold its beer.

Lt. Scrivner, while on his mid-tour leave, became very ill. He got examined by a doctor and was diagnosed with Crohn's disease. He would remain on rear detachment and stay at home in the States to begin treatment. This was yet again another loss Two Charlie would face, but not a big one. Upon getting the word the platoon leader wasn't coming back, SFC Santos was instructed by the CO to pack up all his belongings and gear to be sent back to rear detachment.

"We need to pack up Squeak's shit to be sent back to the States. Make sure you get an inventory of everything, and make sure nobody steals shit," SFC Santos said to SSG Rosa. "Knolly, you can help him."

The two men went to Scrivner's room and began packing things into duffle bags. SGT Knollinger stumbled across his laundry bag. It looked like the clothes inside hadn't been washed since they had gotten to the Arghandab. He threw the bag at SSG Rosa. "One laundry bag full of dirty ass clothes."

SSG Rosa opened the draw string to the green bag to examine its contents. He reached in and pulled out a tan Army undershirt, the armpits and neck stained from sweat. "God damn!" he exclaimed, as the smell filled the room. He quickly threw the shirt back in and recinched the bag. Gagging, he held out the bag back towards SGT Knollinger. "We got to wash this shit. We can't send it back smelling like this."

"I ain't washing shit," SGT Knollinger declared. He leaned away from the bag like it was infected. SSG Rosa leaned in closer with the bag and extended his reach farther. SGT Knollinger inched away each time SSG Rosa inched closer with the bag. "Fuck no! I'm gonna get Crohn's," SGT Knollinger playfully said as he stood up to walk away. SSG Rosa laughed as he threw the bag in the corner with the other inventoried equipment.

Lt. Scrivner's bags were packed and sent back home to join him. The platoon picked up their new soldiers and new platoon leader as the month of February continued. Lt. Farrington was not the normal second lieutenant "butter bar" a line platoon usually gets. Sure, he was still an officer, but he had been with Alpha Company since the beginning of deployment, so he wasn't a freshly graduated West Point Cherry.

He immediately saw that the Two Charlie men were hardened and seasoned from their time in country so far. The Joes knew their stuff and had their gear prepped at all times, so they were ready to go at a moment's notice. They were a very tight-knit group, and it was easy to see SFC Santos was the cornerstone of that. It was very rough living at COP Tynes, as everything was pretty much constructed from dirt; anything that wasn't dirt had a fine layer of dirt and dust over it. The men worked hard daily and were all constantly covered in dust and dirt as well. For some, the only time they probably got a good wash was when they crossed the canals. It was prevalent they showed feral signs, as inside the COP they would be in PT shorts and flip flops but, if shit hit the fan, they would be in full uniform and kit ready to go out and kill someone in minutes. This dynamic worked for the men. The things that could be feral were feral, but the things that absolutely mattered were squared away. Lt. Farrington dared not change that.

"What's the patrol schedule like?" Lt. Farrington asked SFC Santos as he unloaded his things in Lt. Scrivner's old room.

"Straight to business. We usually patrol twice a day, then set up a LP/OP at night. That changes if company needs us to be their bitches and do a Thunder Run for them in the trucks. But, for the most part, two a day and one at night," SFC Santos said.

"Thunder Run?" Lt. Farrington asked as a smile grew on his face. Whatever it was, the name was hilarious.

"Yeah, FSC clips don't really come out this way too much so sometimes we are tasked to do them for company or battalion. Having trucks is kind of a double-edged sword," SFC Santos replied.

"Did you and Scrivner switch out on patrols?" Lt. Farrington asked.

"Lt. Scrivner would rotate, I liked going out on as many as I could. Someone's got to keep these guys in line," SFC Santos said with a smile.

"I'll go out too then. I've got to play catch up anyway. You guys have a couple months' head start on me," Lt. Farrington said.

SFC Santos nodded in approval. He had a good feeling about this new platoon leader. He began to leave him to his own to unpack his things when he stopped himself. "One more thing," he said, pointing to the far wall corner. "Your roof leaks in the corner over there."

"Good to know," he said as he moved his ruck away from the corner.

SFC Santos smiled. "That may or may not have been by design." He turned to leave the room and go to the TOC to check out the other new soldiers.

The new Cherries grabbed their bags out of the vehicles as well and lined up along the outside of the wood structure. The seasoned Joes and team leaders all swarmed around them. They were fresh meat and needed to be toughened up. You could pick them out of the crowd like a sore thumb, with their brand-new uniforms that had only been in country a week or two. You could still see the colors and digital pattern on the fabric. Their kits were still clean too, like they had just been issued to them from the Central Issuing Facility.

"Damn," one of the guys said, looking each one of them over. "Too bad none of you are going to Third Squad. We'd fix that real quick."

"Roger, Sergeant." Vasquez, one of the Cherries, replied.

"Sergeant?" the soldier replied, "How about we get started now on seasoning those uniforms. Do push-ups! All of you."

The Cherries got down and started to do push-ups in the dirt. It sucked, like they were back in basic training. "Flutter kicks, go!" another soldier yelled. The three men rolled over on their backs in the dirt and began kicking their legs six inches above the ground. Sweat started dripping from their foreheads.

"Vasquez, Dunlap, Blevins, get in here!" another voice shouted as they opened one of the doors to the wood structure. The three men got up off the dirt and started to walk single file toward the door. "Hurry up!" the soldier yelled, "Didn't they teach you to move with a sense of urgency?! Damn!" The three men began to sprint past the soldier into the hallway, another soldier was at the end of the hallway to corral them into the TOC where SFC Santos was waiting.

He looked the three men over. "Who was the one that got caught smoking in the barracks?" The men knew exactly what he was talking about but didn't know SFC Santos knew of the incident. Dunlap had been partying in the barracks on rear detachment back at Fort Bragg before they were shipped out to Afghanistan. He was underage and was drinking and smoking spice. He just received a slap on the wrist at Bragg and was shipped out to Afghanistan the next week. Dunlap slowly raised his hand. "You're in Second Squad. Your squad leader is SSG DeMeo. Go introduce yourself," SFC Santos said. One of the soldiers in the hall called for Dunlap and he sprinted out of the TOC.

"Vasquez," SFC Santos said as he looked over the new soldier. "That's your Dad right there." He pointed to SSG Craumer, who was going over something on the small boxy government computer.

SSG Craumer stood up and walked out of the TOC. "Come on, I'll introduce you to the rest of the squad," he said in the most monotone voice Vasquez had heard. They both left the TOC.

Blevins was the last of the new soldiers to remain. He stood there, unsure of what to do as SFC Santos just stared at him. "Blevins," SFC Santos finally said.

"Roger, Sergeant," Blevins said, locked in the position of parade rest, hands behind his back and shoulders spread, eyes straight forward.

"You're in Weapons. I hope you are good at rucking," SFC Santos replied.

SSG Rosa came into the TOC. "Is this my new Joe?!" he asked with a smile. "Come on, let's go." He waved Blevins to follow, and they exited the TOC.

One of the initial things Lt. Farrington noticed about his platoon's new AO was how big it was. The area the Two Charlie men were responsible for covering was the typical size of a company AO for the rest of the battalion, extending several kilometers along the north side of the Arghandab River. Getting to the Shuyens was going to be quite the task, especially if they didn't take vehicles.

Lt. Farrington continued the initial phase of patrolling in the area where Lt. Scrivner left off, documenting everything. They would continue to take the ANP out and conduct a kind of a census of the area. Take a picture and note the grid location of each front door to every building, figure out and document who was supposed to be living in those buildings, and photograph and document them in the HIIDE system.

Lt. Farrington would learn and talk with the elders of each village and ask them what they needed and if they felt represented in their district-level shuras. Basically, cover the politics of the area. He was just as stumped as the other Two Charlie men were when it came to where the enemy was in the valley. The reports he had read from the 2nd ID guys of the year prior were full of fighting. They had rarely even come across fighting-age males in the valley; just older farmers and their families. Children would line the streets of the villages. It was odd.

During a shura meeting, the lieutenant finally asked one of the village elders, "Where are the fighters?"

The old man listened as the platoon's interpreter translated the question. He smiled at the question, then gave his reply, pointing down at the thick pomegranate orchards to the south. The interpreter, Gucci, nodded, then said, "He says, you see those trees down there?" motioning to where the old man had pointed. "When the leaves return to those trees, the fighters will return to the valley."

Captain Razuri and Lt. Farrington decided Two Charlie needed to step out and pursue the three villages of the Shuyens more frequently, to try to see if the fighters were using the villages further away from the American forces. Lt. Farrington and SFC Santos took out First Squad to dismount to the area. It was a seven-kilometer movement one way, so they decided that would be the only patrol for the day, as it would take all day to get there and back. Shuyen days were long ones for the squad that got stuck going out there. The best strategy they found was to take the orchards on the way out, then march back north of Red Dog through the desert. The way out was the typical slow-moving travel of making their way through the maze of orchards, and the men felt very vulnerable once they pushed further east of Babur. The further they moved from COP Tynes, the further their Quick Reaction Force (QRF) would have to travel to get to them. It was like being on the moon when they were in the Shuyens, nobody was going to help you. If they were ever to get in a fight out there, they would be on their own with only Close Air Support if it was available.

It made the men feel uneasy being that far away, especially since the commander was wanting them to do more extended stays out there. SFC Santos and Lt. Farrington came up with a solution for this uneasiness. They would take the trucks and set up a vehicle patrol base up north in the open desert, just out of reach of RPGs. The men could run dismounted patrols out of there and come back to the trucks to resupply. If the dismounted element came in contact with the enemy, they would have the trucks just north as an armored QRF force. They also requested a sniper team be assigned to them. The battalion's sniper section leader, SSG Farnsworth, sent out his most solid team, SGT Rush and Moon. They both had come from Charlie Company before becoming snipers, so he felt it would be a good fit for them as they knew a lot of the guys already.

The men executed this plan three times, once with each squad, and each time would spend a couple days patrolling the Shuyens. They would drive to set up their patrol base, then throughout the day would dismount as a squad to the village, with Moon and Rush covering them. At night they would send out multiple mini-patrols, four-man teams, to patrol the village to see if there was any traffic they could intercept.

As sketchy as it was being that far away from the COP, the Shuyens made up for that feeling with a sense of beauty. There was something about their fields, their canals, their people, that made it kind of a beautiful place out there. Each time First Squad would go out, the children would rush from the khalats and fields. Neenan, with his heart of gold, would always have candy for them. Neenan was the kind of guy that one would introduce to their sister. It was hard to think he was capable of great violence, but he hated bullies and always stood up for the little guys. He would fill his pockets, handing out candy as children came. Sometimes it would cause the children to swarm the men, begging for any last piece of candy they had.

SGT Bragg would get on him. "Stop doing that. You're gonna draw unwanted attention one time."

"It's alright, Sergeant. They wouldn't shoot at us with their kids around, would they?" Neenan replied.

SGT Bragg thought about that for a minute. Maybe it was good to have the kids around, if not only for that reason. "Just keep an eye on them. They are pretty good at pickpocketing and swiping stuff. Keep them away from your gear." The children were obsessed with pens and would swipe them out of the men's sleeve pockets every chance they got. SGT Bragg couldn't care less about a pen—his worry was a kid walking away with NODs. "And Neenan, don't get too attached. We aren't taking any of them home."

Neenan laughed. "Roger, Sergeant."

Third Squad would have a crazy encounter of their own in the Shuyens. One day, while they were on their patrol down one of the river paths, SSG Loredo caught a glimpse of something out of the corner of his eye. "Did you see that?" he asked as he sprinted around the corner.

"See what?" SGT Lachance shouted, running to catch up with him as he came to the corner of the mud wall along the path. SGT Lachance grabbed his hand mic, ready to call in the Kiowas on station.

"Look," SSG Loredo whispered while putting a finger over his mouth to signal SGT Lachance to remain quiet. "It's a lynx."

SGT Lachance reclipped his hand mic to his rig. Just when he thought they were about to see some action, SSG Loredo and his ADHD was over here chasing a mythical creature. He sighed, letting the spike of adrenaline running through his body settle, then peaked around the corner. Sure as shit, there it was. A large cat stared at them from the middle of the path, with large black pointy ears and big paws. It stared right at them. Startled, it took one leaping bound and was up and over the 12-foot mud wall.

SSG Loredo and SGT Lachance looked at each other in surprise. Neither of them had ever seen a lynx. It was not what they had expected to see on a patrol in Afghanistan. But they hadn't seen anything they had expected up to this point.

Despite the increase in patrols in the area, the men of Two Charlie still found no evidence that backed up what the units there before them had experienced. Where they initially found old IEDs and stashes, no one had come back to check on them or replenish them. The men had free reign of the AO and moved uncontested wherever they wanted. It allowed them to learn the area well but made each day very uneventful.

The villagers in the valley, especially the Shuyens and Babur, weren't always the most welcoming. They would more likely than not turn a cold shoulder to the men and weren't welcoming of them being in their villages. To try to mitigate this dislike towards the men, a Humanitarian Aid operation was planned alongside one of the company clearance operations. An Army psyops unit was called in to take part in the matter, bringing with them female soldiers and doctors to provide examinations to the local women. The men were given blankets to hand out to the locals, along with bags of beans and rice for them to eat, and coloring books and crayons for the children. It was intended to be a kind offering to the people, an invitation to break bread and show them the American forces were not all bad and just wanted to help the people. The children loved the coloring books, but the elder villagers didn't buy in. They continued to be hesitant towards the men and refused to answer all their questions.

After a failed shura meeting with the elders of the Shuyens, the psyops unit mounted up in their vehicles and headed back to Terra Nova. The Two Charlie men began their walk back down Route Red Dog.

"What's that?" Young said pointing in the sky from the direction they had come from. The men looked back down the road, and they noticed a plume of black smoke across the sky. They quickly turned around and started heading back to investigate. By the time they had returned, all that was left was a pile of ash in the middle of the road; a couple of half-burnt coloring books stuck out of the pile. The villagers had gathered the blankets, food, and whatever else was given to them by the troops and burnt them.

The men were going to have their work cut out for them in the villages in their AO. They continued to patrol the Shuyens, Babur, the Khosrows, and Torak Kolache throughout February and into March, until the leaf buds in the valley began to bloom.

CHAPTER 6

# 22 Mar 2010

The morning started out just as any other morning. SGT Knollinger and SGT Brown were rounding up Third Squad guys and getting them prepped for their morning patrol, making sure they got a quick breakfast in while preparing their gear for the day. Men in First and Second Squad continued pulling guard in the towers and those not pulling guard got ready for the arrival of the new battalion sergeant major (SGM) at COP Tynes. The battalion had received new leadership after the battalion commander and battalion SGM had been relieved of their duties for a politically incorrect Powerpoint slide, or at least that is what the men were told. They had liked the old command and were unsure of what to make of the new one. The new SGM was making his rounds of the battalion's AO, and today First Squad was going to pick him and his entourage up and bring them to COP Tynes. Initially, One Charlie was going to escort them from COP Nolen on a dismounted patrol, allowing him to see the area, but that all got changed at the last minute. Guess the new SGM didn't feel like walking. Regardless, this meant everything had to be spick and span, dress, right dress for his arrival. Team leaders went around, making sure the guys' rooms were neat, and they were in the proper uniform.

"Roll down those sleeves," SGT Knollinger said to Jackson and Godard, referring to the sleeves of their camouflage uniform they had rolled to their elbows. The men had gotten used to the relaxed uniform and grooming standards they had been following the last couple of months. Rolling up sleeves, unblousing boots, a little five o'clock shadow, became kind of the norm; as long as you were squared away with your gear and how you conducted yourself on patrol, little things like that could slide. But not today.

"Better shave before we go out, Winston, don't know if we will be back before the sergeant major gets here," SGT Brown said as he checked Winston's things.

"You too, Ryan," SGT Knollinger barked. It seemed Ryan always had a five o'clock shadow going. He had one of those faces that even if he had just shaved it just naturally looked scruffy. It didn't help he had failed out of the Q course for special operations before he got sent to the 82nd, so any chance he got to look the cool guy part he would take full advantage of. Looking cool was half the battle for him.

Nguyen walked out of the wood structure and past the men of Third Squad. He was wearing only his PT shorts and flip flops and had a toothbrush in his mouth.

"Jonny Nguyen, put some clothes on!" SGT Knollinger barked, "You can't be walking around like that today. Sergeant Major is on his way."

Nguyen walked back into the wood structure and returned, this time wearing his tan battalion PT shirt. White foam was dribbling from his mouth as he brushed his teeth with his brush.

"Shoes? PT belt? And tuck your shirt in!" SGT Knollinger continued to harp on him.

Nguyen removed the toothbrush from his mouth and spat a large pile of white spit on the ground so he could speak, "PT belt?" He ogled SGT Knollinger's face trying to determine if he was fucking with him or not. "Are you fucking serious?" he finally asked after not being able to tell.

"Yes!" SGT Knollinger replied.

The men continued to scurry, cleaning up messy areas, hiding things from sight that would probably get brought up if seen and making sure everything was dress, right dress. Men shaved if they hadn't already done so and got in their best uniforms which, after months of filling sandbags and patrolling around the valley only to hand wash them in buckets, weren't exactly the most presentable. At this point, if there wasn't a hole in the crotch from ripping the seam hopping over a mud wall, that was considered a presentable uniform.

SFC Santos had just finished his workout as he walked into the TOC to flex in front of SGT Knollinger. "You get your sets in yet?" he asked as he flexed his triceps.

"Nah, not yet. Getting ready for Sergeant Major and today's patrol," SGT Knollinger replied.

"Got to get those sets in, Knolly, if you want to get big and strong like me," SFC Santos said with a smile. He had been hitting the gym regularly now, trying to get in shape for his mid-tour leave coming up. It was he and his wife's anniversary.

"Yeah?" SGT Knollinger replied with a laugh.

"COP Tynes, this is Charlie One Five, is Charlie Two Five available? Over." A call came over the radio.

SFC Santos grabbed the mic from SGT Knollinger. "Roger, this is Charlie Two Five."

"Roger Two Five, just checking on your ETA to pick up Two Fury Five."

"We'll SP at 0900 as initially planned," SFC Santos said irritably.

"Roger, we'll let him know. One Five out." The radio transmission ended and SFC Santos handed the mike back to SGT Knollinger.

"Why are you even going on that stupid patrol? They don't need you to go pick him up. First Squad has it," SGT Knollinger asked jokingly.

"You got to send in the big dogs to pick up the big dogs," SFC Santos replied as he flexed one more time then went to his room to get ready for the convoy. SGT Knollinger just shook his head.

SFC Santos passed Lt. Farrington in the hall as he was doing final radio checks for the dismounted patrol. "You got this?" he asked.

Lt. Farrington nodded. "Yeah, I got this. I'd rather not deal with Two Fury Five anyway."

"Alright, see you when you get back," SFC Santos said as he walked back into the wood structure to grab his gear and help First Squad get the trucks ready.

"See ya," Lt. Farrington said, then turned to join SSG Loredo and the rest of Third Squad outside. They did their patrol brief and exited through the front ECP. Lt. Farrington picked up his hand mic to call in his start of patrol. "Charlie Six, this is Charlie Two Six, SP COP Tynes. En route to Lower Babur, time now." He reclipped his radio hand mic to a strap on his shoulder and walked out with Third Squad.

SFC Santos got the guys of First Squad to get the trucks ready in a hurry, as he didn't want to keep the new SGM waiting. They quickly went through all the preventative maintenance checks and services. Each truck was running a skeleton crew, or the bare minimum number of men required to operate the truck, so there would be empty seats in the vehicles to pick up the men. Trucks One, Two, and Three all had drivers, Truck Commander (TC), and gunners. Truck Four, SFC Santos's truck, would be the only full one. He would have Doc Chandler, who was taking Doc Taylor's place while he was on leave, and another dismount in the back seat. They would be towing a small M1101 cargo trailer to help transport some gear and supplies from Terra Nova.

Truck One had one of the platoon's new Cherries, Vasquez, occupy one of the rear dismount seats. He was to help SGT Bragg clear the route once they reached Route Phillies. Route Phillies had been known historically for having IEDs placed on it. Although it was not a long route, maybe only two to three hundred meters long from Red Dog to COP Nolen, it had spots that were out of sight of Terra Nova's "eye in the sky" and COP Nolen. There was a kind of tricky little bend in the road after a small bridge over the first canal where other mounted patrols had hit IEDs in the past. One and Three Charlie had conducted numerous dismounted night overwatches of the area out of COP Nolen to try to catch the enemy placing these bombs but were yet to be successful. The plan discussed in the patrol brief was that prior to the small bridge, SGT Bragg and Vasquez would dismount, search the bridge and road for any possible IEDs, and then continue to walk the route in front of the trucks looking for any signs of buried explosives.

SGT Bragg was okay with having Vasquez along, as he and SGT Maher had been training him up for the past few weeks at COP Tynes. However, SGT Bragg also had the other new Cherry, Blevins, assigned to gun for his truck. He used that to protest and make a last-minute change to the load plan. "Hell no, two Cherries in the lead truck with me. Nuh-uh. No way. Give me Rostran as my gunner."

SFC Santos knew SGT Bragg and Rostran were pretty tight knit, as they had both been in Weapons Squad together and worked well with each other before Bragg moved to First Squad after the drug deal trade, so he allowed the last-minute change. "Whatever. Blevins, you're with me," he replied.

Rostran wasn't too thrilled that he would have to trade spots with Blevins. He would much rather be gunning for SFC Santos in the rear truck than the lead one. He grabbed his things and put them in the turret of Truck One.

"If I'm gonna die in the lead truck, you're coming with me, Rostran. We die together," SGT Bragg said jokingly with a big smile on his face. Rostran put on a fake smile in response, not exactly thrilled by the notion.

The men loaded up the trucks and began their final radio checks and ready.

"Truck One up," SGT Bragg said over the radio.

"Truck Two, we're good," SSG Craumer replied.

"Truck Three up," SGT Maher said.

"Truck Four, good to go. Let's roll," SFC Santos said, signaling to SGT Bragg's truck to lead them out.

They began to snake through the back exit of COP Tynes and were just making the turn onto Route Red Dog when Neenan slammed on the brakes of the truck. His face turned pale like he had seen a ghost as he looked around his seat frantically.

"What's wrong?" SGT Bragg asked, confused.

"Sergeant, I think I left my rifle against the Hescos," Neenan admitted.

SGT Bragg's jaw dropped. No way that just happened. A soldier's rifle is practically part of their hand. One doesn't just forget their rifle. "Go get it!" he lashed out. Neenan opened his door and ran back through the back entrance, past all the other vehicles.

"Truck One, what's the hold up?" SFC Santos said over the radio.

"Forgot something, running back to grab it real quick," SGT Bragg said as discreetly as he could, trying to keep his Joe out of getting into any unnecessary trouble. He would deal with him later.

But SFC Santos noticed everything. It's impossible to sneak one by him. He watched as Neenan came running back past his truck, now carrying his rifle. "Did he have that when he ran by the first time?" he asked his driver, Rae.

Rae, not wanting to get a fellow Joe in trouble, acted unsure, "I don't know, Sergeant. I wasn't paying attention."

Santos knew he was lying by the tone of his response. "I'm gonna smoke the shit out of that fucker when we get back," he said and then the trucks began to move again.

The convoy rolled up to the turn off for Route Phillies. Truck One made its way south on the road and pushed up to the bridge across the first canal. It was a very short and narrow bridge, only long enough to cross over the five-foot-wide canal and maybe wide enough for a single vehicle to pass at a time. From the looks of it, it would be very difficult to get one of their big MATVs over. Directly after the bridge was the awkward bend in the road. It was definitely a point at which the vehicles would have to take it slow, making it a good spot for a bomb.

SGT Bragg opened his door and ordered Vasquez to hop out of the truck with him. "Let's go. It's time to leave the safety of the armored vehicle to walk out in front of it and get blown up. Neenan, I'll wave you over the bridge once we check it out. You think you need any help clearing that thing? It's kind of narrow."

"I think I got it, Sergeant," Neenan replied confidently.

"Alright. If you need me to ground guide you, yell at Rostran to get my attention," SGT Bragg said as he climbed down and slammed his armored door closed behind him.

Vasquez and SGT Bragg approached the small bridge. It was wider now they were on the ground than when they were in the vehicle, but it was still pretty narrow. It just cleared the top of the water by about a foot or two. The MATV might just be able to squeeze over it.

Vasquez took the left side of the bridge and SGT Bragg took the right. "What are we looking for exactly?" Vasquez asked.

"Wires. Cords. Yellow plastic jugs. Turned up dirt. Anything that doesn't seem right really," SGT Bragg replied as he kneeled to peer under the bridge, almost dunking his head in the water to get a good look. He studied the bottom of the bridge looking for anything out of the ordinary. With no discovery of anything odd, his search then turned to the opposite bank of the canal where the bridge met the dirt. Seeing absolutely nothing of suspicion, SGT Bragg was satisfied enough to cross the bridge, Vasquez followed closely after. They scanned the other side of the bridge, overturned a large rock to maybe uncover a hidden wire. Nothing. They pushed into the grape vineyard on the east side of the road. The leaves were now blooming from the vines, filling the mud walls with a very appealing green. It was like there was a little life in the valley now. They found nothing and proceeded to push further down the road.

Confident they had cleared enough of the area for the first truck to get over the bridge safely, SGT Bragg waved Neenan to move forward. It was slightly terrifying as he wanted to be close enough to watch the vehicle cross the bridge and guide Neenan over if he had any trouble, but also far enough away so, if the truck did explode from a bomb they had missed, he wouldn't be hurt or killed from a piece of it flying through the air. SGT Bragg figured 20 meters might be far enough, though the blast that killed Tynes and Nolen still playing in his head made him very uneasy about that decision. He knelt in the ditch beside the road, hoping for the best.

Neenan flawlessly drove the MATV over the bridge and around the bend. He was a pretty good driver and SGT Bragg really liked having him drive for him. Neenan didn't mind driving either. Driving a MATV was like driving a monster truck. It was kind of like a childhood dream come true.

SGT Bragg motioned for Neenan to slow his roll so they didn't get too far ahead of the other vehicles as they crossed the difficult spot. He and Vasquez continued to walk about twenty meters in front of Truck One and continued to clear the road. One by one the trucks made it over the bridge and around the bend. SGT Bragg was confident it was clear as he watched the front two tires of the last vehicle contact the bridge. He turned to keep walking down the road.

"Sergeant Bragg, I got something," Vasquez shouted as he lifted his rifle. He was pointing it at a motorcyclist that was rolling up on them on the road. The motorcyclist stopped when he saw Vasquez had his rifle dialed in on him and kicked his kickstand down. SGT Bragg started to walk over to Vasquez to help.

BOOM.

The concussion from the blast hit the backs of Vasquez and SGT Bragg. They could feel it shake their spines through their body armor. Vasquez fell to a knee, keeping his rifle pointed at the man on the motorcycle. SGT Bragg flinched, driving his chin into his chest. He was a little closer to the blast than Vasquez, but not by much. He sat there all tense, standing in the middle of the road waiting for a tire or some other piece of shrapnel from his truck to hit him in the back of the head, killing him immediately. Nothing happened, nothing had hit him. He turned to see what happened and, to his surprise, his truck was staring right at him, untouched. He saw the massive plume of smoke and dirt well behind his vehicle, and he saw debris and the M1101 trailer flying through the air. The tire he imagined impaling him in the back of the head was flying through the air too, and it landed a good hundred meters from the dust cloud.

"What do I do?" a fearful Vasquez called out to SGT Bragg.

This snapped SGT Bragg out of his daze. "Keep that guy on the motorcycle there, don't let him go anywhere. Rostran, if he tries to run, shoot at him." He turned to look back at the blast. He couldn't see the truck. Maybe it had just gotten the trailer, he thought hopefully.

SGT Maher had just jumped down from the truck commander's (TC) seat of his truck and slammed the door. SGT Maher glanced at what was left of the truck behind him and then looked back at SGT Bragg. He waved "Let's go" to SGT Bragg and began running to the wreckage. SGT Bragg followed. It had not just gotten the trailer.

Lt. Farrington and Third Squad were taking a short halt in the shade of one of the orchards. It was just another typical patrol, they were monitoring the local traffic in the fields and roads, just listening and watching from their secluded hiding spot. The leaves blooming on the trees were great to conceal their position but made it quite difficult for the men to see far distances now. There was a break in the trees that allowed them to get a good view of the river, so the men decided to set up there. Lt. Farrington and SSG Loredo were sitting next to each other when a bizarre call came over the radio. "IED, IED, IED." It was definitely SSG Craumer, but it was weird because the men hadn't heard anything.

SSG Loredo heard the transmission as well and was equally puzzled by it. Just as he was about to say something to the lieutenant, a dull roar erupted through the orchard, like thunder in the distance. Only there was no rain. Lt. Farrington and SSG Loredo's eyes widened and they snapped to look at each other. Without a word, SGT Knollinger and SGT Brown ran over to their location. They knew that noise and they knew it was from something big. Third Squad immediately got on their feet and started to run.

SGT Brown took point, hurling himself over a mud wall into a narrow alley with mud walls on each side that ran directly to the second canal. He sprinted as fast as he could, clearing every break in the wall he passed with his rifle as quickly as he could. His men were quick behind him, giving everything they had to stay on his heels. The narrow alley ended, and SGT Brown started sprinting west along the dirt path that skirted the canal.

"Where are they at?" SGT Knollinger yelled up to SGT Brown, not knowing exactly where they were heading, they were just going west as fast as they could.

"Just get to Route Phillies!" SSG Loredo yelled up to SGT Brown.

His feet couldn't carry him faster.

Dust filled the air inside the truck, making it hard to see. Rae could feel the sharp pain in his back when he removed his seatbelt and fell against the center radio mounts of the truck. They must have been on their side or upside down or something, he couldn't tell as he was disoriented from the blast. He couldn't hear anything but an annoying ringing sound that eventually faded to the painful screams of the other guys in the truck. In a daze, all he could think to do was what they went over in training after hitting an IED, which was just yell IED three times. "IED, IED, IED." He groaned each time he said it as the sharp pain pierced his back like a knife stabbing him.

"No shit, Rae!" McCune screamed through the dust. He was bent over the now sideways gunner's platform inside the truck.

"Ahhhhh, fuck!" Doc Chandler yelled. He had been buried by the .50-caliber ammo cans that had broken loose in the blast. Each one of them probably weighed about thirty pounds so he couldn't move.

SGT Maher ran up to the wreckage. The truck was lying on its side facing the opposite direction from the way it had been traveling, meaning the thing probably did a flip in the air before landing on the TC's side of the vehicle. The back end was a mess of mangled metal exposing the frame of the vehicle. The rear tires were gone, but it appeared the hull was intact. SGT Maher could see Blevins dangling from the turret and he could hear the other guys screaming inside. He ran over to Blevins, grabbed him by the arms and started dragging him from the turret.

"Ahhhh," Blevins moaned as his legs came free. His ankles were obviously broken, as they were both at abnormal angles. SGT Bragg arrived at the scene and grabbed an arm to help SGT Maher drag Blevins to the ditch on the side of the road for cover.

"We need to get a Nine Line going," SGT Maher shouted over Blevins's painful screams.

"Craumer is already on it. I saw him on the radio as I ran by," SGT Bragg reassured him as he started to run back to the truck.

"Stay down!" SGT Maher barked at Blevins and then ran after SGT Bragg.

McCune was the next closest one to the turret, so SGT Maher used his big ogre arms to reach in and grab him, yanking him out of the turret. McCune's rig was larger than the other guys, since he carried the SAW, and it got caught in the opening. They struggled to get him free and couldn't figure out what it had gotten caught on. SGT Bragg could feel the hot metal of the truck radiating heat through his gloves. The guys in there must be roasting; he had to find another way to get them out. He climbed up to the top of the vehicle to try to open one of the doors, to give the guys inside another path of escape. He stood prying on each door with all his might, but they didn't even budge. They must have been combat-locked from the inside. Noticing the soles of his boots were beginning to melt, he quickly climbed down to continue to help SGT Maher.

"Cut him free!" SGT Bragg snapped.

SGT Maher pulled out his knife and the two of them found the strap from his rig that was stuck around the turret crank handle. SGT Maher cut it and they yanked him free from the turret. The sergeants both fell flat on their backs with how easy McCune came out. They got up, dragged him over by Blevins, then went back for the others.

Rae had already been grabbing ammo cans and throwing them out of the truck, trying to unbury Doc Chandler. He was at an awkward angle, so it proved rather difficult for him and he only managed to get two cans out of the way before SGT Bragg came flying in through the turret. His skinny frame made it easy for him to maneuver within the confines of the vehicle. He started grabbing the cans and handing them outside to SGT Maher. Can by can, Doc Chandler was freed from his tomb. Doc pushed SGT Bragg out of the way and got out of the truck on his own accord, gasping the cool air and crawling away from the wreckage. SGT Maher grabbed him and brought him to the others. In a daze, Chandler began treating the guys in the ditch, triaging them.

"Sit down," Maher shouted at him, "You're a casualty."

SGT Bragg went climbing back into the truck to help free Rae. He was in the driver's seat and had to squeeze through the small gap between the radios and his seat. Rae took off his helmet and started climbing through as SGT Bragg assisted by pulling and removing anything he got caught on. Rae powered through the opening and then followed SGT Bragg out of the truck. The feeling of the airflow over the sweat on his face felt good as he looked up to the sky and breathed. The adrenaline was wearing off and the pain in his back had returned. He ignored it as he staggered back to the wreckage to help SGT Bragg get SFC Santos out of the wreckage.

SGT Bragg caught Rae as he was about to fall to the ground. "I got this. You're done, Rae," he said as he walked him to the rest of the casualties. SGT Maher had been treating the guys in the crude casualty collection point they established and was trying to get Doc Chandler to relax. SGT Bragg laid Rae beside them and returned to the vehicle for SFC Santos.

He climbed back in the turret and looked down. He could see the 82nd patch on SFC Santos's shoulder. He grabbed him to start pulling him out, but he didn't budge. SGT Bragg wasn't the strongest of guys and SFC Santos was one of the larger guys in the platoon, but he knew he could at least get a guy to budge. This felt different though. He looked to see if he was caught on something and noticed how still he was. In the chaos and urgency of the whole situation, for the first time it seemed to be calm for a moment. SGT Bragg sat there studying him, noticing for the first time just how quiet it was inside the vehicle now. He slowly followed his arm up to his shoulder and the 82nd patch. That is when he noticed it. SFC Santos's head and arm were outside the door, underneath the truck. He slowly climbed back out of the turret. Sure enough, SFC Santos's arm and crushed helmet were sticking out from underneath the truck, his head was still in the helmet. His door must have been blown open in the blast and he had been partially outside the vehicle when it landed on him.

SGT Bragg took a step back, as he had almost stepped on him. It made him very uneasy and he felt sick. He looked back at SGT Maher and the other guys. None of them knew. He couldn't let them see it. He grabbed the camo net from the turret and was going to use it to cover him. The damn net was caught underneath the truck as well. He struggled and he fought the thing, trying to free it.

SGT Maher saw SGT Bragg struggling fighting the net. "What are you doing?" he asked.

"Help me, Maher!" SGT Bragg said as he motioned to the bottom of the truck. SGT Maher looked to where he was pointing, and his shoulders and jaw dropped. He slowly walked over to SGT Bragg, his eyes focused on SFC Santos the entire time. "Help me cover him up," SGT Bragg said again.

SGT Maher grabbed the other end of the net and with one tug they ripped it free, and slowly placed it over SFC Santos.

Third Squad continued sprinting down the dirt path along the second canal. They had probably already run for at least four kilometers and were only a hundred meters from Phillies. Nichols was dying at this point, as his SAW and 1,000 rounds on his rig were really weighing him down.

"You got to keep up!" Godard shouted at him as he passed him carrying his M4 rifle. He had been giving Nichols shit ever since Jackson took his spot as SAW gunner and he took over RTO. Nichols didn't want to hear it right now, he was too exhausted from the run.

The men pushed further down the path and came across a squad from One Charlie. They had responded from a warm base they had established as soon as they heard the blast. Third Squad ran up on them so quickly it startled them, and they were met with raised weapons. Upon recognition of friendly forces, rifles were lowered, and the One Charlie guys waved Third Squad on. They had detained a couple of locals seen fleeing the vicinity of the grape fields close to the blast site. "Go on, we got these guys," they said to Lt. Farrington who, with the rest of Third Squad didn't hesitate as they pushed on to Phillies.

More of One Charlie men had arrived at the site and were helping secure the area and treat the casualties. SGT Brown and SGT Knollinger set their guys in to help with security and to take a breather. They found SGT Maher among the One

Charlie men securing the wreckage. SGT Maher saw SGT Knollinger approaching from the fields and he walked to meet him, his head hung low.

"How bad?" SGT Knollinger asked.

SGT Maher paused and shook his head. "He's gone."

"Who's gone?" SGT Knollinger asked, confused. SSG Loredo, SGT Brown, and Lt. Farrington joined him by his side.

"He's gone," SGT Maher repeated, as if he didn't say his name then maybe it wasn't true.

"What?" SGT Knollinger said, still confused by SGT Maher's vagueness.

"He's under the truck right there," SGT Maher said, pointing to the camo net.

SGT Knollinger looked at the small portion of net covering the truck under the turret. His eyes started to tear up as he looked at the men on the stretchers being loaded into the MedEvac Birds landing in the field and putting two and two together. SFC Santos wasn't among them. He was under the truck.

SSG Loredo approached the net and lifted it. He couldn't believe SGT Maher and needed to see for himself. The four of them could almost physically see his heart sink in his chest. He lowered the net and slowly backed away. SFC Santos was gone.

CHAPTER 7

# The Only Thing Necessary

The remainder of that day Third Squad went kicking in doors in the town of Jelawur, looking for possible squirters from the scene. The Kiowa helicopters on station at the time thought they saw a male in a green tunic and pants running from the fields immediately following the blast. The Birds followed him all the way until he took shelter in a khalat north of Jelawur. They kept an eye on the compound and began to guide the Two Charlie men in.

The ANP officers linked up with the men as they passed them in their pickup trucks. Bismullah waved the men in from the driver seat of one of the trucks. The Third Squad guys hopped in the beds and some rode standing on the side running boards of the vehicles, directing the Afghans where to go based on what the Birds were telling them. They finally made their way to the entrance of the compound.

Part of the rules of engagement was that Afghan forces needed to enter buildings first when not in direct contact. "ANP has got to be the first ones in!" Lt. Farrington made clear, yelling over the trucks to the men as they rolled up to the front door of the compound. SGT Knollinger grabbed one of the police officers as soon as the vehicle came to a stop and basically threw him through the front door of the compound as they all flooded in afterwards. They found the Afghan male the helicopter pilots described and took him to the ground, throwing flex cuffs on him as they detained him. They searched the rest of the compound, but ultimately found nothing else. No explosives. No bomb making material. Nothing. All they did find were weird old photos of Mujahideen soldiers. The men had the ANP take the suspected trigger man into custody and back to COP Tynes until he could be investigated.

The dismounted element followed the ANP back to COP Tynes. SSG DeMeo and SSG Rosa were waiting for them outside the gate. The anticipation was killing them, and they didn't want to wait in the TOC any longer. They had a dismounted radio clipped to their waist and greeted the Third Squad guys as they came in through the wire. The Third Squad men had their rifles all hung low by their sides in their hands. They had a look of defeat across their faces and walked with a sluggish demeanor.

"What's going on? Who is it?" SSG Rosa asked; Everyone that remained at the COP was still unaware of exactly what happened. They had only been able to put together bits and pieces from the radio chatter over the platoon and company nets, and they didn't want to believe some of the pieces.

Lt. Farrington looked at SSG Rosa. "It's Santos," was all he said. SSG DeMeo and SSG Rosa couldn't believe it. SSG DeMeo stumbled as he walked back into the COP in shock. SSG Rosa didn't follow him. He just stood there in disbelief.

The mounted patrol returned to COP Tynes with one less vehicle that evening. Now the platoon was together, the leadership made the announcement to everyone. SFC Santos was dead. Three Charlie had conducted a BDA while waiting for the wrecker to recover SFC Santos's body. They found a lamp cord buried a foot under the ground, so the bomb was not a pressure plate but a command-wire detonation. The cord ran buried for a hundred feet until it reached the other side of a grape orchard perimeter wall, where it ran along a furrow into the adjacent field. There was a notch cut out of the mud on the top of the wall that the triggerman used to time the detonation so the vehicle was right over the homemade explosives (HME) buried in the road. No one could tell how long the explosives or the wire had been there. The blast had gone off as the rear tires of the vehicle were directly over the main charge, causing the vehicle to flip and land on its side. While the vehicle was airborne, the truck commander's door was blown open and SFC Santos began to slide out before the vehicle landed on top of him, crushing him instantly.

It was unbelievably quiet that evening as men dealt with the news. They all were distraught and trying to make sense of it. Questions ran through the men's heads. What did they do wrong? How could SFC Santos die? He was Dad—the glue that held everyone together—the cog that made the machine turn. He was the man who was supposed to get the first cut of turkey at the dinner table but, in reality, always took the last. He looked out for them and protected them from a lot of shit that rolled downhill from battalion and company command, some of which was their own doing, but he stood up for them nonetheless. Now he was gone. He was the highest-ranking non-commissioned officer in the platoon; he wasn't supposed to die. If he could die, what kind of odds did that leave them? If it could happen to him, then it could happen to any of them. But the most asked question was a somber one—for what? The battalion sergeant major didn't even end up coming to COP Tynes that day after what happened. So, what was it all for? A lot of the men put a lot of the blame on the SGM that day.

SGT Bragg placed a lot of the blame on himself. He was the one clearing the route; how did he not see it? How did he miss it? He looked for all the signs and details he was taught to look for and he still missed it. Even though the wire was a foot under the ground, he should have somehow seen it. He had taken point every time he had been on patrol since he had moved to First Squad. He told himself it wasn't going to happen again. Not on his watch. He was going to keep taking point, every patrol his squad would go on, and he was going to find the next one. No one was going to die on his watch again.

SGT Knollinger was mad. They did everything they were supposed to and somehow it still happened. He started to realize he didn't have as much control over things as he thought he did. He decided then and there that if there was one thing he could control, it was his guys, and he was going to do anything he could to make sure they were going to be alright. He was going to do anything to ensure they were going to make it home. He started to see just how much the higher leadership and brass didn't care about Two Charlie. They were pawns in this game they were playing. Santos cared, and he took care of the guys in the game. Now who was going to take care of them?

The men all had that same question. Who would be the one to take care of them now, who was going to fill Dad's shoes? Nobody could fill that man's boots. Nobody.

The next few days the men didn't go out. They just pulled tower guard and remained back at COP Tynes. They convoyed over to Terra Nova to pick up a few of their guys returning from their mid-tour leave, but that was about it. Those men had gotten word of Santos's death and were eager to be back with the rest of the Two Charlie men. Everyone was trying to do things to take their minds off of the day. Some men gathered in rooms and watched newly released bootleg movies on their laptops together. Others spent the day by themselves.

SGT Lachance kept reflecting on the fact he wasn't there that day. He was one of the soldiers returning home from his mid-tour leave when it happened and found out in the airport on the way back to Afghanistan. He always rode in SFC Santos's truck, and always sat in the seat behind him. He kept wondering what it would be like if he was there that day, how it would have been different. The thought pissed him off that he wasn't there, to be with his friend during his final moments, to be in the truck with him. He could play the "what if" game all day, but that wouldn't make anything change. Santos was still gone.

Neenan was one of the men who preferred to be alone with his thoughts as well. He snuck around to the south side of the outpost, a box full of candy in his hands. He liked to give out candy to the children of the villages. It made him feel a little better, lightening up the children's day, and he needed to feel better. He saw a group of children playing in the field down the road, "Dalta Raasha!" He shouted, calling the children over while shaking the box of candy in the air. The kids ran at the sound of sugary joy bouncing off the walls of the cardboard. The whole scene was like someone feeding ducks at the park. They ran up to the concertina wire and put their hands in the air, begging Neenan to throw a piece over. Neenan obliged and threw a handful to the begging children. They all smiled as they unwrapped the candy and put it in their mouths and then begged for more. The children's smiles made Neenan smile, if only for a moment.

SGT Bragg walked around the corner of the Hesco wall to find Neenan emptying the box over the wire and the children going crazy, grabbing the pieces of candy off the ground and filling their pockets. He slowly walked beside him and joined him, watching the entire spectacle.

"How you doing?" SGT Bragg asked.

"Alright, Sergeant," Neenan lied.

SGT Bragg saw right through it. "How are you really doing?" he asked him again.

Neenan looked towards the ground for a moment. "That should have been us, Sergeant, shouldn't it have? We were Truck One."

SGT Bragg was quiet, then broke the silence with a somber, "Yeah, it should have." SGT Bragg placed a hand on Neenan's shoulder. "But it wasn't."

Neenan started to tear up. "What did we do wrong, Sergeant?"

SGT Bragg searched for the words to help cheer up his soldier. He couldn't think of anything to say, all that he could muster was, "Nothing. We didn't do anything wrong." Even after saying it, he didn't believe it himself. He could tell Neenan wasn't pleased with this answer either. "It just wasn't our day to go."

SGT Bragg took his hand off Neenan's shoulder and started to walk back into the outpost, leaving him with his thoughts. He stopped just before he was about to round the corner of the Hescos. "Oh, Neenan," he said and waited for Neenan to turn towards him. "Don't get close to those kids, they've been known to bite."

Neenan let out a short-lived laugh and a faint smile. "Roger, Sergeant."

Back at the gym, SGT Knollinger and SSG Rosa wanted to get their usual workout in before the sun got too high in the sky. The temperature during the day had definitely started to increase, and it was no longer the cold, damp river valley they had been introduced to.

"It's twenty-two." SGT Knollinger said.

"Whatchu talking about, you're on eight?" SSG Rosa asked as he spotted SGT Knollinger doing his bench sets.

"No man, it's twenty-two," he said as he placed the bench bar back on the shaky wooden rack and sat up to look at him. "That's not a good number for us."

SSG Rosa, not understanding what SGT Knollinger was getting at, just stared back at him. He waited for him to go on.

"November twenty-second. March twenty-second. It's twenty-two, man. That shit just isn't our number," SGT Knollinger explained.

Rosa thought about it for a second. "Dang. You're right." It was kind of spooky thinking about it.

"Shit, even SSG DeMeo's call sign is Charlie Two Two. That says something right there," SGT Knollinger smiled, and the two men laughed. It felt good to laugh again.

"Yeah, maybe we don't go out on the twenty-second anymore," SSG Rosa said, only somewhat joking, as he took the bench and started his set. He finished and the two men hopped up and started flexing in the broken mirror hung on the dirt wall.

SGT Knollinger noticed as SSG Rosa flexed that he had a fresh tattoo on his right ribs. "What's that?" he asked, pointing to it.

SSG Rosa looked down at the scabbed over letters. "I had Chancy give me that the other night when he got back from leave. It's the last one Santos got." The two men stared at it, reading it over. "The only thing necessary for the triumph of evil is for good men to do nothing. 22 Nov 09, 22 Mar 10." The men sat in silence, admiring SGT Lachance's work.

SGT Knollinger wasn't the only one to notice SSG Rosa's tattoo. A lot of guys saw it and started lining up to ask Lachance to get it. Rostran and Doc Taylor got it wrapped around their bicep, Lt. Farrington on his inner bicep, Bowman on his forearm, and SGT Knollinger on his thigh. SGT Bragg asked to get it right where SFC Santos got his, wrapped around his right forearm.

The other tattoos the men had gotten were different from this one. This one had evolved past more than just a simple tattoo. It was a badge of honor. It was Dad's last tattoo, and it was kind of a last message to his men. They knew they had to get back on the horse, that they couldn't quit, if not for their own reputation, then for his. They were Santos's boys and they always would be. They needed to keep his legacy going, and sitting back at COP Tynes doing nothing wasn't going to do that.

The men started to become quite superstitious of the number twenty-two. They would plan patrols around that day if possible, wouldn't listen to the twenty-second song on a playlist, and some would even go as far as skipping the twenty-second page in a book.

One and Three Charlie marched to COP Tynes along with the Company Headquarters element a few days later for Santos's boots and rifle ceremony. A lot of higher enlisted from battalion wound up also attending the ceremony, including the new SGM. Word travels fast when an SFC dies in combat, especially one of SFC Santos's caliber. The SGM addressed the men, but his words landed on deaf ears. They didn't care for what he had to say. A lot of them believed that, if it wasn't for him, Santos would still be there. But he wasn't, hence the gathering of the brass pretending they gave a damn.

The Two Charlie men paid no attention to all the brass. Their focus was on the boots and rifle display, and the picture placed below it. The chaplain gave his typical speech, and SSG DeMeo and SSG Rosa followed with a few somber words of the man Santos was to them, how he made them grow as NCOs, and how the platoon grew under his command. First Sergeant did the roll call, and Taps was played as the 21-gun salute rang out. The men, tears in their eyes, stayed focused on the display and rendered their slow salute as the rounds were fired into the air and the bugle began to play. It was all background noise as their focus was the picture at the foot of the boots, and the stinging of the raw flesh where they had gotten Santos's tattoo. The pain was a reminder he would never be gone, that he lived through them now, and it was up to them to keep his legacy going.

The men of Two Charlie could not be without a platoon sergeant forever. The men all looked to SSG Rosa at that point. He was like the big brother that became the man of the house. He had been part of Two Charlie for longer than any of the men and was the next senior NCO. He was a natural leader for the men and had been good to them in the past, always looking out for them. He was close with all the guys, as he would go out on every patrol with every squad along with one of his gun teams. He realized the men had been looking for someone to follow ever since Santos's death, someone to lean on, to lead the way. He was "Dad adjacent" and took it upon himself to be that man. He never was up front about it or outright came out to the men, saying he was in charge now. Instead, the transfer of the Dad role just organically fell on him. His credentials didn't need to be questioned, and he already had the men's trust. They gravitated toward following him now and he stepped up to that plate.

Team leaders and squad leaders all stepped up to help fill the void as well. SSG Loredo, SGT Knollinger, and Lt. Farrington all stepped up. There was even a noticeable difference in the Joes of the platoon after Santos's death. Each man didn't just know the role of his superior, they started to do it, and look out for their peers and subordinates. Not only did they grow stronger as a platoon from losing SFC Santos, they grew as a family.

Regardless of Two Charlie's ability to self-govern and manage their own hierarchy, the Army was not going to let them run amuck without a proper platoon sergeant. They sent over another Sergeant First Class, SFC Cartwright.

SFC Cartwright arrived at COP Tynes the day after Santos's boots and rifle ceremony. He had come down from working for Battalion as the Air NCO, a role he had held for a while now, a very different role from leading men in combat. He had done his squad leader time in Alpha Company, but that was some time ago.

He pulled SSG Rosa aside. They were both from Jersey, so they bonded immediately and SFC Cartwright knew Rosa was the man of the house now. He wanted to learn as much as he could from him before he presented himself to the rest of the men. "What's the dynamic of the platoon like?" he asked.

"You got yourself a platoon full of fighters, Sergeant," Rosa replied. "It's a pretty crazy bunch of dudes, but they are some of the best fighters I've ever fought besides and work extremely well together. We are a pretty tight-knit group. It's a pretty heavily team-leader-run platoon, and you got a good bunch of team leaders. They take charge and get shit done. Any one of them would make a good squad leader one day. And the Joes know their stuff. They don't really need to be told much anymore and are pretty much all capable of filling a team leader's role. We have a few new guys, but the guys are getting them along and they are figuring it out rather quickly. If these men trust you, they will do anything for you, but first impressions are kind of important."

SFC Cartwright nodded. "How can I make a good first impression on these guys? What do you recommend I do to not come in hot and overstep what you guys already have?"

SSG Rosa thought for a moment. "Just be up front with the guys. Don't try to sugarcoat anything or beat around the bush. We are all men here."

SFC Cartwright nodded again. "Alright, go get the boys. I want to meet the platoon."

The men gathered in the clearing outside the gym so SFC Cartwright could introduce himself. He stood in front of the group of men, they all looked upon him with wary eyes. He was a short, skinny man, not quite what you would expect a combat soldier to look like. He looked the men over and saw in them the well-oiled machine Rosa had talked about. He could tell they had established their own internal hierarchy and a way of getting things done. He knew better than to throw a wrench in that.

SFC Cartwright stood in front of the group of men sitting on the gravel. He seemed very relaxed for the position he had just been thrown into. "I'm Sergeant First Class Robert Cartwright, and I'm going to be your new platoon sergeant," he said in a stereotypical Jersey accent. The men all stared at him blankly, not knowing how to react, like they had been given something that they had not asked for. "Now look, I'm not here to fill anyone's shoes. I'm not here to change things up. This is you all's platoon. I'm here to do a job as your platoon sergeant."

The men looked at each other, surprised. They weren't expecting that, but it was kind of exactly what they needed to hear at the moment, especially from an outsider being forced in. Content, the men went around introducing themselves to their new platoon sergeant.

After the introductions were made, they broke up the gathering and went on to doing whatever it was they had been doing before. As they walked away, McDaniel took this opportunity to lighten the mood once again. "I'm not calling him Dad," he said, "even if there is a firefight!" The men burst out in laughter, as he was quoting a line from the movie *Step Brothers*. "Robert better not get in my face, cuz I'll drop that motherfucker."

## CHAPTER 8

# So, It Begins

The Men of Two Charlie started the month of April off with an air-assault operation into none other than the Shuyens. It was not clear as to why the men were air-assaulting in, as they had spent the past couple of months as a platoon walking or driving to the villages, but the company commander got the air assets for the operation anyway, so why not? Perhaps the whole purpose was to flex the capabilities of the Coalition forces to the locals, or maybe it made someone higher up in the brass leadership look good having an air-assault operation under the battalion's belt. Regardless, the men of Two Charlie thought it was ridiculous. One Charlie and Three Charlie would join them in the operation. They had never been to either village, so it was a little more exciting for them, but to the men of Two Charlie it was unflattering. Just another logistics nightmare. The men would air-assault in CH-47 Chinook helicopters with the ANP forces and clear the villages door to door, looking for any weapons, explosive making material, etc. After the clearance operations of the Shuyens and Upper and Lower Babur were completed, they would exfil to the north through the desert on foot.

The scout-sniper element was supposed to be sent out early under the cover of darkness to cover the men's infill and overwatch the Landing Zone (LZ). However, the weather didn't cooperate with them that day, and the operation timeline was pushed back until Air status turned green again. The sniper team: SSG Farnsworth, SGT Rush, and Moon, along with SGT Lachance, all staged outside the outpost in their gear waiting for the word to head out. Of course, they didn't receive the word until the last minute.

"Birds are en route to Terra Nova to pick up the guys, you guys need to go!" a soldier from the TOC came running around the wall of Hescos to announce to the four men.

"Oh shit!" SSG Farnsworth replied, "Let's go!" He, SGT Rush, SGT Lachance, and Moon grabbed their gear and began heading east. They had a lot of ground to cover so they began a slow jog, which turned into a run as the sound of the Birds got louder and louder in the valley.

The four men ran through the orchards until they finally made it to Babur, but had a hard time finding a good overwatch position for the infill. The trees were so thick, and the valley consisted of pretty flat terrain for the most part, leaving no high ground to get a good, elevated position. By the time they established somewhat of a hasty LP/OP on top of a building in Lower Babur, the Birds had already set down and Charlie Company had already infiltrated the villages.

The clearance operation went as planned and, like in the past, they came up with nothing. No weapons, no explosives, nothing. There was one thing the men did start to notice and found odd—no one occupied Lower Babur. It was abandoned, a ghost town. They had noticed this in one other village as well, Tarok Kolache. Whenever they asked the villagers why this was, they never got a straight answer from them. The men just figured that when the farmers would come back into the valley to start farming they would start to reoccupy them. It always felt a little eerie walking through them though.

After the operation was complete, the men pushed north to the desert clearing and marched their way back to COP Tynes.

The company First Sergeant had been gunning for SGT Thomson for some time now. He hated 2nd Platoon for some reason, and he hated SGT Thomson the most. When SFC Cartwright took over the platoon, he was told he would have a deadbeat E-5 on his hands; in fact, it was quite the opposite.

"You're going to have to start going out on patrols now," SFC Cartwright said to SGT Thomson as he pulled him aside into the TOC.

"What are you talking about?" SGT Thomson replied, a look of confusion on his face. "I go out on every patrol."

SFC Cartwright looked to Lt. Farrington for confirmation. "Yeah, he's been going out every single day. He works with the ANP on patrol. We've had some drastic improvements since he started."

SFC Cartwright nodded. "Really?" he said, surprised by the answer.

"Yeah. Before Tommy, they didn't even wear uniforms. They'd be walking around the COP in their damn man dresses, coming and going as they pleased. One of our guys almost shot one of them cuz all they saw was a man in civilian attire with an AK approaching," Lt. Farrington explained. "Now they are at least in uniform. They still come and go as they please. And we are still working on getting them to go out on patrol not high as fuck."

SFC Cartwright smiled. "Alright. I apologize. From what the First Sergeant said, I thought I was going to have a shitbag on my hands. Now I see that there isn't anything to worry about."

SGT Thomson turned red. He hated the First Sergeant almost as much as the First Sergeant hated him. He mumbled something under his breath in anger.

"First Sergeant really doesn't like you, huh?" SFC Cartwright laughed.

"No, he does not," SGT Thomson said and left the TOC.

SFC Cartwright was able to block the First Sergeant's attempts at getting rid of SGT Thomson for about a month, however, due to a Mass-Cal situation in Bravo Company, soldiers were moved from the battalion Headquarters element to fill their spots. This left space in the Battalion Personal Security Detachment (PSD) and a request for soldiers was put out. First Sergeant jumped on the opportunity and offered up Thomson. Once Battalion accepted, it was out of SFC Cartwright's hands.

With SGT Thomson gone, the amount of supervision on the ANP decreased. Lt. Farrington and SFC Cartwright would meet with Bismullah and his men regularly to go over possible patrols and objectives in the area, sometimes even cooking and sharing dinner with the officers, but other than their meetings and the patrols, they were unsupervised. Bismullah and his men seemed very loyal to the Two Charlie men, but they were also rooted in the reality of the whole war. The Americans weren't going to be there forever. They had to look out for themselves.

When Thomson left, Bismullah's men stopped pulling guard duty in their tower on the roof. The Two Charlie men had built their three towers so they didn't need to rely on the ANP for security, so it wasn't a major concern for the men. It was more of a lack of discipline on their part. They barely pulled security as it was when they did man their tower.

The first major concern the men had was during an afternoon meeting with Bismullah. Lt. Farrington had just finished explaining to them the plan for the next day. "Alright, is there anything that you need before tomorrow?" he asked and the platoon's interpreter relayed the question.

Bismullah said something back in Pashto and the interpreter looked at him. "He said 'Yes, sir,' they would like to have more bullets for their rifles, some of his men, they have no more rounds."

Lt. Farrington looked surprised. "What?! They don't have ANY rounds?"

The interpreter asked Bismullah again to confirm he had gotten the message correct. "Uh, yes, sir, he said that some of the men don't have any more rounds."

"What do you mean? We gave them plenty of ammo a month ago and they've only been to the range once. What did they do with it all?" Lt. Farrington asked angrily. The platoon interpreter relayed to Bismullah, who didn't answer. "Did they shoot it all?" Farrington continued. "When?" Bismullah still had no response.

Lt. Farrington thought for a moment. "Tell him they can have enough for three magazines each. They don't get any more unless they bring back the casings. Is this understood?"

The interpreter relayed the message and the two of them both nodded. "Yes, sir, this is good."

Lt. Farrington ended the meeting and frustratedly walked back into the TOC. "What's wrong?" SGT Maher asked him.

"I think we have been supplying ammo to the Taliban." Lt. Farrington replied.

"Hey, help me clear some of this shit out of the MRE room." SSG Rosa said to the scouts snacking in Loredo's kitchen. He was sick and tired of all the clutter the room had in it and had been meaning to clean it up for some time now. It initially was where the men had been storing their boxes full of MREs, but slowly became the place where they would just throw items picked up on Thunder Runs or delivered to them on FSC clips. The men followed him to the room, each grabbed a box to put in the gym building.

"What is this stuff?" Moon asked, setting down the large, heavy box he had just picked up. He pulled out his knife to open the box and examine its contents. It was full of the Humanitarian Aid (HA) blankets they had attempted to give the locals in the past.

SSG Farnsworth did the same with his box, and it too contained wool blankets. "So much for these. Might have been nice to have them for ourselves a few months ago," he said as he folded the blanket and replaced it in the box.

"Oh, shit!" SSG Rosa said as he opened his box. "Check these out." The men came over and didn't know what to make of what was in SSG Rosa's box.

"What the fuck?" SGT Rush said slowly as he tried to make sense of what he was looking at. Moon just laughed.

The box was full of the ugliest hot pink Crocs the men had ever seen. Rosa opened another box of similar size and shape and, like the other, it was full of glowing pink shoes. The three men started opening boxes to reveal more and more of the ugly shoes of all different sizes.

"What the actual fuck?" SGT Rush said again with a big smile on his face, trying to understand why Crocs of all things would be sent to Afghanistan, especially in pink. "What, they couldn't sell them in the States, so they try their luck in Afghanistan as HA?" he laughed.

SSG Rosa had already put a pair on. "You know, they aren't bad," he said, holding one of his now pink-covered feet in the air and turning it to examine it from different angles.

SSG Farnsworth and Moon laughed and searched for a pair to try on themselves. "You think we were supposed to give these to the locals?"

The four men thought for a second, then laughed. The thought of hot pink Crocs falling into the hands of the Taliban much like all the other HA they had distributed was hilarious. They couldn't picture being in a firefight and seeing the Taliban running around in pink Crocs, that would be ridiculous.

"Nah," SSG Rosa said, "These are ours," he said, walking away wearing the ridiculous shoes and taking the box with him.

It wasn't long before the other men noticed Rosa's Crocs, and it wasn't long before they all had a pair of their own. Hot pink became a very prominent color around the outpost. It was quite the sight to see, battle-hardened men in a battle-hardened combat theater wearing pink plastic shoes. The men thought it was hilarious and it became a sort of Two Charlie trademark. Lt. Farrington and SFC Cartwright even had a pair. If they weren't on patrol or in the guard tower, the men were wearing their Crocs.

Spring in the valley didn't come alone, it brought with it the heat. It was like someone turned the switch to the furnace on, and all the mud and rain turned to dust. The men had spent a day installing tin roofing on the wood structure after enduring the monsoon season, only to have the whole thing ripped off in the first sandstorm. Sandstorms are a crazy thing to experience. One minute the sun is beating down on you, and the next it's not. There is no hiding from them either. All one can do is watch and wait as the wall of dust and earth approaches like the slowest-moving tidal wave. When it finally hits, it's like a hurricane had a child with sandpaper. All you can do is hunker down and breathe in dust until it's over. Then it gets calm again.

With the changing of the seasons also came the changing of the patrol style. The men cut down on the number of patrols they were conducting per day and increased the time in which they were out on patrol each day. Their focus also shifted from census information-gathering patrolling to more "Hunter Killer"-focused patrolling.

There was a lot more activity in the valley as the fields began to become lush with leaves. The pomegranate trees were fully leafed, and the grape vines reached over the three-foot mud walls of the vineyards. The distance the men could see through the brush shrank drastically, and the valley became a thick jungle. More and more farmers were out tending their crops, and more and more farmers were digging to move water. The Afghan people are masters at irrigation. They had an impressive network of canal systems branching off the Arghandab River, leading to all their fields. It was like the valley woke up one day and it wasn't thrilled to have the men of Two Charlie at its front door.

Third Squad was on their way back from a particularly hot Hunter Killer patrol. They had spent a lot of time wandering through the orchards and grape vineyards of Lower Babur. Despite the increase in farmer activity, there was no increase in anyone occupying the village, and it remained barren.

The jungle of leaves and undergrowth does an amazing job of keeping all the water from escaping. When the men would venture south of the second canal, it was like they were in a sauna, sweating bullets through their combat uniforms and practically breathing in the humidity under the foliage canopy. When they were north of the canal, it was scorching dry heat with the sun beating down on them and no escape. They had to choose their poison.

SGT Brown had chosen to take the northern path through the desert on their way back from patrol that day instead of climbing through the orchards. There was a large dried-up riverbed that lay between the village of Upper Babur and the village of Druia. It was extremely exposed, but the closest cover and concealment the enemy would have to shoot at them from was far enough away that it was worth the risk. It was much faster than going through the obstacle course the orchards presented. They had climbed enough walls on the way out there and just wanted to get back to COP Tynes.

SGT Brown noticed Nguyen falling behind in their wedge formation in the open desert. Nguyen was the patrol's acting medic, filling in for Ryan who was on leave and giving Doc Taylor a break from patrolling that day. He had the heavy aid bag with all the medical equipment on his back weighing him down. "Keep up, Johnny Nguyen," Brown shouted at the soldier falling behind.

This made Nguyen angry. He hated carrying the aid bag but didn't really have a choice in the matter. He and Ryan were chosen by Santos to go through EMT training before deployment to help the platoon medic with treating casualties. Ryan was chosen because he was one of the older and more mature men in the platoon, as a majority of the men were only 18–21, and Nguyen was chosen because he was Asian and Santos thought he was smart. Santos picked him and trusted him, and he wore that like a badge of honor, but Nguyen was also kind of a rebellious soldier and sometimes hard to handle. For some reason he liked his team leader, SGT Bragg, and listened to him, for the most part. He bounced his aid bag in an attempt to readjust the weight, picked up his pace, and threw up a big middle finger SGT Brown's way. SGT Brown shook his head and turned to continue on. That is when it went off.

Katunk!

The loud, odd sound echoed in the openness of the dried-up riverbed. It wasn't a boom like something blowing up, but more like the sound a firework makes when being launched into the air. SGT Brown turned to see a small cylindrical object being propelled from the ground into the sky between Nguyen and Dru. "Oh shit," he thought to himself, "what the fuck is that?"

"Bouncing Betty!" SGT Cornelius thought to himself as he hit the deck. He too saw the object flying straight into the air and could only think of it being one thing. The other men instantly followed suit and got prone. They cringed anticipating a secondary blast that would send shrapnel in all directions through the air.

Precious seconds went by, nothing happened. The only sound they heard was a dull thud, as the cylindrical object fell back down to earth. They scanned in all directions, looking for anyone watching them or a possible trigger man.

Pop! Pop! Pop!

Shots rang out from the trees along the second canal and whizzed by the men. Dru immediately responded by launching his 203 grenades into the tree line. He was insane with the grenade launcher and got three rounds off before anyone could even react. The rounds splashed at the base of the trees where the shots had come from, ripping the leaves off the branches and engulfing them in a cloud of dust.

"Move to cover!" SSG Loredo yelled, pointing at a mud wall 100 meters from where the men lay in the direction of where the shots had come. Jackson laid into the trees with his SAW to cover their movement. The men pushed past the wall and to the canal, they were no longer receiving enemy fire, but continued to lay down covering fire until they got to the canal wall.

"COP Tynes, this is Charlie Two Six Romeo, troops in contact over," Godard sounded off over the radio, letting the men back at COP Tynes know their situation.

"Roger, Two Six Romeo, standing by," a voice over the radio responded.

SSG Loredo and the men got along the wall and pushed further south into the orchards, maneuvering past where they had been receiving fire. They bound through the fields, searching as they moved, but whoever had taken the shots at the men were gone.

The men reestablished security along the second canal, SSG Loredo took the hand mic from Godard to give their situation report. "COP Tynes, this is Charlie Two Three. Sitrep as follows: We encountered what we think was a failed IED. When the explosive didn't go off properly, we received fire from the canal, brake." He scanned the fields to the south like a hawk as he talked, his eyes focused on the distance. "The enemy has broken contact. We have no casualties but are going to need EOD assets to come and take a look at what's left of the IED and possibly blow it in place. We are currently holding security to the south. Prepare to copy grid location."

"Roger, send it," the radio replied.

"Quebec Romeo 0592 4321. How copy?" SSG Loredo said.

"Good copy, EOD happens to be at Terra Nova and is heading our way. They will join the QRF and be out there shortly. Are you on site of the IED now?" The radio replied.

"Negative, the IED location is about one hundred meters to our north in the wadi. Just have the QRF bring EOD out to the edge of Druia. We can link up there and walk them in. Over," SSG Loredo replied.

"Roger, hold tight and we will have EOD out to you. COP Tynes out."

The men pulled security along the canal for about an hour, waiting on the EOD assets to be escorted out to them. The whole thing was no firefight by any means, just a couple of pop shots, but it still got them riled up. It felt good to have the thrill of firing their weapons again at the enemy, even if it was only for a moment. Their spike in adrenaline had begun to wear off and the men started to feel the effects.

Finally, First Squad arrived with EOD at the outer edge of Druia. SSG Loredo left SGT Brown's team along the canal to continue to pull security while he and Bravo team rendezvoused with First.

"What took so long?" SSG Loredo asked SGT Bragg.

"You know how it is, EOD doesn't do anything fast," SGT Bragg replied. He walked over to Nguyen to check on his soldier. "You alright, Johnny Nguyen?"

Nguyen had the biggest grin on his face, "Oh, fuck yeah," he said, trying to hide the fact he was a little shaken by almost getting blown up as he rejoined First Squad. Young laughed as he patted him on the helmet as he walked by. They were happy to see him in one piece. They were happy to see everyone in one piece.

"Got something for ya," SGT Bragg said to SSG Loredo as he pointed over to SGT Knollinger, who had been on mid-tour leave and had just returned. While at Terra Nova awaiting a ride to COP Tynes, he heard that Third Squad had gotten hit. He demanded he go with the EOD guys to COP Tynes to join the QRF.

"Welcome back," SSG Loredo said, glad to have his Bravo team leader back.

"Where is it at?" the EOD soldier asked SSG Loredo, who pointed at the small black object lying on the ground about a hundred meters away from the men. The EOD soldier approached it cautiously and examined the object. When they were convinced it was inactive, one of the guys picked it up and began his further examination. He walked back to the men, object in hand.

"This is a pretty sophisticated bomb," the EOD soldier said to the men as he approached. Third Squad finally got a good look at the object that almost mangled them. In the man's hands was a freaking Folgers Coffee can.

Jackson didn't know what to think. "Dude, that's a freaking coffee can."

"Yeah, and it's full of nuts and bolts and nails. You're lucky the second charge didn't go off. It would have sent all that shit flying everywhere. It was definitely designed to shoot into the air and then blow up. That's pretty sophisticated if you ask me," the soldier replied.

Jackson couldn't believe it. They had literally made a sophisticated bomb out of a coffee can and nails. They were at war with some real MacGyvers and at that moment the same thought crossed the minds of everyone, what do they even look for now? If they can make an IED out of that, they can make it out of anything. They had been told to look out for jugs, as that was the common item used by the enemy because it was easy to fill with HME, and transport. But now, anything and everything could be a bomb.

"We are going to take this one in. I removed the secondary charge so it's inactive, but we definitely want to document this and report it to higher," the EOD soldier explained, putting the device in his pack.

SGT Brown picked up his security and linked up with the rest of the men. First Squad took point and headed back to COP Tynes, avoiding any coffee cans along the way.

Second Squad headed out to patrol the grape vineyards southwest of Babur along the first canal. The men were a little more cautious now they had received their first direct contact from the enemy in the valley since they had been there. SSG DeMeo had his teams bounding through the vineyards slowly, scanning for any possible ambushes. "Move up, Two Two Bravo." He said to SGT McPherson.

SGT McPherson signaled to his guys to pick it up and follow him across the canal. He waded into the waist-deep water and climbed up the bank on the other side. The bank led to a small berm with a three-foot wall on top. It was just high enough to block the view of the fields that lay ahead. He took a knee by the wall, using it for cover and started pulling security for his SAW gunner to cross.

To his right, he noticed two men digging. It seemed odd, as they weren't in one of the fields but along the path on the other side of the short wall. He waved at the men to get their attention. "Wadarega!" he yelled, instructing the men to stop.

The men were surprised. They both dropped behind the other side of the wall behind them. SGT McPherson raised his rifle. To his surprise, the men both popped AK-47s over the wall and began firing at him.

Pop! Pop! Pop! Pop! Pop! Pop! Pop!

SGT McPherson dove behind the short mud wall he was taking cover behind as rounds smacked the dirt and trees around him. Luckily the men weren't really aiming, just hectically blind firing. McPherson came up and began returning fire. The two men ran, retreating through a hole in the mud wall behind them and escaping into the orchards.

Barthel hurled himself against the mud wall next to SGT McPherson. He was halfway through the canal when the shots started to ring out. He walked on water the rest of the way and flew up the berm. "Where are they at?" he yelled, readying his SAW.

"Through that hole!" SGT McPherson replied, pointing at the break in the wall with his rifle. Barthel began sending short bursts through the opening with his machine gun as the rest of Bravo team got online on the berm, but the two men were nowhere in sight. They had disappeared into the thickness of the orchards.

Third Squad prepped for another patrol, this time north in the open desert. The men liked to break up their patrols in the jungle and every so often spent a day in the village of Druia and in the desert to the north, where they knew nothing would happen to them. They picked up their gear and headed out of the front entrance of COP Tynes for a short late-afternoon patrol.

As soon as they had gotten out of the wire, SGT Knollinger noticed a man pushing another man in a wheelbarrow. It was like the men had been waiting for the Americans to come out and, as soon as they saw them, they began waving them down.

SGT Knollinger took his team to go see what all the fuss was about. As he got closer, he noticed blood on the man in the wheelbarrow's tunic. "Hey, Two Three, this guy has blood all over his man dress, I think he might be fucked up," SGT Knollinger said over the radio to SSG Loredo. "Can you send Doc up here?" Knollinger searched the men to make sure they weren't hiding weapons or wearing explosives and then examined the man in the wheelbarrow. There was blood all over his clothes. He raised his tunic to reveal the man's right leg, gone below the knee with bright white bone sticking out of the bloody mangled stump. "Oh shit, yeah, this guy's fucked up," he said as he pulled the man's tunic back down over the mangled limb.

Doc Taylor began tending to the man's wounds as SSG Loredo, Lt. Farrington, and the platoon's interpreter began questioning the other man to find out what happened. Apparently, the two were tending to their field and were heading home for the evening. As soon as they stepped through the doorway of their field, the man blew up and lost his leg.

"Can you show us the field?" Lt. Farrington asked the man.

The man replied, shaking his head, waving his arm for the men to follow. "Woo, woo."

The men followed the local through the fields, the whole time wondering if he was about to lead them into an ambush or possibly another IED. They kept the man close until he finally pointed out the place his friend had stepped on the bomb. Sure enough, there was a small crater right in front of the doorway to the field. There was blood on the ground next to the hole and a chunk of bright red flesh lay beside it. The man's heel was still sitting there next to the hole.

The men established security around the location, being extra cautious to try not to trigger any other IEDs in the area. When security was established, Lt. Farrington picked up his radio hand mic to call it in.

"Wait!" SSG Loredo cried, grabbing the mic out of the platoon leader's hand. "Before we call this in and have to sit here all night waiting for EOD, let me take a look." He took out his knife and began to crawl towards the hole.

"What the fuck is he doing?" Lt. Farrington asked. Loredo was already gone before he had the chance to ask him what his plan was.

SSG Loredo crawled up to the small hole in the ground and picked up the man's heel. He threw it in Lt. Farrington's direction. It almost hit him, he had to move out of the way to avoid it. Loredo began poking the ground with his knife, probing like a World War II soldier clearing a minefield.

"What the fuck are you doing?" Lt. Farrington shouted.

SSG Loredo's eyes widened when he thought he felt his knife strike something in the ground. He slowly pulled it out and noticed a yellow cord sticking out from under some of the small rocks in the blast hole. It was a detonation cord that hadn't gone off. He slowly crawled back to the men. A look of disappointment on his face. "Call it in," he said, mentally preparing himself for a long night.

The men called in the IED, letting Company know they believed the bomb hadn't completely gone off and they would need EOD to conduct a BIP (Blow in Place). Unfortunately, EOD assets weren't going to be available that night, so they would have to secure the site until morning.

SSG Loredo was pissed. "Set the guys in security positions, we aren't going anywhere tonight," he told his team leaders. SGT Brown and SGT Knollinger got to it, letting the guys know they would be out there for the night.

"What about him?" Lt. Farrington asked, referring to the local Afghan that led the men to the site. "We can't just let him go, he could tell the enemy where we are and they could ambush us, or put out another IED for our exfil."

SSG Loredo thought for a moment. He then turned to the platoon's interpreter. "Gucci, tell this man he is going to stay here with us tonight. If he tries to leave, we might mistake him for the Taliban and shoot him. He is to stay by your side until we say he can go." The interpreter relayed the message. The man was not very thrilled.

An hour went by, and the sun left the valley. The men put on their NODs and started alternating security. They went to 50 percent security, meaning for every man up pulling security, there was a man down trying to get some sleep. They would switch every hour until dawn, where they would go back to 100 percent.

SSG Loredo and Lt. Farrington sat slouched along one of the mud walls, staring down the small canal that skirted it. Even though both were extremely bored, neither could sleep, as the night sky robbed the hot air and replaced it with the cold. Then, all of a sudden, SSG Loredo perched up as if he had seen or heard something.

"What's up?" Lt. Farrington whispered, looking in the direction SSG Loredo was looking at through his NODs.

"Do you see that?" SSG Loredo replied. He quickly put his finger over his mouth to signal to the platoon leader to be quiet. He slowly got off the ground and began tip-toeing his way along the canal path. SGT Knollinger saw him and raised his rifle in that direction, ready to engage anything that moved.

The men started to realize Loredo's attention was focused on something on the ground. They watched as he inched his way closer until finally, he pounced. Like a cat on a mouse, his hands pinned something to the ground. A squeak rang out through the silence of the night. "I got it!" SSG Loredo whispered, as he walked back to Lt. Farrington with something in his hands. He opened them to reveal a small hedgehog. "I caught the Weeble Wobble!"

"Weeble Wobble?" SGT Knollinger queried, walking over to look. He laughed through his nose when he saw the thing. "That's a hedgehog."

"It's a Weeble Wobble!" Loredo protested.

SGT Lachance walked over to see what was going on. When he saw the hedgehog Loredo had caught he just smiled and laughed as he walked away, back to where he had come from.

"Charlie Two Six, this is Terra Nova," the radio chirped. The men had turned the volume down on their hand mics so they barely heard the transmission.

"Go for Charlie Two Six," Lt. Farrington replied.

"Roger, our friends down the road, the Beast element, said they might be able to assist and bring out their Charlie to come clear that bomb for you," the company soldier over the radio said. He was referring to the ODA element down Route Red Dog. They must have been bored because the guys had asked them to assist in the past to no avail.

"Roger that, what is their ETA?" Lt. Farrington asked, not wanting to sound too excited to get the hell out of there over the radio.

"They said they can be there in about fifty mikes. We've given them your platoon frequency so they can get into contact with you," the soldier said.

"Roger, good copy, I'll pass it on. Charlie Two Six out," Lt. Farrington said then turned to SSG Loredo, playing with the Weeble Wobble that he now had fashioned a leash for out of parachute cord. "Did you catch that?"

"Roger. Alpha, Bravo, you guys copy?" SSG Loredo said quietly over the radio.

"I copied," SGT Knollinger said.

"Me too," replied SGT Brown.

About an hour went by, and the ODA guys finally linked up with the Two Charlie men. They looked kind of like boogeymen, sneaking through the darkness and fog of the night, beards jetting out from under their expensive NODs. The Two Charlie men weren't jealous.

The group's engineer sergeant made his way to speak with Lt. Farrington and SSG Loredo. "What do we got here?" he asked.

"We think a local stepped on a toe popper that was supposed to set off a bigger bomb still under the ground," Lt. Farrington replied.

"Where is it at?" The man asked.

They pointed out the hole next to the doorway. The man nodded and put down his pack to retrieve something. He pulled out a brick of C4 explosive and tied some parachute cord around it. He also shoved the blasting cap into the brick and unraveled some of the wire. He paused for a moment. "Where is your security located?"

"We got a team along the canal here and another on the south side of the field on the other side of that wall," SSG Loredo replied.

The man nodded, confirming there were no friendlies within the vicinity of the bomb. "Tell them that they are about to hear a loud boom and not to be alarmed," SSG Loredo nodded and relayed the message over the radio to Knollinger and Brown to pass on to their men.

The man tossed the brick of C4 down the alley past the hole. He began to pull the cord, dragging the brick into the bottom of the hole. "Fire in the hole!" he shouted, initiating the blasting cap wire.

BA-BOOM!

The men could slightly distinguish the two explosions that went off almost simultaneously, one being the C4, and the other whatever was under the ground. The blast echoed in the quiet night sky. When the dust cloud finally settled, the ODA engineer sergeant walked up to examine the new hole, then returned to the men. "I think we are good here."

The men just looked at each other. That was pretty easy, and seemed a lot safer than what EOD was doing when they responded to their BIP calls. SSG Loredo looked at Lt. Farrington. "Why can't we do that, sir?" he asked, bending over to pick up his new pet and put it in one of his rig pouches.

"You're taking that thing back?" Lt. Farrington asked.

"It's my Weeble Wobble," Loredo replied.

As days went by, things started to pick up in the valley. The men received more and more pop shots while on patrol until it started happening daily. They would return fire and try to maneuver on the men shooting at them, but the enemy seemed like they weren't there for a fight. They would just dump a magazine into the men and then run away.

The short engagements did start to evolve, however. The fighters began to test the Two Charlie men by unloading a magazine then running to another location. When the men would maneuver on their first ambush spot, they would shoot at them again from another. They repeated this process until the Two Charlie men stopped following them. It didn't take long for the Two Charlie guys to figure out what the enemy was trying to do. They felt like they were being baited, and the enemy was trying to lure them into something.

First Squad had been out on patrol all morning when they heard the familiar thunder in the distance. It rumbled throughout the valley.

"You hear that, Sergeant?" Rae said to SGT Maher. Rae had returned to the platoon after he had been cleared of his injuries in KAF. Everyone thought he was crazy for coming back, but they were all happy to have him. Rae, Young, and Munoz all had a ticket out of there, but they chose to fight through the pain and come back. That said a lot.

"I heard it too," Rostran said. He had taken McCune's place as SAW gunner in the team after McCune got injured on the 22nd.

"Yeah, I heard it. Anything on company net? Couldn't tell what direction it came from. Could be from B co," SGT Maher said, walking to SSG Craumer and Godard to see if they had any radio chatter.

"Nothing yet. I'll get ahold of COP Tynes and see if they have any information," Godard said, then turned to speak into the radio hand mic.

The men took a short halt in a pomegranate field and waited. The morning sun started to warm the cool air as it pierced through the leaves of the canopy above them. Rays of light beamed the tropical paradise and lit up some plum trees with ripe fruit, which the men all picked and ate. It was actually a really pretty place, if it wasn't Afghanistan.

"Let's keep pushing," SSG Craumer said. The men had spent all morning pushing south to the river and were going to loop around to go through the Khosrows. They didn't want to be stagnant for too long.

"Roger," SGT Bragg acknowledged. He signaled his guys to fall back in on him as he took point. Just as he was about to hop over the first wall, a radio transmission from COP Tynes came in.

"Charlie Two One, this is COP Tynes," the radio chirped.

"Go for Two One," SSG Craumer replied.

"You guys have the medic with you, correct?" the soldier asked.

SSG Craumer looked at Doc Taylor who was listening in right beside him. "Yeah, he's right here, what's up?"

"Can you guys get him back to COP Tynes, ASAP?" the soldier asked.

SSG Craumer looked at Doc and Maher, who had just walked up to listen to what was going on. "Roger, you don't want us to continue to push into Khosrow Sofla?"

"Negative, we need the medic here now," the soldier replied, sounding a little distressed.

SGT Bragg heard that last transmission; SSG Craumer gave him a head nod to change course back to COP Tynes. They had no idea what the situation was and why it was so urgent. Perhaps someone got hurt in a dumb way that they didn't want to say over the radio in case company was monitoring? Who knew? All they knew was they asked for the medic, not Doc. It's an unspoken rule that if you want your platoon medic for something non-medical, you refer to him as Doc. If you used or said the words "medic," it was serious. They hurdled wall after wall and made their way until they broke free of the jungle and crossed the second canal. Bragg made quick work out of the grape vineyards and was soon on the south side of the village of Jelawur. He got on Route Red Dog and the rest of the squad staggered the road behind him.

When he got sight of COP Tynes, he noticed there was a large group of villagers at the front gate, all of them seemed upset. Lt. Farrington was out front with the interpreter and a few other soldiers.

SGT Bragg and the rest of First Squad made their way through the crowd to Lt. Farrington. "What's going on?" SGT Bragg asked him.

"Where is Doc Taylor?" Lt. Farrington enquired, pointing to a small child one of the villagers was holding.

Doc Taylor heard his name and ran over. He took a knee to seem less threatening to the young boy who was probably only five or six years old. He was crying and covering his face with his hands. His hands were covered in blood that ran down his forearms. It had dripped all over the front of his small tunic. He wouldn't move them to let Doc Taylor inspect his injury. "I need to see," he said softly to the little boy. "It's okay. I need to see."

He grabbed the boy by the wrists and pulled his hands away from his face. The boy let out a scream as his face was revealed. The boy had a large laceration on his face leading to where his right eye should have been. The eye was hanging out of its socket, completely destroyed. There were smaller laceration and puncture wounds all along the boy's right half of his body, like he had been peppered by rocks and other debris. Doc Taylor got out his dressings and started wrapping the boy's head with them. "What happened?" he asked the platoon leader.

"Apparently the kids found an IED and were playing with it when it went off is what I've gathered so far," Lt. Farrington replied.

Another local man made his way up to the front of the group with a wheelbarrow. It had a black cloth draped over it to hide its contents. SGT Bragg stopped the man and removed the cloth to search the wheelbarrow. Another young boy lay in the barrow, only it wasn't a whole boy. SGT Bragg looked in horror as he realized the boy's body was missing entirely from the ribs down. He was staring at the kid's liver and lungs, mangled like hamburger meat. The boy's skin was pale, as white as paper, and he was literally floating in his own blood.

SGT Flannery walked up to Bragg to help search and have a look. "Oh shit!" he said, "That kid is dead as fuck."

McDaniel walked over to investigate after seeing SGT Flannery's reaction. "Jesus, is it take your kid to work day in the Dab today?" he said, trying to make light of the situation.

Neenan joined them and stood behind SGT Bragg, staring at the small boy. SGT Bragg replaced the cloth over the boy and turned to Neenan, whose gaze didn't leave the cloth. "One of yours?" SGT Bragg asked.

Neenan's eyes began to water as he processed what he just saw. "Yeah," was all he could muster shakily. He swallowed deeply to keep the tears at bay.

SGT Bragg put his hand on his shoulder to try to comfort him. "I told you not to get close," he said somberly.

The men treated the boy with the eye injury and MedEvaced him along with his father. The villagers begged for them to take the other boy also, but there was nothing they could do. Flannery was right, that boy was dead as fuck. Lt. Farrington spoke with the group of villagers, told them this doesn't have to happen to their children, all they needed to do was tell the men where the ones who were putting these bombs in the ground were. None of them answered. It was quiet as the villagers left COP Tynes and headed to the graveyard.

CHAPTER 9

# Don't Trip

The men of Two Charlie continued to patrol the valley and continued to see an increase in enemy activity. Farmers tending their fields would pick up and leave when they saw the men climbing over a wall heading their way into the fields. Some would even pass right by the men on their way out. Lt. Farrington would always ask them, "Where are you going? Why are you leaving?" To which they would always have some fabricated excuse: "I have to meet my uncle for tea" or "I am breaking for lunch." Each villager acted like they didn't want to stay around the men long and definitely did not want to be seen talking with them.

Like clockwork, each time the farmers were seen abandoning their fields, the men would get shot at. It wasn't super effective, as it seemed like only a few men with rifles were engaging them, but the rounds would always land close enough to send the men ducking for cover. They would return fire each time, chasing them into the orchards where they would lose track of them, and the CCA helicopters would be unable to support. It was like a big game of cat and mouse, however it was unclear who was the cat and who was the mouse.

First Squad set out midday on another patrol to the village of Lower Babur. Initially, the patrol headed east along Route Red Dog. The men staggered along the road as they walked through the early June heat. They would sweat buckets through their gear as the heat of the day usually reached around one hundred twenty degrees. This day had been a particularly cloudy one, something very unusual for June in the valley.

It wasn't long before First Squad came to the end of the large walls that ran along the road and opened to reveal a clearing for a cemetery. SGT Bragg changed direction and started heading south. He had been point man on every patrol with his squad and was constantly trying to switch things up, pick different routes, different paths, different walls to jump or climb over. The point men of Two Charlie kept the enemy guessing as to where they were going and tried to never take the same path twice. They even drew their routes on a map on the computer in the TOC so they could track their movement through certain areas, varying their paths as time progressed.

It seemed impossible, after months of patrolling the valley, to find somewhere they hadn't been or a route they hadn't touched. Bragg and the other point men did their best, but there were only so many different ways they could go.

It felt like someone was constantly watching them, from the time they left the ECP to the time they got back. Sometimes the interpreters would even intercept transmissions over their ICOM radios, radios that scanned frequencies to pick up on enemy chatter. They would say things like, "The Americans are leaving their base now" or "They are heading south down the road." They even picked up some transmissions on when they were about to be shot at—"Do you see the three men standing together? Shoot at them!"

SGT Bragg's efforts to avoid IEDs and confuse the enemy did not go unnoticed, especially by his men. They would constantly make fun of him, joke around about his routes, even complain that he was lost. He didn't care what they said, he was going to do what he had to do to keep them from stepping on a bomb or getting shot in the face.

SGT Bragg led his men through the cemetery, around the piles of rocks with rudimentary colored flags sticking out of them covering the shallow graves of the villagers that had died before them. It reminded him of the Tibetan prayer flags that are flown at base camp on Mount Everest. There were so many graves, and they were arranged in no particular order like the cemeteries back home in the United States. This made it impossible to determine if one was out of place. He figured any one of them could have been a fake grave the enemy could have created the night before and planted a bomb in to remotely detonate. SGT Bragg didn't like that thought and felt an urge to exit the cemetery as soon as possible.

There was a break in the wall that led to a small alley. SGT Bragg didn't like it, as it was a possible choke point, but it would get the squad out of the openness of the cemetery and away from the graves. He decided to climb over one of the walls of the alley and dropped into a grape field. SGT Bragg and the other soldiers had grown quite fond of the grape fields. They not only provided great cover, but amazing concealment from the enemy now the vines started to grow their leaves and fruit. It was a good spot to lose anyone that may be watching them or, if they were to get ambushed, it was a good spot to fight from. Plus, it was an opportunity to snag some grapes that were just becoming ripe.

SGT Bragg turned to see if Young needed any help coming over the wall with his SAW. He didn't give SGT Bragg the chance as he just dropped like a bag of rocks off the wall into the field, cursing on impact. He was still upset SGT Bragg wouldn't let him and Neenan switch, allowing him to carry the M203 and give Neenan the SAW. SGT Bragg figured that they were both proficient with their weapon systems, and the beginning of the fighting season wasn't the time to be switching things around.

Neenan climbed over the wall next, and then Nguyen. They pushed into the grapes to pull security for the rest of the squad as they climbed over the wall. Vasquez practically fell off the wall, as he tucked and rolled his landing. He helped Rostran with his SAW over. The gun team handed the 240 machine gun over the wall to SGT Maher and then one by one climbed the wall themselves. Once everyone was over, the patrol continued.

"That wall might have been a little tall," SGT Bragg thought to himself as he pushed through the grape fields. He exposed guys to possible enemy fire each time they came over that wall, but it was better than the alley. SGT Bragg had a sixth sense for things like that, and he did not like the look and feel he got from that alley.

The patrol maneuvered through the grape fields until they came to the first canal. One by one they crossed the canal at a point where it was maybe ten feet wide and waist deep. It felt good cooling off in the water, but it was a luxury the men couldn't enjoy for too long. Each man pulled security for the next, as one by one they made it across the canal and filed into the grape fields.

SGT Bragg led the patrol to an elevated path that had two grape fields on each side. The path ended at a short wall that dropped down onto a path perpendicular to it. SGT Bragg climbed over this wall and dropped to the other side. He landed right in a drainage ditch that paralleled the path. He didn't want to know what was in the mud and water he was standing in; he just hoped it was mud and water.

The ditch he was in made the path next to him about waist height. On the opposite side of the path was another wall. SGT Bragg heard something to his right. An old villager was walking down the path towards them, swinging his shemagh around his neck like a scarf. SGT Bragg looked down at the path and noticed a circular area of dirt that looked odd compared to the rest of the dirt on the path. It was more like dry clay and wasn't as compact. He didn't think too much of it at first and turned to the old man to motion to him to stop. Then he noticed the same crumbly dry dirt form a trail along the wall and lead to a tiny bush that stuck out of the wall about halfway up.

Young plopped over the wall to join SGT Bragg in the ditch. He saw the old man approaching them on the path and raised his SAW to stop him. He took a few steps down the path to the right and took a knee to pull security on the old man.

SGT Bragg continued to examine the strange areas along the wall and path. It had not registered to him yet. Not until the clouds parted and revealed the final piece. The light from the sun reflected off something next to his left shoulder. It shimmered in the ray of light as it reflected the beam. It reminded him of a spider-web strand reflecting light in the woods when it caught the sun just right. However, SGT Bragg realized this was no spider-web strand.

"Fuck! Nobody move!" he yelled. It had just registered with him as he added it all up. There was a trip wire across that path just over his left shoulder. The tripwire led to the piece of vegetation on the wall which was placed there to hide the initiation device. If that tripwire was pulled, it would send a current down a wire hidden by the dried clay along that wall. That wire led right to whatever bomb was buried just feet away from him and Young.

Neenan and Nguyen were coming over the wall and could see SGT Bragg's face. Nothing but fear and a sense of urgency. "Get back over that wall, now!" SGT Bragg shouted to everyone and Neenan and Nguyen did so immediately. They knew from his tone that he wasn't playing around.

SGT Bragg helped Young get back over the wall and then climbed over himself. He motioned to the old villager to stay put where he was and not continue down this way. The old man did as he was told and leaned against the dirt wall. Young, Neenan, and Nguyen all took up security positions as SGT Bragg started walking back to SSG Craumer and SGT Maher.

"What's the hold up?" SSG Craumer asked, a look of confusion on his face. SGT Bragg was pretty hectic with his routes, but backtracking was out of character for him.

"Tripwire," is all SGT Bragg said.

"No way," SGT Maher said with a smile of disbelief on his face. "Show me."

Bragg led Maher to the wall and they both climbed on top of it. SGT Bragg pointed out the tripwire running across the path. It was wrapped around a stick on the left side of the path and led to the piece of vegetation on the right. SGT Maher could see the ant trail of dried clay that ran from the small plant to the path, right to the two-foot diameter circle of dirt in the middle of the path.

"No shit," SGT Maher said with a look of happy disbelief. "Good job. How did you see that?" He smacked SGT Bragg's helmet in approval.

SGT Bragg just shook his head, a little queasy from the thought of being less than a foot away from dying a horrible death, still in denial he was still alive, and that he had actually found it.

"I'll call it in, get your guys set up," SSG Craumer said.

The men set in security very carefully in the grape fields on the other side of the wall. They needed to provide an overwatch on the bomb until they could get EOD out to them for a BIP. They had no idea if there were any more bombs in the nearby area and didn't want to find out the hard way.

After their search of the grapes came up empty, they set in for the long wait for EOD. SGT Maher took the interpreter and searched the old man on the path. They found nothing on him, and it appeared he was just walking home after prayer. The men couldn't let him go though, as he could warn possible fighters in the area of their location and that they had found the bomb. They kept him in the grapes with them and had the interpreter keep an eye on him. The old man did as he was told; he was honestly thankful because, if the soldiers hadn't stopped him, he would have walked right into it.

"Alhamdulillah," he kept saying, or "Praise be to God" as the interpreter said. He thanked the men. The tone of his voice made it feel like it was all bullshit.

SSG Craumer walked over to Maher and Bragg who were hunkered down in the middle of the grape field. "We're in luck," he said. "EOD is at Terra Nova. Third Squad is going to pick them up and bring them out to us. Looks like we won't be here all night."

That was a relief. The men hunkered down as they awaited the arrival of Third Squad with EOD. The interpreter constantly scanned the ICOM radio for any chatter. After about an hour of nothing happening, it was pretty apparent the enemy wasn't out to play with the men that day, and the farmer activity in the surrounding fields added to that sense of security.

The men grew bored, trying anything to keep from dozing off and causing a lapse in security. Setting in a patrol base and being stagnant was a double-edged sword as it allowed the men to rest from carrying all their gear in the hot sun, but it also allowed for them to get too comfortable and possibly fall asleep. SGT Bragg and SGT Maher were constantly checking in on their guys, making sure this didn't happen. The men picked and ate some of the grapes, the sour and sweetness kept them awake for the moment. Nguyen, as a joke, picked some of the leaves off the grape vines and put them in the band of his helmet. "Look, I Second Squad," he said loud enough for the rest of Alpha team to hear him but quiet enough that his voice didn't travel far. He was referring to the time SSG DeMeo made his squad wear camouflage face paint on a patrol. They returned, miserable, as the oils from the paint made it even hotter for them. The other two squads made fun of them for it and wouldn't let it go.

SGT Bragg smiled and shook his head at Nguyen but grabbed a few leaves himself. Wouldn't hurt to have a little more camouflage, he thought. Soon, all of Alpha team was covered in grapevine leaves as they ghillied up their gear.

"Charlie Two One, this is Charlie Two Three," SSG Craumer's radio chirped. It was SSG Loredo.

"This is Two One," SSG Craumer replied.

"Roger, let your guys know we are approaching you from the north and are about a hundred meters out," SSG Loredo said, informing them of their imminent rendezvous.

"Roger, see you soon." SSG Craumer replied.

The men watched as Third Squad emerged from the grape fields north of the first canal. It was easy to tell the difference between the Third Squad guys and the EOD soldiers. The Third Squad guys would move tactically, bobbing in and out of the cover of the grape furrows, emerging only for a second to disappear amongst the leaves again. The EOD guys just walked behind them like they were on a stroll in the park.

They finally reached the canal and crossed it one by one. SGT Bragg and his team overwatched them as they crossed. "Took you long enough," SGT Bragg said to SGT Brown as he crossed the canal and perched along the wall to pull security right beside him.

"Jesus," SGT Brown said; Bragg had scared him half to death. He didn't see the men at first with all the leaves. He laughed. "Take a play out of Two Two's book?" SGT Bragg smiled and shifted his guys' security to make room for Third Squad's men.

"Where is it at?" one of the EOD soldiers asked as they made their way to the center of the patrol base.

"Bragg, you want to show him?" SSG Craumer said.

SGT Bragg waved the men to follow him. He led them down the path and climbed atop the wall. "Right there," he said, pointing at the wire across the path. "There is the wire, and you can see the ant trail along the wall to the main charge."

The men leaned forward and squinted, looking for the wire. SGT Knollinger and SSG Loredo joined the men on the wall. They too had a hard time seeing it. "Damn, Bragg, how did you see that thing?" Knollinger asked as he finally caught a glimpse of the wire.

SGT Bragg didn't answer. He just threw his arms up and dismounted the wall back on the other side to rejoin his men. The other guys did the same and let EOD do their work. They photographed everything they found and did a small search of the surrounding area for any other signs or possible secondaries the Two Charlie men might have missed.

When they were complete, they climbed back over the wall. "Have your guys take cover, we are about to blow this sucker. Maybe have them get back a little too," one of the EOD guys said.

"How far should we be?" SGT Lachance asked.

"You're probably good along the north side of the grape field, just stay down below the mud walls when we blow it," the soldier said, pointing to the north side of the field about thirty meters north of the bomb.

The men moved accordingly and gave the EOD guys a thumbs up to signal they were ready. The EOD soldier returned the thumbs up then turned to his supervisor who was taking cover below the grapes. "Fire in the hole!" they yelled. "Fire in the hole!" another responded.

BOOM!

A thunderous roar rang out throughout the furrows, the concussion of the sound shook the men's bones. SGT Bragg looked up from his cover, he wanted to see what could have been Alpha team's demise. He watched as the plume of dust rose into the air, blocking out the sun. It grew and grew as the dirt spread through the sky. He listened, as small pieces of metal, dirt, and rocks began to plummet down on the men and the leaves of the grapes they were taking cover in. He closed his eyes, it sounded like the beginning of a summer rainstorm. A hot piece of metal landed on the back of his neck. He quickly swiped it off before the metal could char his skin.

McDaniel saw the piece of metal land next to his 240 machine gun. He bent over to pick it up to examine it, only to drop it as soon as he picked it up. He shook his hand off, trying to alleviate the pain from the heat. "Ow," he said, still shaking his hand. He began to think what that would feel like lodged inside of him as he stared at the piece of metal on the ground.

SGT Bragg thought of that too, and he walked over to the blast site after the dust settled. He looked at the hole the blast had left in the ground; it stretched across the entire path. One of the EOD guys had found a rather loud chunk of metal on the ground and was examining it. He pulled out his camera and took a photo of the metal. "Russian anti-tank mine," he said as he threw it to Bragg.

SGT Bragg caught it and examined the piece. He could see the Russian text on one side of the metal. "How much charge did you put on that to blow it?" he asked the EOD soldier. He wanted to know how much of the explosion was from the EOD guys' C4 and how much was from the mine.

"Charge?" the soldier replied, confused by the question. "We didn't put any. We just pulled the wire."

SGT Bragg's stomach sank to the ground as he stared at the hole. His face was less than two feet from that thing. He had heard stories of guys getting completely obliterated from IEDs to the point where they couldn't find anything left of them. It was called getting "Pink Misted." Up until this point, he didn't believe the stories to be real. Staring at the hole in the ground and thinking how close he was to it made him a believer.

The EOD guys wrapped up their work and gathered everything they needed from the site and the Two Charlie men picked it up and began the journey back to COP Tynes. SGT Bragg took point and crossed the canal as the sun began to hit the horizon. "Great," he thought to himself, "We'll be heading back in the dark, and now I have to worry about trip wires."

The next day, Second Squad prepared to head out on a patrol through the village of Druia. They conducted all their Pre-Combat Checks (PCCs) and Pre-Combat Inspections (PCIs) and went through the patrol brief.

"Any other questions?" SGT Flannery asked. The men stood silent. "Alright, get on your stuff and let's go." He released the men from the brief to start dawning their gear. "Oh, one more thing," he added, "Watch out for trip wires."

The men smiled and shook their heads as they grabbed their gear and made their way out of the compound. As soon as they cleared the wire, SGT Rush came over the radio. He and Moon had been on the roof of Tower One to provide overwatch while Second Squad moved through Druia. They could cover the men the entire time from the outpost and felt it would be better to have a bird's-eye view of the area while they were out instead of being on the ground with them.

"Hey Two Two, Viper Four. You see that jingle truck coming down Red Dog?" SGT Rush said, referring to the old Hino truck driving toward the outpost down Route Red Dog. The truck was heavily decorated, painted brightly with every color, chains and pendants dangling from the bumpers that jingled as it hit each bump in the road, hence why the troops referred to them as "jingle trucks." SGT Rush wasn't so focused on the truck as he was the contents of what it was carrying in the bed. It was hauling at least twenty men. Usually these trucks hauled rice, beans, and other cargo. This was the first time they had seen one carrying people for transport outside of Kandahar City.

Second Squad stopped the truck and motioned for the men to get out of the back. The men followed the instructions, and they all squatted along the side of the road. SGT Flannery and his team searched the vehicle while SGT McPherson and his team searched the men. Lt. Farrington and the interpreter asked the men where they were going and where they were from. They replied they were coming to farm the valley, and they all gave different locations as to where they were from.

"Let me see your hands," Lt. Farrington asked one of the men. The man smiled and held out his hands to the platoon leader.

Moon and SGT Rush could see the smooth baby skin hands from where they were perched. "Those don't look like farmer's hands to me," Moon said to SGT Rush as he examined them through the scope of his rifle.

"Yeah, those guys don't look like they've farmed a day in their lives," Rush replied.

"Anything in the truck?" SSG DeMeo asked.

"It's clean," SGT Flannery said.

"Nothing on the men either," SGT McPherson added.

"Well, we don't have anything to hold them on," Lt. Farrington said, looking at the men staring at him. They had a look in their eye like a child that was about to get away with something, except their faces were more sinister. They followed the instructions of the soldiers with malicious smiles on their faces; they didn't seem to fear the men. They did this until they were let go and, one by one, climbed back into the back of the jingle truck.

The last man to get back on seemed to be somewhat of the leader of the group. He turned to look at the soldiers and saluted them as he climbed back on to the bed of the truck. The truck driver fired up the engine and continued its slow clunky ride around COP Tynes and down Route Red Dog.

"Did you fucking see that?" SGT Rush asked over the radio.

Wreckage from the IED blast on 22 November 2009 resulting in two KIA and three wounded. (Supplied by Thanhtrung Nguyen)

SPC Marcus Tynes. KIA 22 November 2009. (Supplied by Ethan McDaniel)

SGT James Nolen. KIA 22 November 2009. (Supplied by Brendan Neenan)

Bare bones COP Tynes as the men of Two Charlie received it from the 2nd ID men in December 2009. (Supplied by Lucas Rae)

Leadership discussing the plan forward to build up COP Tynes. (Supplied by Lucas Rae)

Parachute canopy the men would gather under to relax and reconcile after long days of patrolling and filling Hescos. (Supplied by Lucas Rae)

Christmas came early for the men of Two Charlie. Soldiers unboxing all the accessories to their new MATV vehicles. (Supplied by Lucas Rae)

If the men weren't out on patrol, they were filling sandbags to fill Hescos. Soldiers pictured building Tower One. (Supplied by Lucas Rae)

The wood structure built by the men to make their home away from home feel more like one. (Supplied by Nick Thompson)

The gym constructed by the men with all the "tactically acquired" workout equipment. (Supplied by Dale Knollinger)

SGT Thomson covered in shit after falling into the shit can. (Supplied by Thanhtrung Nguyen)

The grape fields south of the first canal. The rows of three-foot mud walls covered in grape vines provided excellent cover and concealment for the men of Two Charlie, especially during firefights. (Supplied by Cody Cornelius)

Some of the children of the Shuyens. (Supplied by Cody Cornelius)

Leadership discussing the patrol's next move while on a patrol in the Shuyens. (Supplied by Cody Cornelius)

Men of Two Charlie on patrol heading into the Devil's Playground. (Supplied by Cody Cornelius)

The platoon's adopted dog, Nepal, out on a patrol with the men. (Supplied by Thanhtrung Nguyen)

Wreckage from the IED blast on 22 March 2010 resulting in one KIA and four wounded. (Supplied by Jared Moossy)

Soldiers of Two Charlie mourning at a boots and rifle ceremony. (Supplied by Ethan McDaniel)

SFC Carlos Santos-Silva. (Supplied by Brendan Neenan)

A soldier walking with an Afghan child in the Khosrows. (Supplied by Ricardo Garcia Vilanova)

A soldier looking out into the orchards south of the second canal. (Supplied by Brandon Young)

One of Two Charlie's team leaders on point in the orchards south of the second canal. The vegetation was very thick, and visibility was sometimes limited to less than fifty feet. (Supplied by Cody Cornelius)

Soldiers walk through the orchards south of the second canal. (Supplied by Ethan McDaniel)

SSG Loredo scanning the trees of the orchards on a patrol after word that enemy in the area were watching them. (Supplied by Ricardo Garcia Vilanova)

SSG Loredo formulating a plan with his squad to maneuver on enemy fighters in the area. (Supplied by Ricardo Garcia Vilanova)

M240 machine gun team engaging the enemy south of the second canal near the village of Babur. (Supplied by Ricardo Garcia Vilanova)

The blast from a tripwire IED that was luckily found by one of the men of Two Charlie rather than triggered. (Supplied by Thanhtrung Nguyen)

Men of Two Charlie crossing one of the many canals in the Arghandab River Valley. (Supplied by Ricardo Garcia Vilanova)

Afghan National Police officers refused to patrol south of the second canal on 7 June 2010. They knew something the men didn't and would not tell them. (Supplied by Ricardo Garcia Vilanova)

Men of Two Charlie treating casualties in the established CCP as red smoke marks the HLZ after an IED blast on 7 June 2010. (Supplied by Ricardo Garcia Vilanova)

Men of Two Charlie load wounded onto stretchers and carry them to MedEvac helicopters. (Supplied by Ricardo Garcia Vilanova)

A Two Charlie squad leader reading the Bible to one of the casualties of an IED blast. (Supplied by Ricardo Garcia Vilanova)

SPC Brendan Neenan takes a break during a short halt in a compound in the Shuyens. (Supplied by Brandon Young)

SPC Christopher Moon geared up and ready to go out on a patrol to help provide sniper support for the men of Two Charlie. (Supplied by Christopher Rush)

SPC Moon scanning the tree line along the second canal for possible enemy targets in the area. (Supplied by Brian Mockenhaupt)

Two Charlie team leader calling over the radio to give a sit rep after an IED blast along the second canal near Babur. (Supplied by Brian Mockenhaupt)

The men of Two Charlie try to calm their nerves after evacuating a wounded soldier out of the battlefield. (Supplied by Brian Mockenhaupt)

A soldier scans along the canal for parts of a soldier's weapon lost in an IED blast. (Supplied by Brian Mockenhaupt)

One of the Two Charlie team leaders addressing the 101st replacements about the reality of the situation they are in after a soldier was severely wounded by an IED blast. (Supplied by Brian Mockenhaupt)

A sniper shooting at enemy fighters from Tower One. (Supplied by Brian Mockenhaupt)

The dog team lifting the bomb dog Dix over a mud wall south of the second canal. (Supplied by Brian Mockenhaupt)

Soldiers helping with heat casualties in the compound the patrol was taking shelter in. (Supplied by Brian Mockenhaupt)

A medic treating heat-casualty soldiers in one of the mud rooms in the compound. (Supplied by Brian Mockenhaupt)

Soldiers getting on the roof of the compound to push back enemy fighters in the area. (Supplied by Brian Mockenhaupt)

The platoon FO coordinating with air support while the compound they are hunkered in is surrounded by enemy fighters south of the second canal. (Supplied by Brian Mockenhaupt)

Soldiers of Two Charlie take a break from the heat of the day in the compound. (Supplied by Brian Mockenhaupt)

Two Charlie soldiers prepare to secure the landing zone for helicopters to evacuate wounded soldiers. (Supplied by Brian Mockenhaupt)

QRF element arriving at the compound to resupply and reinforce the position. (Supplied by Brian Mockenhaupt)

Two of the Two Charlie Joes happy to be alive after a hard-fought battle. (Supplied by Brian Mockenhaupt)

First Squad. (Supplied by Christopher Moon)

Second Squad. (Supplied by Dustin Barthel)

Third Squad. (Supplied by Dale Knollinger)

Weapons Squad. (Supplied by Edward Rosa)

Two Charlie men showing off the tattoos they got in honor of their fallen brothers. (Supplied by Brian Mockenhaupt)

"Yeah," Lt. Farrington replied, watching the slow vehicle disappear down the road. "I think the first of the fighters have entered the valley."

The men continued their patrol, but it wasn't long before they could hear the faint sound of shots fired in the distance. It sounded like someone was test firing their rifles or celebrating. Or maybe a little bit of both. Regardless, there was no doubt in the men's minds—the real fighters were here.

CHAPTER 10

# The Day Lovelace Got Shot in the Face

The men of Charlie Company started out the month of June with the word that their Company Commander, CPT Razuri, was being reassigned as the new HHC Commander. The officer side of the Army works differently from the enlisted, especially in the infantry. Each officer is given an allotted time to serve as a platoon leader (PL), company executive officer (XO), company commander (CO), and so on. When they reach the end of their time in a position, the Army moves them and they are off to fulfill their next position regardless if the unit is in the middle of a deployment or not. CPT Razuri had served his time as Charlie Company's commander; it was time for him to move up the ladder.

Getting used to a new leader was always a little stressful, especially on a deployment where things were starting to pick up and get hairy. However, replacing CPT Razuri as commander was the company's Mortar Platoon PL, CPT Christmas, so the men at least knew the man and he them, and the transition was hoped to go smoother.

Third Squad left COP Tynes before sunrise one early morning to push down and observe activity along the actual Arghandab River. The intent was to get south before the enemy was awake and then push north and get eyes on the village of Tarok Kolache, attempting to surprise the enemy as they were placing IEDs in that area. Tarok Kolache was like Lower Babur in that the men always got an eerie feeling while patrolling through it in the earlier months. It seemed the enemy would engage the men more often from south of the second canal near those two villages. The enemy had gotten used to the soldiers coming from the north and having the river to their backs. The men had hoped they would catch them off guard coming from the south, and sneak in their back doors.

Unfortunately, for some reason unknown to the men, air assets' status went black that morning after they had reached the river. This meant the men couldn't rely on any help from Kiowa helicopters and wouldn't be able to get a MedEvac helicopter out to them if they received any casualties. Since IEDs were a growing concern in the area, and the more they walked around the more likely they were to step on one, the men decided to hunker down in one of the pomegranate orchards and wait for air status to turn back to green.

As they climbed over the mud wall into the orchard, Lovelace couldn't help but realize the morning sun rays piercing through the canopy. It was pretty, and he could feel the warmth as he laid in them to pull security next to Dru.

"You know, this is what old people do when they want to get exercise," Dru said quietly to Lovelace as he took off his NODs and stowed them in one of his pouches on his rig.

"What?" Lovelace said, slightly confused by the statement. He placed his SAW bipod legs down to support the weapon on the ground and pull security.

Lovelace and Nichols had just swapped their positions in the team when Nichols got back from his mid-tour leave. Nichols couldn't be happier to not be carrying the SAW anymore. He had the biggest shit-eating grin as he climbed the wall with ease with his rifle and underbarrel M203 grenade launcher. It might as well have been a pistol. "Hi, buddy," he said, still smiling as he reached out to run his hand over Lovelace's helmet, rubbing it in.

"We are doing old people exercises. We are just walking around, waiting for someone to shoot at us," Dru went on, frustrated. Dru was one of the less stable guys in the platoon. He was a hell of a fighter, and definitely one the men wanted on their side, but no one ever really asked or dug into what went on in Dru's head. It was just better not to know. He had become flustered with the lack of fighting he was promised before they deployed. He thought they were going to be cutting off the Taliban's heads every day, not take morning walks in the woods waiting for the enemy to fire a couple of rounds at them and run.

Jackson heard the frustration in Dru's voice. "I don't think that old people do that last part."

"Hey, let me get one of those," SSG Loredo said to SGT Knollinger as he found a spot to take cover next to him.

Knollinger handed him one of his Starbursts he retrieved out of his pocket. "No more, this is all I got left till we get more mail," he said.

They continued to pull security and wait for air status to change. The activity in the area seemed typical for the valley. As the sun, rose plumes of smoke could be seen on the horizon coming from the kalats of the villages. The farmers were boiling their tea over their kitchen fires before they ventured into the fields to begin the day's work. As more time went on, more and more farmers passed by. Some pushing wheelbarrows, some leading goats, or a donkey cart. The valley began to wake up and the workers flooded the fields.

"Air still black?" SFC Cartwright asked Godard.

Godard got on the radio to check the status with Company. A few moments later, he got his reply. "Roger, it's still black," he finally replied to SFC Cartwright.

SFC Cartwright sighed and turned to Loredo. "Well, what do you want to do? We can't sit around here and wait all day."

SSG Loredo thought for a moment and then motioned for SGT Brown and SGT Knollinger to come to him. The two men walked over to join the small huddle. "Air isn't turning for some reason, so let's get out of here. Brown, let's push a little more west as we head north, try to get away from Tarok Kolache a little more and get closer to COP Nolen. Once we make it to the second canal, we should be golden," he suggested. SGT Brown nodded in agreement. "Keep an eye out," SSG Loredo said as SGT Brown and SGT Knollinger went to gather their men to move.

The men pushed through the thickness of the orchards slowly, keeping a close eye out for anything suspicious. As they moved, the farmers in the fields started to notice the men were there and began to leave.

"Not a good sign," SSG Loredo whispered over his hand mic. The rest of the men noticed the fleeing farmers as well and could feel their stomachs drop. "Eyes open, stay low, and get ready," Loredo said to the men around him. They continued to push through the thick orchards and fields.

Ca-Chink!

The men all got down behind cover. It was the strangest noise they had heard, like metal clunking and slamming against something. "What was that?" SSG Loredo asked over the radio.

"Sounded like an RPG misfire," SGT Knollinger suggested. They sat in the orchards motionless, as low as they could get listening for any other sound.

"Could have been a shot or something to signal to the others that we are here," SGT Brown came over the radio.

"Keep moving," SSG Loredo said, and the men got their dicks out of the dirt and pressed on.

SGT Brown came to a small dirt road that ran east to west, perpendicular to the men's direction of travel. To the east it ended at a road that ran north to south into the village of Tarok Kolache. That road had a wall paralleling it on the east side. North of the east-to-west road in front of them was a clear field. It stretched all the way to the grape fields along the second canal and consisted of only knee-high grass.

SGT Brown took a knee for a moment to determine his best path forward. He noticed a small drainage ditch that ran through the middle of the field that could provide some cover. It had some short thick brush along it. It wasn't much, but it was better than standing in the middle of the field. He started towards the brush and noticed a small tree he and Lovelace could pull security down the road from while the other soldiers crossed. He figured that was where they were most likely to take contact from and he wanted his most casualty producing weapon to be pointed in that direction, so he signaled for Lovelace to take his SAW and follow him there. The rest of the team pushed into the field along the small ditch.

"Sir," the platoon interpreter said to SFC Cartwright as he ran at him with his ICOM radio. "Sir. They said they are set in," SFC Cartwright and the rest of the men took a knee.

Lovelace watched as an adolescent boy came onto the road from behind the walls by the intersection to the east. It looked like he was pointing at the men for someone who was out of sight in the orchards. Lovelace stood up and raised his SAW to get a better look through his optic. "Wadarega!" He yelled at the boy. That is when all hell broke loose.

Pop! Pop! Pop! Zip! Pop! Whiz! Pop! Pop! Snap! Rat tat tat! Pop! Pop! Zip!

Lovelace's head snapped to the side as he spun and fell to the ground. Dirt started kicking up all around him and the other men of Alpha team. They could hear the rounds snap past them. They could almost feel them. SGT Brown ran towards Lovelace. "Lovelace is down!" he shouted over the storm of machine gun fire pinning the men to the ground. The other men of the squad began to fire back, but it wasn't effective at slowing the enemy volley of gunfire. The wall along the road had an array of small holes, only about a foot in diameter. The men of Two Charlie had come across these before, not knowing what they were used for. Now they knew. The murder holes were just large enough to get the barrels of the enemy's AKs and PKMs through, and each hole had a barrel sticking through, spitting fire and lead into the field.

SGT Brown came to the tree Lovelace was behind and began firing at the enemy. "Lovelace!" he screamed to his soldier laying face down on the ground only ten feet away. "Lovelace, give me your hand!" He reached for him as the enemy continued to unload on them as dirt kicked up all around them. It almost looked like it was raining, there were so many rounds hitting the ground.

Lovelace lifted his head to look at SGT Brown, who could see the fear and dread in Lovelace's eyes as he hopelessly reached his hand out to him, blood spilling from his face and out his mouth. SGT Brown looked into Lovelace's eyes; he couldn't just let his soldier sit there like that and possibly get shot up more. He ran out from behind the small tree, out of cover to go retrieve his soldier. He grabbed Lovelace by his body armor handle and began dragging him, hoping the enemy would take interest in the other men shooting at them for a moment.

Lovelace wasn't exactly the lightest guy in the squad, especially when you added all the SAW ammo he was carrying in his rig. SGT Brown dragged him a couple feet before the enemy started laying into them again. He fell to the ground and rolled back behind the cover of the tree, the enemy rounds narrowly missing him and Lovelace. "I need a medic up here!" he yelled as he started returning fire once more.

The next lull in the fire came and SGT Brown ran back out to try to drag Lovelace the rest of the way behind cover. He ran and grabbed Lovelace by the handle again, and to his surprise SFC Cartwright was right there with him. The two men dragged Lovelace back to the drainage ditch where a lot of the rest of the squad had been taking cover. SGT Cornelius, Ryan, and SGT Knollinger scooted over next to SFC Cartwright in the ditch, and the men started working on Lovelace. Knollinger, Cornelius, and Cartwright began ripping off all of Lovelace's gear, exposing his injuries for Ryan to begin treating. He had blood all over his face and under his arm.

"I can taste blood," was all Lovelace could say, his tongue now feeling that his teeth were missing on one side of his face.

SGT Brown returned to his tree to get back in the fight. "Nichols!" he yelled, "Get that SAW up!" Nichols came running over with his M4 and M203. Brown was so used to him being his SAW gunner that he forgot he and Lovelace had switched.

At that moment, SGT Knollinger came running up with Lovelace's SAW. It was like he had read Brown's mind. He threw the SAW through the air to Nichols, "Nichols!" he shouted. Nichols turned and, like a scene from a fucking movie, caught the machine gun and immediately began cyclically laying waste into the holes in the wall. SGT Brown watched for a moment, like a proud father watching his boy play a sport for the first time, as Nichols laid into the enemy. He quickly snapped out of it as they began receiving fire once more. "He needs more ammo!" Brown thought to himself, as Nichols only had one drum of ammo in the SAW.

"Winston, get over here!" SGT Brown called. Winston came running to join the two behind the tree. "Stay here with Nichols and cover him. I'm going to get more ammo for him," SGT Brown said as he ran back through the fire, back to the drainage ditch where he had taken Lovelace.

SGT Knollinger had begun the Nine Line as SFC Cartwright and Ryan treated Lovelace. He saw SGT Brown running up and grabbed Lovelace's rig and threw it at him. Again, SGT Brown was amazed how SGT Knollinger was just able to read his mind. Knollinger got back on the radio to continue the Nine Line. SGT Brown ran back to his men with a full load of SAW ammo.

"Get up! Get up!" SGT Maher yelled as he kicked in the doors of the rooms of First Squad. Vasquez had just gotten his eyes closed after getting off tower guard. "Get up, we got to go!"

Vasquez jumped out of his cot and threw on his pants and boots. He grabbed his gear that he had set in the corner of his room. He threw his body armor on and followed SGT Maher into the hallway. First Squad had been assigned QRF for the patrol this morning, so the men were instructed to have their gear ready.

"Let's go!" SGT Bragg called as he exited the wood structure, his men following shortly behind.

Vasquez followed SGT Maher outside and linked up with the rest of their team. Maher conducted a quick radio check with SSG Craumer and the TOC. SGT Bragg and his team were already outside the front entrance.

"What's going on?" Vasquez asked SGT Maher as they ran to catch up with Bragg and his team.

"Third Squad is in trouble. They have casualties. Air is black. They need our help," SGT Maher yelled back so all his men could hear him. "Bragg, do you have the grid?" he asked over the radio.

"Roger," SGT Bragg replied.

The men pushed south, practically hurdling the walls of the grape fields. The rest of the men were having trouble keeping up with SGT Bragg as he made his way to the second canal.

Rostran, with the SAW and all its ammo, was falling behind. His short legs couldn't keep up. Vasquez pushed him from behind, trying to help him. "Come on, come on," he kept saying to Rostran as he nudged him forward.

SGT Lachance caught up to the two and decided to help. He took the SAW from Rostran, and they picked up the pace. "Tell Bragg to slow the fuck down!" SGT Lachance yelled up to Lt. Farrington and SSG Craumer.

"Bragg, slow down. We are no good to them if we are smoked by the time we get there," SSG Craumer said to him over the radio.

"Roger," SGT Bragg replied. He had just gotten to the second canal.

Ratatatat! Snap! Ratatatat! Zip!

SGT Bragg started taking fire from a two-story structure to the south. He dove into the canal. It was neck deep and he had to hold his rifle over his head to keep it from getting waterlogged. He could hear the other guys in the squad as they started returning fire. He climbed the bank on the opposite side and slammed into a dirt wall to take cover and engage the enemy. Young was right behind him and plopped next to him along the wall.

"See that second story building?" SGT Bragg said over the gunfire.

"Yeah," Young said as he let out another burst.

"They're up there. Light it up, keep them pinned!" SGT Bragg said. Young started unloading his SAW over the roof of the second-story structure.

"Bragg, we don't know where Third Squad is. You might be engaging them. Hold your fire," SSG Craumer said over the radio.

SGT Bragg looked at his wrist Garmin. Third Squad's grid they gave him was a few hundred meters to their southwest, but he decided to cease Young's fire, since they were no longer taking fire. They were going to need the ammo. Neenan and Nguyen joined the two along the wall.

Maher saw Bragg's team on the south side of the canal set in to cover his team and the rest of the QRF element as they crossed the canal. He jumped into the cold water as he submerged all the way to his chest. Rae and Vasquez were right behind him. They sank completely, Vasquez using his lips as a snorkel as he moved through the water. Maher reached out to help Rae from the bank and pulled him to shore. Vasquez swam to him and grabbed a tree root. He turned back to look for Rostran. The only thing he could see was Rostran's little hands holding up the SAW above the water. He grabbed him and dragged him over to SGT Maher, who pulled him ashore. Vasquez continued to help people through the deep water until everyone was on the south bank.

"Maher, I got a good support-by-fire position here if you want to bound along the canal with your team. We will follow," SGT Bragg said.

"Roger." Maher was already on the move.

Jackson and Nichols were now rocking their SAWs at the enemy, along with Dru launching grenades over the wall. The men had gained a little superiority in the fight, which provided a lull in the enemy fire and gave them a minute to think.

"How we getting him out of here?" SGT Knollinger asked SFC Cartwright. The air was still black as far as they knew, so their only option would be to get him to COP Nolen which was only a few hundred meters away, But Knollinger didn't know if he could carry Lovelace the whole way. He was strong, but he wasn't that strong.

Ryan grabbed his litter out of his med bag and began unfolding it. They rolled Lovelace on the litter and picked him up. They might as well have put him in a trash bag as the litter hung flaccid, dragging across the dirt.

"This isn't going to work. I won't be able to maintain his airway like that," Ryan said as the men set Lovelace down on the other side of the road, behind a little more cover.

Jackson overheard the men contemplating their options. He remembered seeing a donkey strapped to a cart down the road before the chaos started. He looked back to see if it was still there. Sure enough, the damn donkey was still standing there in the middle of the road strapped to the cart. The dumb thing just stood there, rounds probably flying all around it, no fucks given. "Hey, we got to get that fucking donkey cart!" Jackson yelled over to the men.

SGT Knollinger and SFC Cartwright turned to look at the cart. They then looked at each other and shrugged. "That will work. We can pull the cart to Nolen," SGT Knollinger said. He picked Lovelace up and headed toward the cart, the other men covering him.

SGT Knollinger flopped Lovelace down on the cart and watched as his face winced. The hot metal of the cart had been baking in the sun and did not feel good against his skin. SGT Knollinger felt bad but told him to stay down, as he began pushing the cart down the road in the direction of COP Nolen.

"Knolly!" Cartwright yelled. He was holding the hand mic from Godard's radio to his ear. "They got us a Bird!" The relief in his voice spread to all the men that heard him. Knollinger stopped pushing the cart. Cartwright, still with the hand mic to his ear, shouted, "It's the PJs! They are coming to get him out!"

The PJs, or pararescuemen, were one of the Air Force's elite units. They are trained to jump in and rescue pilots shot down behind enemy lines, but in Afghanistan they acted as a high-speed MedEvac unit. Someone somewhere must have pushed it up and gotten them to fly. The men were relieved to hear the PJs were on their way. Perhaps they might get out and help them fight if they truly were the Billy Badasses everyone hyped them up to be.

SGT Brown, SSG Loredo, and SGT Knollinger pushed the donkey and cart behind some cover as they were still getting shot at. The rest of the men had moved from the field to the berm along the road. They needed to figure out where they were going to land this Bird, as it was coming in soon.

"They're two minutes out!" SFC Cartwright shouted.

SGT Knollinger grabbed a smoke grenade from Loredo and threw it as far as he could into the open field.

Pop! Psssssssssss!

As soon as the red smoke started to billow in the field, the enemy erupted with gunfire again, as intense as they had during the initial ambush volley.

Pop! Pop! Pop! Zip! Pop! Whiz! Pop! Pop! Snap! Rat tat tat! Pop! Pop! Zip!

SSG Loredo stiffened up like a board of wood and fell backwards onto the ground. Knollinger looked at him and asked, "You good?!"

"That motherfucker almost shot me!" he replied, lying flat on his back. SGT Brown and SGT Knollinger laughed.

The men could hear the roar of the Bird's rotors as it got louder and louder and slowly overpowered the noise of the enemy fire. The men still knew the enemy was shooting, as they could see dirt kicking up all around the Bird as it touched down in the middle of the field between them.

"Let's go!" SSG Loredo said as he and SGT Brown started to push the cart. SGT Knollinger started pulling, but the donkey began to lock up. It wasn't going anywhere near that helicopter.

The PJ opened the sliding cabin doors to the Bird and stared at the men as they struggled with the donkey. It was probably an odd sight to see, three men fighting a donkey with a man sitting in the cart bleeding from the face. The PJ motioned for the men to bring him over.

Jackson ran over to help. The four men pushed and pulled, but the cart didn't budge. Jackson waved to the PJ to come and help the men, or at least bring them a spine board or something to get him on. The PJ didn't leave the cabin of the helicopter. He just waved back at them to bring the cart to him. So much for them being Billy Badasses.

The men struggled until they got the cart close enough to carry Lovelace the rest of the way. SGT Knollinger threw him over his shoulder and plopped him down in the Bird next to the PJ. The PJ saluted the men and went to work, assessing Lovelace's injuries as Knollinger rejoined the rest of the squad behind cover. The helicopter took off and, as the roar of the engine faded, the sound of enemy fire took its place.

Nichols started to get nervous. He had already gone through most of the SAW's ammo and knew the rest of the men were running low as well. They couldn't keep this up for much longer.

Ratatatatatatatatata! Pop! Pop! Pop! Ratatatatatatata!

Fire started erupting from the north, but this time it wasn't directed at them.

"First Squad is here, shift fire to the south!" SSG Loredo called out. First Squad had arrived on QRF and was already on the enemy's flank, engaging them with their SAWs and the 240 machine gun. It was a beautiful sound to the men's ears, and the enemy fire stopped completely as they began to flee.

"Move up!" SSG Craumer said over the radio. They could see the Black Hawk MedEvac helicopter as it quickly left the ground and flew high into the sky.

SGT Bragg and his team picked up and started pushing towards where they had just engaged the enemy. He and his men's rifles were at the high ready as they pushed through the orchard, ready to shoot any fighters they may come across in the face. He took a knee as he noticed a pool of blood on the ground, kneeling to touch the blood to see if it was still wet. It was actually still warm. The dirt around the puddle looked like they had dragged the wounded fighter away, down a narrow alley. The alley had mud walls about chest height on each side with pomegranate branches from the neighboring fields draping over it, blocking out the sun. The drag marks transitioned to a single tire track, where the other fighters probably loaded the wounded man onto a motorcycle or wheelbarrow to get away. The alley itself was dark and felt angry; SGT Bragg didn't want to push down it. The trail of blood ran by a pair of AA batteries lying in the dirt. One of the enemies must have dropped them while switching out his radio. SGT Bragg grabbed his hand mic. "I got a blood trail and drag marks."

"Any bodies?" SGT Maher asked.

"Negative. If we killed any of them, they got 'em out," SGT Bragg replied.

SGT Maher moved up with the machine-gun team. They began to push past Bragg's team, past the batteries, and down the alley. You could almost hear the men groan as they entered the narrow alley, nothing about it felt good.

At the end of the alley, a man popped out from around the corner. He had an evil smile on his face, and he seemed almost excited to see the men. His face lit up as this was his chance to kill an American infidel; they were lined up for him. He raised his PKM machine gun to his hip and pulled the trigger.

Kakakakakakakakk!

Maher began returning fire at the man. The branches were snapping right above his head and the leaves began helicoptering down to the ground around him. His rifle malfunctioned right as the rest of his team got beside him in the alley. "Scunion!" he yelled as Rae, Rostran, and Vasquez began unloading on the man. The man tucked tail and popped back around the corner.

"I'm hit! I'm hit!" Rostran called out. He felt a burning sensation on his neck as he threw his hand over it to cover his wound.

Vasquez's heart sank. He and Rostran had become close, and he didn't know what he would do if he lost his friend. "Let me see! Let me see! Let me see!" he said, trying to pull Rostran's hand from his neck. He pulled down Rostran's collar and a brass casing fell out from underneath. It must have slid under his collar after being ejected from one of their rifles and burnt his neck. Vasquez laughed as he removed the casing. "You're fine."

SGT Maher and his team chased the man down the alley and SGT Bragg's team moved in behind them. Maher pied the corner the man disappeared around which opened to a road. The road ran through the middle of the village of Tarok Kolache. Maher hadn't realized they had pushed that far south. The village was abandoned like usual, so it wouldn't be hard to find the man. Maher's team pushed down the road and into the surrounding fields. They searched the area and any possible exits he might have taken, or holes he might be hiding in, but he was nowhere to be found. He had gotten away.

SGT Maher pushed into one of the pomegranate orchards and found a small mud shed in one of its corners. He raised his rifle and walked to clear it, Rae by his side. He fixed his rifle on the door, "Open it," he instructed. Rae flung the door open to reveal the contents of the shed to Maher, who was ready to shoot anyone hiding in it in the face.

The shed had no one in it, but it wasn't empty. Maher lowered his rifle and his eyes widened. "Fuuuuck," he said as he stared at jugs of HME, detonating cord, old Russian grenades, toe poppers, AK-47s, and a ton of ammo. The men started to look around the shed and noticed more materials stashed in the trees of the orchard. More detonating cord hung from branches along with toe poppers and jugs drying in the sun. SGT Maher picked the hand mic up and brought it to his mouth to speak: "Two One, this is Two One Bravo. We have a slight problem."

CHAPTER 11

# The Lion's Den

"What do you want to do?" SGT Maher asked Lt. Farrington and SSG Craumer as they examined the stockpile of explosives and weapons.

"It's too much to carry back." Lt. Farrington said.

"Charlie Nine Two, this is Nine Five," the radio hand mic chirped on SGT Lachance's shoulder.

He covered it to muffle the loudness as he adjusted the volume. They didn't want radios to give away their location. He turned to talk into the mic. "Go for Nine Two." He listened as the voice over the radio replied. "Roger that," he said into the mic then turned to look at Lt. Farrington and the rest of the men. "Air is back. Longknife will be on station momentarily." It was nice having the Kiowa helicopters overhead. Lachance had many uses for them. They could be used as recon of the surrounding area, or at least what little movement they could see through the thick orchards. They would conduct gun runs on the enemy if possible, or at least reduce the enemy's freedom of movement and deter them from attacking the men in the first place. The enemy didn't like to shoot when they knew they would take a rocket to the face in return.

"Not sure they will be much help for us down here," SGT Maher said. It seemed the further south the second canal the men went the thicker the orchards were. The canopy over the men was blocking out most of the sun.

"At least we got 'em," Lachance shrugged.

"Two Three, this is Two Six," Lt. Farrington called for SSG Loredo over the radio.

"Two Six, go ahead," SSG Loredo replied. They had been holding their position, waiting for word on the plan to rendezvous or return to base (RTB).

"Go ahead and push your guys this way to us. We can consolidate and reorganize ammo here. We just found a huge weapons and explosives cache. I think we are going to have to call EOD to blow it," Lt. Farrington said.

There was a pause. "Roger that. Send us a grid and we will be en route." SSG Loredo said, and Lt. Farrington sent him the grid to their location.

Farrington switched his radio to the company net and began to call in the cache and request EOD assets. He turned to SSG Craumer. "Sounds like we lucked out finally. EOD is at Terra Nova. They are gonna scrap up someone from Headquarters to escort them out to us," he said.

SSG Craumer nodded. "Bragg. Maher. Set in security. We are waiting on EOD. Hold your fire to the north until Third Squad gets here," he said over his radio.

First Squad set in security and Third Squad linked up with them in the middle of the orchard. Vasquez handed a few of the guys water bottles he had stashed in his assault pack as they passed him and made their way into the orchard. They were drenched in sweat. Nichols took a water bottle and poured it over Lovelace's rig, which he was now wearing. It was covered in blood and the flies wouldn't leave him alone, swarming him as he swatted them away.

"You hit?" Maher asked.

"It's not my blood," Nichols replied.

Third Squad took cover in the orchard with the shed while First Squad formed an outer cordon around them. Maher took his team and put Rostran, Rae, and Vasquez on the walls to the west. Bragg and Nguyen watched the south and the southeast, while Neenan and Young went with Maher to the north to watch the road. The machine-gun team went with them. The men hunkered down and remained quiet. They didn't know how long it would take for EOD to get to them and they didn't want to attract any attention to their location.

The interpreter's ICOM radio started to hiss with static and then chatter as the enemy started to communicate over it. He quickly turned the volume down and put the radio to his ear. "What are they saying?" Lt. Farrington asked as the man listened to the chatter.

"Many different speakers, sir. They are asking if everyone is okay." He paused and listened some more. The guys of Third Squad that were lounging around him all perked up, they were curious to learn if they had killed or hurt any of the enemy in their fight. "You injured a few of them." The interpreter continued. You could see the small victory in the eyes of the men around him as they relaxed and went back to lounging in the orchard. "They are regrouping now. They don't seem happy." He paused to listen some more. Lt. Farrington could see the fear build behind his eyes. "They know we are here. They know we have found their supplies. They say they see some of us!"

"Everybody down," SSG Craumer said over the radios and Bragg and Maher got their guys down. It was quiet. The men listened for anything that might alert them of the direction of the imminent attack.

Nothing happened. The interpreter continued to listen. "They can't see us anymore," he said.

The men sat quietly, waiting for an attack. The attack came, but not for the Two Charlie men. A dull thunder echoed throughout the orchards. An explosion in the distance. A big one.

"Charlie Six, this is Charlie Six Romeo. IED!" The transmission came over the company net. The Headquarters squad escorting EOD had hit an IED and received casualties, one of them losing his leg. They started their Nine Line and called in their grid.

SGT Bragg checked his map to see where they were. "Hey, Knolly, I think they just hit that bomb on the same road you guys got hit on."

Knollinger looked at the map. "No shit," he said. The ambush they walked into was probably set there to bait them into the bomb. They had walked all around it getting Lovelace out of there. It spooked him to think about how close they had come to having an even worse day.

The ICOM radio started hissing again with transmissions. Apparently, the fighters were celebrating. The company radio was also busy with traffic, as the Headquarters element and leadership at Terra Nova was figuring out the situation on the ground and formulating a plan of action moving forward. Three Charlie had another squad out in the area. They would assist with the MedEvac and another squad from COP Nolen would QRF to pick up EOD and continue to escort them to the Two Charlie men hunkered down in the orchard.

"Well, sounds like we are going to be here for a minute," Lt. Farrington said after acknowledging the new plan over the company net.

The men spread the word and hunkered down. Neenan took a knee along the road facing Tarok Kolache. The road had a mud wall on one side and a drainage ditch on the other that opened into a small field. There was a break in the wall about twenty meters in front of him. A man wearing a blue tunic and brown pakol hat emerged slowly from around the corner and stopped in the middle of the dirt road. He looked Neenan right in the face, standing there like an outlaw in old western movies challenging the sheriff to a shootout.

"Wadarega!" Neenan yelled as he stood and raised his hand to motion for the man to stay put. The man just looked at him with the same satanic smile on his face as the man back in the alley. Neenan put his hand down and began to raise his rifle, starting the duel, except instead of single-shot pistols the men both had semi-automatic rifles. The man whipped up his tunic to reveal an AK and a fighting rig with magazines. The two men started unloading on each other.

KaKaKa! Pop! Pop! Pop! Kakaka!

The dirt wall behind Neenan began to explode as rounds impacted it all around him. The two men must have silhouetted each other with lead, as neither hit the other with a single shot. Neenan fell to his back shooting, and the man sprayed until he disappeared back around the corner.

SGT Bragg heard the commotion and started sprinting to the road. He had both Neenan and Young over there and needed to make sure they were okay. Maher was helping Neenan up and Young was shooting at enemy fighters as they popped in and out of the breaks in the wall down the road. It reminded him of a game of whack a mole, except instead of having a mallet he had a SAW. He fired bursts into the breaks in the walls as the enemy fled.

"You good?!" Bragg asked Neenan between the bursts of SAW fire from Young.

"Roger, Sergeant!" Neenan replied, a little stunned. They withdrew from the road and into the orchard.

Another gun volley erupted from the south, from where Bragg left Nguyen. An RPG whizzed through the treetops and smacked the other side of the dirt wall SGT Brown and Lt. Farrington were behind. The dirt cracked from the impact and shook the men as they stepped away from the wall and got down in a small irrigation ditch. Their eyes widened as they looked at each other in disbelief. SGT Bragg started running back through the orchard to check on Nguyen and engage the enemy. He could see Nguyen shooting over the wall from a tree he had climbed. "God dammit, Johnny Nguyen" he thought to himself as he ran towards him. He reached the middle of the orchard and the ground started exploding in front of him.

Buhdudududududuh!

A line of dirt spit 10 meters into the air right between Bragg and where Godard and Knollinger were laying. It ripped past SGT Lachance, Lt. Farrington, and SGT Brown. They all fell to the ground as the dirt rained down on them. "What the fuck kind of weapon does the Taliban have?" Bragg thought as he looked at Godard and Knollinger. All three men had the same expression on their faces.

A Kiowa helicopter buzzed over the orchard. SGT Lachance noticed the Bird's nose drop and realized they were coming in from an incorrect attack heading different from the one he had called over the radio. He ripped out his hot pink and orange VS17 panel and ran to the road to get the Bird's attention. "Abort! Abort! Cease fire! Cease fire!" he yelled over his radio, waving the panel in the air as the second helicopter pulled off above them. "You're shooting us!"

Bragg didn't have time to figure out what had just happened, so he got up and ran to Nguyen. "Where are they at?" He shouted to him in the tree. "And get down from there!"

"They are shooting through that doorway!" Nguyen replied, pointing to the break in the wall.

SSG Loredo ran up to Lt. Farrington. "They are probing us. Trying to get us to waste our ammo. Harassment fire," he said. "They have us surrounded. We have to conserve our ammo until One or Three Charlie gets here."

The men consolidated and reorganized their security and ammo. Third Squad joined First in establishing security. They were instructed to only shoot at what they could hit.

A few moments went by before the next fire came, this time from the field directly east of them. Nichols sprayed a burst back with his SAW and SSG Loredo ran up to throw a grenade. He unwrapped the electrical tape the men used to secure the spoon and was about to pull the pin when he saw Nichols eyeing the grenade. He paused, then turned to him. "You want to throw it?"

Like a kid at Christmas, Nichols snatched the grenade from his hands, pulled the pin and chucked it over the wall the men had shot at them from. "Frag out!" he yelled as the two men plopped back down behind the wall and waited for the boom.

SGT Bragg saw the look of disappointment in SSG Loredo's eyes as he ran past him checking on his guys. "What's wrong?" he stopped to ask.

"I gave my only grenade to Nichols to throw," he said.

SGT Bragg found it kind of comical that he was butthurt from that. "You want one of mine? I have two," he offered, taking one out of one of the grenade pouches on his rig.

SSG Loredo's eyes lit up much like Nichols's had. "You mean it?" he asked, surprised by the gesture. SGT Bragg just nodded and tossed the grenade to him. Loredo caught it and smiled. "Thanks." Bragg shook his head and continued to go check on his guys.

The next few hours or so continued much like the last few had, with small engagements from the enemy from every direction. They took contact from the north again. More shots rang out from the south and the east. Those fighters were within grenade range so they threw frags over the walls. It was nothing substantial, but the men's ammo was dwindling. Team leaders did their best to resupply their men with ammo. It was getting down to each man only having one or two magazines a piece, and the SAWs were getting down to their last nutsack of ammo. It was hardly enough to sustain an actual fight, and nothing was more terrifying to the men than running out of ammo while being surrounded. They grew very uneasy—they needed that QRF to get there soon.

Another squad from Three Charlie tried to push out of Nolen to resupply the Two Charlie men. That plan quickly fell apart, as they listened from the orchard as a firefight erupted in the distance from the direction of their approach. The enemy had ambushed them en route.

"Jesus. It's getting crazy out here," Lt. Farrington said, listening to their radio transmissions as they maneuvered on the enemy. The fighters must have taken notice of all the movement coming from COP Nolen and shifted their fighters in that direction. They continued to ambush the troops, attempting to bait them into more IEDs. Three Charlie finally made their way to the Two Charlie men in the orchard, but after their engagement with the enemy, they didn't have much ammo of their own to give the men either.

The afternoon sun filled the sky, and the stomachs of the men began to groan. "You got anything to eat?" SGT Knollinger asked. All he had eaten that day was his breakfast and a few Starbursts. Some of the guys had a strip of beef jerky or a granola bar in their pockets, nothing substantial. They needed to get out of there soon.

"Charlie Two Six, this is Charlie One Six, we are about a hundred meters to your north. Hold fire as we are approaching your location with EOD," the radio chirped.

It was music to the men's ears. Finally, EOD had arrived. The men cleared a path for the One Charlie guys to make their way through and Lt. Farrington escorted the EOD soldiers to the shed.

SGT Knollinger, seeing the gaggle of soldiers stacked on the road and in the orchard, started yelling at the other platoon's team leaders and men. "What the fuck are you guys doing? You are all in a fatal funnel. Someone could kill all of you right now." The tired soldiers tried to move but there were just too many of them in the area. Between the four squads, it was getting crowded.

He moved down the road to find a place to push his men. He walked up to the first metal door in Tarok Kolache and kicked it in. He and Ryan flowed into the compound, rifles at the ready, sweeping all the corners. It was clear of people, but as SGT Knollinger opened one of the wood doors to the khalat he noticed it was full of more explosives and mines. HME was drying in the sun on the roof of the khalat structure. Mines were stashed in the building. Ryan looked at SGT Knollinger wide eyed. "Oh, shit!" he said as he inspected the motorcycle in the corner of the compound. The saddlebags were full of more detonation cord and antipersonnel mines.

"Fuck," SGT Knollinger leaned in to talk into his radio. "Two Six, we just found more shit over here. Can you bring EOD over?"

EOD came over to the compound and continued to search the kalat. They found more toe poppers, AKs, and ammo. They gathered it all and moved it back to the original shed that contained the other stash. Knollinger saw one of the EOD soldiers removing the mines from the saddlebags of the motorcycle. "Fuck that, blow up that whole motorcycle," he said, taking the explosives and putting them back into the saddlebags. He pushed the motorcycle to the shed.

"What the heck is that?" SGT Maher asked, wondering why Knollinger was pushing a motorcycle.

"Taliban motorcycle. It needs to go too," SGT Knollinger replied as he rolled it into the shed. Maher just laughed.

"Charlie Two Six, this is Charlie Six," CPT Christmas came over the radio. He was having a hell of a first day as the company commander with three casualties on three different patrols being evacuated on three different MedEvacs, and now this.

"Go for Two Six," Lt. Farrington replied.

"Roger, EOD is saying you guys found more weapons and explosive material?" CPT Christmas asked, trying to get clarification of what was actually happening on the ground.

"Roger, we are consolidating it into a single stash and EOD is going to blow it in place, over," Lt. Farrington explained.

"Okay, roger, break." CPT Christmas paused for a moment, then returned. "We are going to need you to push into Tarok Kolache and clear the rest of the village. We need to make sure there aren't more weapons or explosive material in the area."

Lt. Farrington sighed and looked at SSG Loredo and SSG Craumer who were also listening in on the conversation. They both shook their heads. There was no way they were going to be able to do that with the ammo they had left. Their men were running on empty.

"Look, sir, we are almost black on ammo out here. We don't have the capability to clear an entire village," Lt. Farrington replied to CPT Christmas's orders.

"You mean to tell me between the four squads out there, none of you have ammo?" CPT Christmas replied, irritated by their unwillingness to comply.

"We've been at it for a good ten hours now," Lt. Farrington continued. "Each squad out here has been ambushed, we are constantly receiving fire, and we're surrounded. We are running out of ammo and daylight, sir. We need to RTB."

"Standby," CPT Christmas replied. The radio went silent. The men sat in the orchards as they awaited their fate. The heat of the day had left the valley, and the sun was on the horizon. "Two Six," the radio finally chirped, "Go ahead and blow what you got and RTB. I'll work with the One and Three Charlie elements to establish a clearance of the village. How copy?"

Lt. Farrington mouthed a "Fuck yes" to SSG Loredo and SSG Craumer and then picked up his hand mic to reply. The three men sighed with relief; it was the small victories. "Roger, good copy."

EOD grabbed a charge big enough to blow up all the equipment that the men had gathered in the shed. The men pushed out of the orchard and First and Third Squad moved north, heading towards Jelawur. A faint "fire in the hole!" was heard in the distance, followed by a massive boom that shook the leaves of the trees around them.

Every man was at the high ready on the way back, pieing every hole in every wall and every corner. It was more of a bluff though, as most of them were down to their last magazine and couldn't do much even if they wanted to. It was terrifying as they ran straight line back to Jelawur. They got to the field that Third Squad had been initially ambushed in that started off the whole day. SGT Bragg set in his team to provide overwatch for the others to cross.

"What are you doing? Go!" SGT Maher yelled at him over the radio.

Bragg understood, picking up his men and began running across the open field. What was the point of providing an overwatch when they didn't have any ammo to do it with. They just needed to get the fuck out of there, now.

The men continued running until they got north of the second canal and into the grape fields south of Jelawur. Once they got to the other side of the second canal, it was like a weight was lifted from their shoulders. They followed the furrows all the way north into the village, using it as a type of shield from enemy fire. The men staggered on Route Red Dog and pushed east. The Hescos and mud walls of COP Tynes glowed orange in the late afternoon sunset, welcoming them. They had finally made it back home.

## CHAPTER 12

# 07 Jun 2010

The men had gotten Lovelace out successfully. He was going to make it. The bullet had entered through his face, shattered his teeth and jaw, traveled down his neck, pierced a lung, and exited out his armpit on the opposite side of entry. It had missed his esophagus, his trachea, his carotid, his jugular—basically everything vital. He was as lucky as anyone who just got shot in the face could get.

The Two Charlie men continued to patrol, getting into more fights as the days went. The enemy had established a front line and made it clear the men were not welcome south of the second canal. It also became increasingly difficult for the men to reach Lower Babur, as the usual pop shots they would receive turned into machine-gun fire and volleys of RPGs. The valley was fully awake, and it was angry at them.

Company had received some intel of men wearing fighting rigs and carrying rifles turning villagers and farmers away as they tried to cross the bridge heading south at the second canal intersection on Route Highlife. CPT Christmas decided the men of Two Charlie needed to go check it out. They planned a patrol to establish a traffic-control point (TCP) at the intersection. It would leave early in the morning in hopes of getting there before the fighters did.

The birds began to sing in the orchards as the sun started to light up the valley. It had not quite crested the horizon, so the night chill still lingered in the air. The men of First Squad set their body armor and rigs outside the wood structure and were lounging along the internal Hesco wall, waiting for the patrol brief. Some were sitting, some standing having a smoke, and some were still half asleep. Eventually, once everyone was gathered, the patrol brief began.

The objective was clear and straightforward. SFC Cartwright spoke to the men of the Intel that possible fighters had been diverting locals away from the intersection that lay less than a kilometer south from COP Tynes along the second canal. The patrol was to reach that intersection undetected and conduct a TCP, hoping to beat the enemy fighters to the location and surprise them when they arrived.

SGT Maher would take point for this patrol while SGT Bragg would be the trailing team. It was a huge weight off SGT Bragg's shoulders, getting a break from being on point. He and SGT Maher had spent the night before collaborating to decide on the best route to infill, so SGT Bragg didn't pay attention to the route brief Maher gave, he just stood there eating some cold oatmeal out of a paper cup and looking over his guys' gear.

SGT Maher stood in front of the rest of the men of First Squad, informing them of the route they were going to take. "Initially we are going to head east out of the outpost before heading south in case any early spotters are out," he said. The men of Two Charlie were always being watched. From the second they left the compound walls, their direction and location was constantly being communicated to the enemy fighters in the area in some form or another. SGT Maher had hoped this would psych the spotters out, possibly make them think they were heading east into Babur. "If anyone is watching us, we can hopefully lose them in the grape fields, so stay low as we travel through them."

"Sounds good to me, I'm just glad we aren't going to be climbing any walls or doing any of SGT Bragg's crazy routes," Young joked to the group. SGT Bragg was notorious for taking the guys through some hectic routes. He would climb over things, climb under things, walk through things, basically do anything he could to avoid IED emplacements. The day he almost tripped a tripwire IED still played in his head, and he did whatever it took not to come that close to death for him or his guys again. This didn't stop the guys from giving him a hard time for it, joking about how he was lost or didn't know where he was going.

"You guys don't like the five Ds of the Arghandab?" SGT Bragg asked. "Dodge, Duck, Dip, Dive and Dodge." The men smiled.

They went over the final things that needed to be put out in the brief—what to do if they took contact, what to do if they hit an IED, radio checks, etc. They picked up the remainder of their gear and went to grab the ANP before they headed out. For some reason the police force was very hesitant that morning, and it was even more so like getting children ready for school than it had been in the past. They dragged their feet, as one by one they joined the rest of the men by the front gate.

"Not early risers?" SFC Cartwright asked.

"They haven't had enough time to get high yet," Nguyen responded. The men laughed as another ANP officer joined them. The three officers they could scrounge up slowly put on their vests and loaded their AKs, one even put on his helmet, which was a rare sight to see. The men just shrugged off their behavior to them not being used to being up that early and continued.

The sun had just begun to crest the horizon as the men started the patrol. They headed east out of COP Tynes before dropping into the grape field maze that was the land between the first and second canal. They moved quickly, as they had gotten a late start due to the hesitation and uncooperative police. They stayed low and used the mud wall rows and foliage of the grape fields to conceal their position.

They reached a clearing about the size of a football field north of the second canal, it was just north of the intersection. They did a quick halt to observe it from afar, not to give up their cover and concealment before moving in case any of the enemy fighters had beaten them there. The men had a clear view of the intersection from their position. The canal had a dirt path on both the north and south sides. The southern side had a line of trees that ran along the canal. A knee-high mud wall ran along the south side of its path. There was a break in the tree line where Route Highlife ran north to south. A concrete bridge, just barely wide enough to get a single car over, ran over the canal. The wall to the southwest dropped off to an open field with an abandoned mud structure in it. A thick orchard was just past that. It was a good place to shoot at the patrol from. To the southeast, there was another clearing with an abandoned structure and then more grape fields. The grape fields to the northwest of the intersection ran all the way to the canal. It gave the men good cover and concealment on their approach to the intersection. This was the route SGT Maher would take.

He moved through the rows of grapes west of Route Highlife, SGT Bragg's team and the ANP following behind. SGT Maher and his team reached the last row of grapes and halted. He called for the interpreter. "Tell these fuckers to check under that bridge for a bomb." The interpreter did as he was told and turned to the ANP officers. The officers looked horrified. You didn't need to speak Pashto to know they were saying "Hell no." They hadn't ever been this relentless in the past, usually doing exactly what the Two Charlie men said when they told them what to do.

"Are you fucking kidding me?" SGT Maher exclaimed. He almost grabbed one of the officers close to him and threw them out of the grape field. He was so mad. "Come on!" Maher moved out of the ditch he had been taking cover in and motioned to Rae to join him. He proceeded to approach the bridge with Rae following behind, the rest of the patrol provided overwatch for them as they checked the banks of the canal on the north side. They climbed down the banks to search under the bridge for anything suspicious. After both were satisfied, they signaled to the rest of the patrol and pushed across.

The ANP watched the men and got even more hesitant as they pushed to the south side of the canal. SGT Maher's team took up security positions to cover the south and the east while SGT Bragg's team would push up to positions to cover the north and the west. SGT Maher set Rostran and Vasquez to pull security within the abandoned structure and overwatch the grape fields to the southeast while Rae would watch the road to the south. SGT Bragg pushed up with Young and Neenan, leaving Nguyen in the grape field to the north with SFC Cartwright. Nguyen was their acting medic, so he wanted him to stay put out of the intersection in case something happened. The ANP were acting very oddly; something didn't feel right.

SSG Rosa, Bowman and Stegic moved up to get their 240 machine gun to get eyes on the orchard to the south. He and Bowman rested the gun along the mud wall but noticed the abandoned khalat in the field to the south.

"You think we can get on the roof?" SSG Rosa asked Bowman, who pointed out a wooden ladder along the back side of the structure. Rosa nodded and the men moved.

SGT Bragg saw Rosa move his team and had Neenan take their place. He walked over to set him in behind the mud wall and give him his sectors of fire. It was a pretty good spot, as Neenan had plenty of cover and could help the gun team by raining down his 203 grenades in the orchard if they got attacked. He walked back to set Young behind the canal trees to cover the path to the west, then took a knee along the wall between the two.

"Look at this," SGT Maher said, reaching up into the branches of one of the trees near the intersection. He revealed a broken cellphone that had been hanging from one of the tree's branches by a piece of white cloth. The men had heard the enemy had used things like this to mark IEDs. He removed it and brought it over to SSG Craumer, Godard, and SGT Cornelius, who were examining an odd spring-like switch device they had found by the base of another tree.

"Don't be fucking with that," Godard said to SSG Craumer as he pushed the spring in his hand.

SGT Maher brought the broken phone to the ANP. "You know anything about this?" he asked as he dangled it in front of them. One of the officers reached out to examine it further. The other two's eyes were focused on the mud wall. They had been reluctant to push past the bridge and just stood in the middle of it. One grabbed a few rocks from the road and began to throw them between Neenan and SGT Bragg against the wall.

"What the fuck are these guys doing?!" SGT Bragg yelled. Something wasn't right at all. "What do they know?!" he said as he stood up and turned to Godard who was walking toward him.

BOOM!

A dust cloud erupted from the ground like a geyser of dirt, engulfing Godard, SSG Craumer, SGT Cornelius, and Neenan, and throwing SGT Bragg across the dirt path. SGT Bragg could feel thousands of small rocks pepper his side as the cloud rapidly engulfed him like an avalanche rolling down a mountain. He landed on his side and winced. When he finally opened his eyes, he could see he was a couple meters from where he had been standing and had landed right next to Young. He looked up at Young who was just outside the cloud of the blast.

Young had a slight look of horror in his eyes. He knew someone had just gotten fucked up in that blast, it was huge, and he felt the concussive force rattle his chest and head. He raised his SAW, looking for a possible follow-on ambush or anyone fleeing the area that might have set off the explosion remotely.

"Jonny Nguyen, get the fuck over here! Medic!" SGT Bragg screamed as loud as he could. He didn't know the extent of anyone's injuries, but knew it wasn't going to be good. The ringing in his ears was excruciating.

"My legs," Godard groaned and he started to drag himself out of the remaining dust cloud that lingered in the air. He was missing one of his legs below the knee and the other was covered with lacerations and burns. SGT Maher had emerged from the cloud over him, spinning him on his back to begin applying tourniquets around his legs.

Godard groaned in pain. The pain of his leg being gone and the other one being badly burnt and mangled hadn't registered, but the cinching of the tourniquets hurt like hell. He sat up to look down and examine what had happened to him. SGT Maher pushed him back down. Godard looked to his side, a piece of his foot in part of his boot lay next to him on the ground.

SGT Cornelius woke in a daze. His entire body hurt and he couldn't hear a damn thing. He lay there as he did a quick self-inspection, checking his legs, arms, and body for blood. He could feel blood running down his face, a sharp pain near his right eye. As the dust settled, he rolled over to see SSG Craumer, who had blood all over his face and running down the front of his equipment. He had managed to grab a bandage and was clumsily trying to wrap it around one of the wounds on his leg. SSG Rosa grabbed the bandage and took over his aid. Vasquez helped SGT Cornelius to his feet.

Nguyen had begun sprinting over the bridge, he noticed an unexploded mortar round lying on the ground next to the men. It must have been part of the explosion that hadn't gone off. They began to move the men the best they could to get them out of the intersection and into some cover on the other side of the canal, away from any secondary explosives that might remain in the area, off the X. SFC Cartwright established the casualty collection point (CCP) in the cover and concealment of the grape fields along the road.

"Bravo team?!" SGT Maher shouted, trying to see where the rest of his guys were.

"Bravo team is up!" Vasquez replied. He, Rostran, and Rae had been pulling security in case a follow-on ambush was to pursue. They had been shaken from the blast as well, felt its concussive force rattle their bodies.

SGT Bragg looked around. Young was alright, still pulling security. Nguyen was helping with the casualties. Where was Neenan? He looked along the wall where he had posted him, the spot where he would be able to rain down grenades. He wasn't there. Instead, what took his place was a crater in the ground. "Neenan!" SGT Bragg shouted. There was no reply. "Does anyone see Neenan?" He got up off the ground and staggered to his feet.

"Neenan!" Rostran and Vasquez began shouting from the positions they were pulling security. They quickly cleared the mud ruins around them to no avail.

"Neenan!" SSG Rosa even started to call for him as he led SSG Craumer to the CCP.

There wasn't a reply. SGT Bragg began to panic. He began running up and down the wall where he had placed his soldier, checking the trees, screaming his name. He had to find him. His search became more frantic. Where the hell could he be? There was no way he was just gone, pink misted, that wasn't real. "Young, do you see Neenan?" he shouted.

"No," Young replied, staring down the road he had been pulling security on, "But I see his leg." The pant leg was still bloused in the boot, and it covered the leg up to about where the knee area should have been. Bright-red mangled flesh stuck out from the end of the fabric. It didn't seem real. SFC Cartwright walked past Young and, like a scene out of *Saving Private Ryan*, picked up Neenan's leg.

"He's down here!" Bowman yelled.

SGT Bragg sprinted around the wall, down towards Bowman. He ran right up to him, and the two of them stared in horror. Neenan lay among some of the rubble from the wall above them. Both of his legs were gone above the knees. The two men stared in a horrific daze, unable to move. Then, suddenly, Neenan took a breath of air. It was enough movement to snap the two out of the dazed shock they were in. They both snapped into action, running over to him and ripping his tourniquet off his rig to apply to one of his legs. SGT Bragg used the tourniquet off his own rig to apply to the other. He grabbed his left leg, Bowman grabbed the right. Neenan began to moan with the little air he had in his lungs. As SGT Bragg applied his tourniquet, he noticed the damage extended well beyond just his legs. His right arm was being held on by the skin of his elbow. Bowman grabbed his tourniquet and ratcheted it down on Neenan's arm. There were lacerations all up the back of his legs, and his pelvis was open. SGT Bragg and Bowman grabbed him to try and move him. Bragg could feel Neenan's tail bone exposed underneath. His intestines had begun to seep out. The two quickly put a hand on them to hold them in. They couldn't move him, not without him falling apart more.

"Medic!" SGT Bragg screamed at the top of his lungs.

SSG Rosa and Nguyen made their way around the wall and into the depression. Their stomachs sank as soon as they laid eyes on Neenan. Nguyen worked to establish an airway using an endotracheal tube and began to breathe for Neenan using a bag valve. He grabbed Neenan's hand on his good arm and Neenan began to squeeze. SGT Bragg and Bowman continued to bandage and do what they could with his lower laceration and pelvic area, packing it with dressings and holding in anything that tried to come out. They were going to need a stretcher to get him out of there, to get him to the CCP.

"Let's Go! Let's Go!" SGT Knollinger yelled as he ran through the wood structure banging on the doors of the Third Squad guys' rooms. He didn't need to wake them. They all heard the loud thunderous boom shake the walls at COP Tynes. They had all shot out of bed and were throwing their gear on as they headed out the door. They didn't need to hear SFC Cartwright calling in the Nine Line over the radio in the TOC to know something terrible had happened; they could feel it in the air.

They ran out the gate and started sprinting immediately down Route Highlife. SGT Brown was on point, and his guys were doing everything they could to keep up with him.

SGT Lachance heard one of the battle roster numbers called in the Nine Line and knew it was SGT Cornelius. He immediately started to try to establish communication with him through their Fire Net station on the radio. He didn't get a reply. He picked up his pace, running as fast as he could past some of the other Third Squad men.

It didn't take long for them to reach the men of First Squad. SGT Brown ran right past Godard, SSG Craumer, and SGT Cornelius all in the ditch of the grape fields. SSG Craumer was sitting next to SGT Cornelius smoking a cigarette; blood was seeping through their bandages. Rae was tending to them as SGT Maher and SFC Cartwright were providing aid to Godard. The men had been stripped of their gear which was laying mostly on the road. Godard was pretty much naked, as his uniform was cut off of him to expose all his injuries. That's when SGT Brown noticed his leg was missing and the other one was messed up.

"I can't feel my leg," Godard said, surprisingly calm. "Oh wait, that's because it's not fucking there!" His voice grew increasingly frustrated as he spoke.

"Bring the medic to Neenan!" SGT Maher yelled. "Ryan, you help us." Ryan jumped into the ditch to begin assisting with treating the casualties.

Doc Taylor ran past the men. "Where is he at?" he asked, not knowing where to run to.

"Over there!" SGT Maher replied, pointing to the other side of the wall.

SGT Brown pushed past the CCP and went to set in his men to pull security. Nichols took up a position east along the canal. He noticed something along the path. It was a boot with a pant leg sticking out of it, with red mangled flesh and bone poking out of that. It was Neenan's other leg. "Sergeant," Nichols said as he stumbled on his words.

SGT Brown turned to him to see what was wrong. He saw the leg on the path. "Push past it so you don't have to look at it." Nichols did as he was told, his eyes glued to his friend's leg as he walked past it, avoiding it like it was a snake. Lt. Farrington heard the men and came over to pick it up, taking the limb back to the CCP, where he found Neenan's other leg next to a piece of Godard's foot. "Jesus," he thought to himself, "we literally have a pile of body parts."

Doc Taylor ran across the bridge, SGT Knollinger closely behind him. They made their way down the road and around the wall. They came up to the group of men huddled around Neenan on the ground. Doc Taylor jumped in; SGT Knollinger watched as the men frantically worked on him.

SGT Knollinger looked at Neenan; his skin had turned to a ghostly gray. His eyes stared glossed over into the sky. He knew he wasn't going to make it. SSG Rosa stood up to make room for Doc and made eye contact with SGT Knollinger. "He's gone," is all SGT Knollinger said.

SGT Bragg looked up at him, still holding the gauze under his hip as Bowman began to wrap what he could. Bragg could see the look on Knollinger's face; it was the same look he had on the day Santos died. "He's still breathing!" SGT Bragg yelled at him in protest. "He's still fucking breathing!"

SGT Knollinger left the men to continue working on Neenan. He could hear the MedEvac Birds in the distance. He stood in the middle of the intersection and watched as SFC Cartwright tossed a red smoke grenade into the middle of the open field to mark the landing zone. The smoke billowed and grew in the field and blew across the road towards the men. He followed the smoke with his eyes and noticed the ground all around him was littered with gear. Pieces of torn ACU uniform, parts of rigs, damaged weapons, and helmets lay throughout the dirt, all covered in dust.

The MedEvac helicopter landed in the field marked by the red smoke and SGT Knollinger ran out to retrieve a litter. He found Winston pulling security and handed the litter to him. "Get this to Neenan!" he yelled over the engine of the helicopter. Winston took it from him and disappeared around the wall.

The MedEvac's crew chief medic came stumbling out of the helicopter into the field. His flight helmet was huge on him, making him very top heavy. That and the unevenness of the field made his balance even worse as he waddled over to the men to assess the casualties. There were a total of two Birds that were going to land, and he wanted to determine which patient would go in which aircraft.

SGT Bragg, SSG Rosa, Bowman, and Winston came around the corner of the wall carrying Neenan on the stretcher. They took a knee once they reached the other side of the bridge and waited for the medic's instructions, shielding Neenan from the dust being kicked up by the helicopter's rotary wings. Lt. Farrington approached the men, carrying Neenan's legs in his hands.

"What the fuck?!" SGT Bragg yelled over the roar of the helicopter as Farrington set the legs on the stretcher next to him.

"They got to go with him!" Lt. Farrington responded.

The medic walked over to the men, took one look at Neenan, and gasped. He leaned over and put two fingers on Neenan's neck to humor the men, feeling for a pulse he knew wasn't there. He looked up at the men and shook his head.

SSG Rosa picked the man up by the collar and held him in the air. "You don't do that. Not in front of my boys," he yelled at the man as he set him back down. A look of defeat crept over the men that had just spent the last who-knows-how-long trying to save Neenan.

The crew chief signaled to load Godard and Neenan into the first Bird, then SGT Cornelius and SGT Craumer into the second. They executed, loading the first Bird, then went back with more stretchers to get Craumer and Cornelius.

SGT Cornelius wasn't having the stretcher. He had walked into this damn valley, he was going to walk out. He put his arm down to stand himself up and that's when he noticed the extreme pain. His adrenaline spike had worn off and he could tell something wasn't right in his arm. It was fucked. He screamed as Rae helped him to his feet and cradled his arm as they approached the helicopter. SGT Cornelius plopped right down beside SSG Craumer in the Bird's cabin and, as soon as the other men were clear, the Bird took off.

SGT Cornelius looked over at SSG Craumer; he was holding a picture of his wife he had retrieved from his helmet before they ripped it off him. The two men watched from the helicopter window as the valley got smaller and smaller in the distance.

The dust from the Birds began to clear. SGT Bragg turned to look at SSG Loredo, who was standing right behind him. Loredo had the same look SGT Knollinger had, the same look the crew chief had after they had seen Neenan. SGT Bragg walked up to him, his head hung low. "He's dead, Sergeant," he said as tears began to billow in his eyes. "He's dead."

SSG Loredo didn't look at him, just grabbed SGT Bragg by the collar and pulled him close so that only he could hear him. "Not now," he said. "Not yet."

SGT Bragg understood as he picked up his rifle, wiped the tears from his eyes, and began to head back to rejoin Young and Nguyen.

Bowman stared at all the gear everywhere as his mind wandered. He was close to reaching his breaking point too when SSG Rosa walked up to him. "Bowman," he said, putting his arm around him. "You're good." Bowman nodded and rejoined the ranks as well.

Jackson noticed Rostran who was pulling security by himself to the north. "Hey, Rostran, we don't need to pull security that way, the towers from COP Tynes can cover the north." Rostran didn't even acknowledge him. He started talking to himself, uttering something under his breath.

The adrenaline had begun to wear off for Vasquez as well and he began to feel overwhelmed by the situation. He could feel a slight pain in his back and his feet were going numb. "Sergeant Maher, I can't feel my legs," he said as he lay on the ground. Rostran was moved over to the CCP and he and Vasquez were stripped of their gear. The blast had obviously shaken them.

"I'm going to call in another Bird, we need to get them out of here," SFC Cartwright said as he started another Nine Line over the radio.

Doc treated the two for shock as they awaited another Bird. SSG Rosa read to Rostran from the Bible to comfort him and, when the third MedEvac Bird landed, the two men were loaded up and sent on their way to KAF to join the rest of the wounded.

The remaining men started gathering all the gear. Plate carriers, rigs, helmets, weapons, pieces of uniforms, and radios were all piled in the road north of the canal.

"How the hell are we going to get all this stuff back?" Lt. Farrington asked.

"Call COP Tynes, get Bismullah to bring one of the ANP's trucks down here. We can load up the bed and follow them back," SGT Maher suggested. He too was coming down from his adrenaline high.

SFC Cartwright did just that and the men waited for the ANP to bring their Hilux down the road. They piled the gear in the back of the truck, making sure not to leave a single piece of fabric for the enemy to be able to collect as a trophy.

"Sergeant Bragg," SFC Cartwright said.

"Roger, Sergeant," SGT Bragg replied.

"Take point and take First Squad back home. Third will trail the Hilux behind you." Cartwright replied.

SGT Bragg picked up his men and started north back towards Tynes—Young, Nguyen, SGT Maher, Rae, and Bowman with the gun team all behind him. They all had their heads hung low the entire way. They had been defeated.

CHAPTER 13

# The Triumph of Evil

"Everyone go inside and get into PT shorts, I need to check you out," Doc Taylor said to the men of First Squad as they walked through the wire of the front gate to COP Tynes. Each man slowly made his way to his room to remove his armor and ACUs. They slowly staggered out of the wood structure one by one in their dusty black shorts and pink Crocs. Doc Taylor began evaluating them for any injuries that might have been hidden by their uniforms and any pain that might have been numbed from the adrenaline.

He walked up to Rae and shined a small light into his eyes and then moved it away, observing how his pupils would respond. He covered one of his eyes and repeated the process. He began pushing him in random places all through his body. "Any of that hurt?" he asked him.

Rae didn't look up. "No."

Doc Taylor continued to examine the other men, checking their eye reaction to light, and seeing if any of them had any hidden injuries. He was especially concerned about Rae and Young, as they had already been blown up once before and were more susceptible to blast injuries. He carefully examined them and then had them sit down against the Hesco wall.

SGT Bragg started conducting a self-check while Doc was looking at SGT Maher to help speed up his examination. He ran his hands down his legs; everything seemed to be alright. He slid his right hand down his left arm and was surprised to feel something sharp and foreign. He rotated his wrist to expose the back of his forearm, there was a small trail of blood running down it. A small sliver of something was sticking out of his skin. He removed it using his fingernails and wiped off the blood with his hand so Doc Taylor wouldn't notice.

"Bragg, look at me," Doc said as he completed Maher's examination and started to walk toward him. SGT Bragg lifted his head and looked Doc in the eyes. Doc shone his light into SGT Bragg's eyes, momentarily blinding him. "What is that?" he asked, grabbing Bragg's arm by the wrist.

His attempt to clean off the blood must have failed. "It's just a splinter of something," SGT Bragg explained. "It barely broke the skin."

Doc rotated his arm to get a better look at it, whipping the new blood trail off that had replaced the one SGT Bragg had cleaned. "Keep it clean and let me know if it gets infected," he said as he cleaned the small wound with an alcohol wipe and put a band-aid over it. He continued to the next man.

SSG DeMeo exited the wood structure to join the men outside. He had just come from the TOC and didn't look so happy. "Where is Sergeant Cartwright?" he asked.

"Over here," SFC Cartwright said. He was helping Doc check in on the First Squad guys.

SSG DeMeo walked over to him. "I've got an update on the casualties," he said quietly.

"Well, let's hear it," SFC Cartwright replied. The rest of the men all snapped their attention his way, staring at him and waiting for what he had to say.

SSG DeMeo paused for a second, feeling all the eyes of the First and Third Squad guys on him. He turned towards them and announced, "Goddard, Craumer, Cornelius, Rostran, and Vasquez are going to be alright." He paused to look the men over. The expressions on their faces didn't lighten at the news as he had hoped. They continued to stare, waiting for the next part he was about to share, the part they already knew was coming. The part they didn't want to hear. The part they could deny being true if no one spoke the words. SSG DeMeo looked away from the men. He couldn't look them in the eyes as he spoke the words. "Neenan didn't make it," he finally said.

A few guys from Third Squad threw their helmets against the Hesco wall and stormed off into the wood structure. Others slowly followed in after them to drop their gear in their rooms.

SGT Bragg meandered to the other side of the wall where no one could see him. He had held it together as long as he could. Once he was out of sight of the other men, he let the tears flow. He stared at the stupid band-aid on his arm and ripped it off. He had been right next to Neenan and all he got was a scratch. Neenan was blown to pieces. He thought about the promise he made to himself after Santos's death. He had failed, and another man had died on his watch. One of his men, Neenan. He began walking in circles in the gravel clearing, mumbling to himself trying to clear out all the thoughts in his head.

McDaniel was climbing down from one of the guard towers after being relieved of his tower guard duties and noticed SGT Bragg's erratic behavior. He jumped down from the ladder and went to talk to him. "You alright, man?" he asked as he approached SGT Bragg's circling.

"They're everywhere," SGT Bragg replied, tears still coming from his eyes. "Say goodbye to your legs, because they're everywhere."

McDaniel didn't know what to say. He didn't know what to do. This was a side of SGT Bragg he had never seen. The team leaders in the platoon had been men the rest of them could lean on. They were unbreakable, infrangible, and yet Bragg appeared broken. McDaniel stood and watched as SGT Bragg lost it in front of him. SGT Flannery and Bowman had followed Bragg to the other side of the wall as well. They had intended on comforting him, but listening to the things he was saying, they too didn't know what to do.

"I can tie my boots to my belt with five-fifty cord, that way you guys won't have to look for my legs when they blow off," SGT Bragg said, looking at the ground in front of him.

Bowman didn't know what to think. Part of him thought it was kind of a good idea, and part of him saw SGT Bragg losing his mind. "Okay, man," was all he could think of to say shakenly.

SGT Bragg stopped his circling and sat next to the men. He had to pull it together, he couldn't let anyone else see him like this, especially Young and Nguyen. They still needed him. He began thinking about his promise again. He had failed Neenan, but he still had Young and Nguyen. He couldn't give up on them. He needed to do whatever he could to get them out of this. They were still his team. He stopped crying, wiped the tears from his face, and, like turning on a light switch, went back to being normal Bragg. "Sorry you had to see that guys," he said as he got up and started walking back to the wood structure.

"Where are you going, man?" SGT Flannery asked.

"To check in on what's left of my team." SGT Bragg replied.

Two Charlie had taken a major loss that day. They lost their RTO, Godard. They had lost one of their FOs, SGT Cornelius. First Squad lost their squad leader, SSG Craumer, as well as Rostran, Vasquez, and Neenan. The squad was left with just five out of the original nine men.

After a BDA, it was found Godard had initially set off the IED. He had stepped on a buried antipersonnel mine. This mine was designed to maim soldiers, not kill them, and that is exactly what it did to Godard. It had blown off one of his legs below the knee and left his other burned and riddled with shrapnel. The blast sent shrapnel into the surrounding area, peppering SGT Cornelius and SSG Craumer. The small mine, however, wasn't the only explosive that went off that day. Detonation cord had been wrapped around the mine, and that cord led to jugs full of homemade explosives and old Russian unexploded ordnance. When the mine was set off, it caused a chain reaction, setting off the detonating cord and then ultimately the jugs of explosives. Those explosives had been buried under where Neenan was standing.

The ANP were never brought into question about the IED, though it was clear to the men of Two Charlie that they knew the whole time. The men couldn't do anything about it. Bismullah acted very differently after that day, almost ashamed. A severe distrust resulted between the two groups, and the Two Charlie men stopped bringing the police on patrols with them unless they absolutely had to. The higher ups could shove the COIN operation up their asses.

Rostran and Vasquez would return to the platoon in the valley after their recovery, as their injuries were less severe than the other casualties. SSG Craumer, SGT Cornelius, and Godard would be stabilized and flown out of the country to receive further treatment in Landstuhl, Germany, and later in Walter Reed, Washington, D.C.

The next step for the men of Two Charlie was to begin packing the belongings and gear of the wounded men and Neenan. It was another silent day at COP Tynes, as nobody spoke a word while they packed away the things that reminded them of their buddies they wouldn't get to see again. They had done this too often for their liking, and the reality sunk in, as they quietly packed away Neenan's belongings, that it was probably not going to be the last.

Lachance had to go out of his way to find Cornelius's eye protection. The First Sergeant had threatened that Cornelius was not going to receive his wounded compensation for loss of limb or eyesight that the Army provided because he didn't THINK he had his eye pro on. Lachance KNEW Cornelius had them on. He remembered picking them up that day. He dug through the pile of torn-up gear they had brought back. Luckily, at the bottom of the pile, lay Cornelius's glasses. They had been destroyed from the shrapnel that collided with them. It was all the proof he needed, and Lachance sent up a detailed report just to prove the First Sergeant wrong. Looking out for the guys was something the First Sergeant should be doing for his men, not accusing them or trying to catch them in the wrong. But the First Sergeant was never fond of Two Charlie anyway.

McDaniel took notice of the somber tone of the platoon. This is where he had shone in the past and took the opportunity to help lighten the mood. He, Bowman, and SSG Rosa were taking inventory of Godard's belongings and gear and packing them away to be shipped home.

"One Samsung CD player," McDaniel said as he packed the device into a bag and Rosa added it to the inventory list.

"One Samsung computer," Bowman said.

"One Samsung DVD player. One Samsung MP3 player," McDaniel continued. He looked at Rosa who hadn't said a word the whole time; he was just writing down everything the two men said. Bowman was quiet too. McDaniel took his first shot. "This dude's new leg is probably going to be made by Samsung."

SSG Rosa smiled and held back a laugh. He continued to write the items on the inventory list as Bowman called out more things. They both were trying not to acknowledge McDaniel's joke. McDaniel saw them cracking though and continued. "It will probably play his MP3s too, but only on shuffle." He started to shuffle his right foot back and forth across the wood floor.

"Haha!" Rosa let out as his smile grew. He and Bowman were trying to be serious about the situation.

McDaniel wouldn't let up though; he kept chipping away. The next thing they started inventorying was Godard's socks.

"Six pairs of Army Green socks," Bowman said.

"Don't you mean twelve?" McDaniel replied without missing a beat. The two men began full-blown laughing. He could hear other men laughing through the thin walls in other rooms. The silence was broken, and it felt good to make people laugh again. It felt good to laugh again. McDaniel's soul was warmed, as he was able to take an incredibly dark time for the platoon and lighten it. Outside of being a machine gunner, McDaniel knew his role in the platoon. He took great pride in his ability to bring the guys back. To put a smile on their faces. It was all he truly cared about and he definitely accomplished it that day.

Neenan's boots and rifle ceremony was held at COP Tynes. It was another somber day as One and Three Charlie made their way to COP Tynes to join Two Charlie in remembrance. A Kiowa helicopter did a fly by with an American flag flying behind during the ceremony. The pilot had been trained in flight school by Neenan's father. One and Three Charlie made their way back to COP Nolen, and as soon as they returned the outpost came under heavy enemy attack, wounding some of the soldiers in the guard tower. The enemy had been waiting for their return from the gathering, hoping their guard would be down and morale low. It seemed the valley wasn't going to let up for anything, not even a funeral.

The men of Two Charlie all started to come to terms with the idea they probably weren't going to make it out of that valley. The enemy wasn't going to let up, and the fighting was only going to continue to get worse. More and more booms could be heard in the distance of the valley, either villagers or other forces having a bad day. It got to a point where the men would awaken from their sleep to a boom in the distance. Initially, they were unsure if they had actually heard the sound or if they had just dreamt it. The answer would come as they lay in their bunks, waiting and listening to see if others started to stir or the radios in the TOC would start to chirp. If it woke others, then they really did hear it and it wasn't a dream. If no one else responded, then it was only a dream, and they would lay back in bed and try to get back to sleep.

Knollinger had one of those nights, as he woke up to a dull rumble in the distance. He listened for a moment to see if anyone else responded, and he heard one of the exterior plywood doors to the wood structure swing open and then slam closed. Relieved, he got up and left the structure to join whoever it was that had also been woken by the distant boom.

He saw Lachance climb up the Hesco wall and look out into the darkness of the night towards the second canal. He climbed up to join him. "You heard it too?" he asked.

Lachance just nodded. He didn't turn to look at him. "It's the Devil's playground, man. Everything south of that canal is the Devil's playground."

Losing Neenan hit each man in the platoon hard. He was one of the sweetest people they knew. He had grown into a good soldier, into one of the men, a good friend, and now he was gone. They all lost a part of themselves that day; they had lost their hope. There was only one rule in the valley— in the end, the valley always wins. The valley wasn't going to spare any of them. They were all going to go home with a few less limbs, or in a body bag. There was no IF they were going to blow up, it had become WHEN they were going to blow up. They began to believe that they were not going to ever leave the valley, that they were going to die.

For most of the men, however, that was what fed the motivation to keep going out, to continue to patrol. They all developed the same kind of mentality that if it was going to happen, then they would rather it happen to them, not one of their buddies. If it wasn't going to happen to them, then they would rather be there, to be part of the chaos and carnage, because they'd rather be there to do what they could than sit on the sidelines. Nobody wanted to see their buddy get hurt or ripped apart by an explosion, but it was going to happen. It was a crazy and dark way to think about things, but when in the darkness, the men learned all they really had was each other.

First Squad had taken a major hit and was combat ineffective, but that didn't mean they could just leave it to the other two line squads to continue to patrol the area. Joes from Third Squad and Weapons Squad would volunteer to go out with them, to fill the slots of the guys that were gone. McDaniel filled in. Bowman and

Young would switch carrying the radio as the RTO. They all had friends in each squad and if your buddy was going out, then so were you.

SGT Lachance had to go out on every patrol after losing SGT Cornelius. He was the only FO the platoon had left, and he wasn't going to hang the men out to dry with no air support.

Two soldiers, however, had a different reaction to all the losses. Ryan and Winston had let the fear of death and dismemberment overcome them. The fear of seeing another soldier lose his limbs was overwhelming, and the thought of it happening to them was paralyzing. They voiced their thoughts to their squad leader, SSG Loredo. He saw the look in their eyes and knew he had to do something. Both had been stellar soldiers up to this point, doing what was necessary to get the job done in the chaos of the fighting. He couldn't let their cries for help go unanswered. He pushed it up to SFC Cartwright, who sent the two to talk with Doc Taylor to have him get an assessment.

"Doc, I can't do this anymore," Ryan said. He didn't look at Doc Taylor, just stared at his shaking hands held out in front of him as he sat on the stretcher in the aid station. "I don't want to be the reason they die."

"What do you mean, man?" Doc asked. He walked over to his aid station door to close it to give the two some privacy, leaving Winston waiting outside.

"I didn't sign up for this. I'm not a medic. I don't want their lives in my hands," Ryan squeezed his hands into fists to try and stop them from shaking. He wasn't wrong. Ryan didn't join the Army to be a medic. He was picked to go through EMT training before deployment to help Doc out, but that training hardly made him a medic. It was barely a step up from the Combat Lifesaver course everyone else went through. He didn't feel he had sufficient knowledge to be able to save his buddies' lives, but because he went through the course he now had the title and the responsibilities that came with it. He knew guys were going to turn to him in those dire moments and he didn't want the weight of a friend's life in his hands. He had treated casualties alongside Doc the day Tynes and Nolen died. He had been part of the QRF that responded the day Santos died. He had provided aid to Lovelace after he was shot in the face. And he had helped and seen the carnage the day Neenan died. He was all too familiar with combat injuries. "I need a break."

Doc took his hands and wrapped them around Ryan's shaking fists and pushed them together to steady them. Ryan's gaze left his hands and he looked up at Doc. "Alright, man, I'll see what I can do," Doc said as he helped Ryan to his feet and led him out of the aid station. "Next!" he shouted, as if calling upon the next person in the waiting room of a doctor's office. Winston stepped in and sat down on the stretcher. "What's going on, man?"

Winston's eyes stared at the floor until he finally raised them to Doc. "I can't do this anymore," he finally let out like a sigh of relief.

"Can't do what, man?" Doc Taylor asked him.

"I can't watch them die anymore," Winston replied. He had been part of a lot of the patrols that had guys get injured and killed on as well, however he didn't have the responsibility of working on the casualties like Ryan did; but that didn't mean he didn't see the carnage of a buddy blown to pieces or shot in the face. It weighed on him and he couldn't take it anymore. "Why does God let this happen?" he asked.

"I don't know, man," Doc said. "I don't know."

The two were released and Doc linked up with Loredo and SFC Cartwright in the TOC. "Well," Cartwright asked, "what do you think? Can they go out?"

Doc thought for a moment. "It's not that I don't trust them, it's just that I don't trust that they won't freeze. Do you really want someone out there that may freeze up on your guys?"

Cartwright and Loredo looked at each other and sighed. "Give them a day off. Let them cool down," SFC Cartwright finally said. "I think Second Squad is going out tomorrow anyway. We will see how they feel after that."

The next day, Second Squad made their way through the grape fields southwest of Lower Babur. They were circling around, pushing south to the second canal before finally setting their sights west to head back home to COP Tynes. The grape field they were in ended, and an open unplanted field stretched a good fifty meters until the next pomegranate orchard on its opposite side. To the south there was a mud wall that butted up to the opposite bank of the canal. A few murder holes could be seen along the wall from where the men were halted in the grape field. It was a perfect place for an ambush.

The men scanned the holes through their optics, looking for anyone who might be watching them through the small openings. "Hey, Charlie Two Two Alpha, have the ANP cross first. See if anyone bites before we cross," SSG DeMeo said to SGT Flannery over the radio.

"Roger," SGT Flannery replied. He motioned to the interpreter to come his way. "Tell Muhammad Duis to take his guys and push across this field. We will set in along this wall and cover them."

The interpreter relayed the message and the ANP slowly pushed across the field. Their eyes were glued to the south, watching the holes in the wall, not a single police officer even glanced in another direction. When the last man made it over the short mud wall on the other side, Muhammad Duis waved to the Second Squad guys, signaling they were set in and ready for them to cross.

"Alright, Flan, pick it up," SSG DeMeo said.

SGT Flannery hopped over the waist-high wall into the open field and, one by one, Figueroa, Dunlap, Leonard, and DeMeo followed.

Ratatatatatatat!

A roar of automatic gunfire erupted from the south. Rounds kicked up dirt all around the men in the open field as they scrambled for the closest cover, dirt raining down around them. SGT Flannery and Figueroa sprinted across the field to take cover behind the short wall on the pomegranate side. Flannery felt like the fastest person in the world as he and Figueroa dove behind the cover.

SSG DeMeo and Leonard ran back to the grape field they had come from, Leonard laughing as they were peppered with dirt. "This is not fucking funny, Leonard!" SSG DeMeo yelled as he hurdled back over the wall.

"Yeah, it kind of is," Leonard said and he dove over the wall headfirst. His foot got caught on one of the grape vines, causing him to be stuck behind the wall.

"Get that SAW up, Leonard!" SSG DeMeo shouted as he returned fire.

"I'm stuck in this root!" The root was preventing him from turning towards the fight and engaging the enemy.

"I don't care how you do it, get the goddamn SAW up," SSG DeMeo scolded him. Leonard ripped the vines from the dirt wall they clung to, freeing his foot. He stood up and began firing his SAW into the wall to the south, aiming for the small murder holes. "Flannery! Do you have your guys?!" SSG DeMeo yelled across the field.

SGT Flannery and Figueroa were both behind the mud wall shooting to the south, they were both alright. The ANP were death blossoming their AKs, spinning them over their heads and firing in every direction, but generally to the south. Flannery could see Leonard with SSG DeMeo in the grape field, but where was Dunlap? "Where is Dunlap?!" he yelled back over the field to SSG DeMeo.

"Leonard, where is Dunlap?" SSG DeMeo barked.

"I don't know!" Leonard said between bursts of his SAW.

"Well, find him!" SSG DeMeo snapped.

"He's right there!" SGT Flannery yelled, pointing over towards SSG DeMeo and Leonard. The two looked in confusion, as he wasn't anywhere near them. Then Leonard poked his head over the wall, and sure enough Dunlap was lying in the prone, on the wrong side of the wall, behind the smallest twig of a plant sticking out of the ground. Rounds were kicking up dirt all around him as the enemy fired upon him. "Dunlap, get over the wall!" Flannery yelled at him, and Dunlap stood up and threw himself over the wall behind Leonard.

"Second Squad's in contact!" SGT Maher yelled from the TOC.

"Let's go!" SGT Knollinger said as he kicked the door open and ran out of the wood structure. He was still throwing his gear on; all his guys closely behind him were doing the same. One by one they all quickly filed out of the building, donning their armor, buckling their rigs, and throwing on their assault packs full of ammo. They didn't need to hear the radio to know that Second Squad was in trouble, they could hear the gunfire in the distance. They all met up along the inner Hesco wall, waiting for the word to head out, all of them but two.

Ryan finally made his way out in his gear and was carrying his aide bag, a look of terror in his eyes. "Is anyone hurt? Is everyone OK?" he asked, a little trembling in his voice.

"Not sure, no casualties have been reported as of yet and no Nine Line requests over the radio either," SGT Knollinger said as he did a quick check of his guys' gear.

"They haven't requested a QRF yet, but get ready," SGT Maher yelled as he leaned out of the doorway of the wood structure.

Ryan looked down at his gloved hands; they were shaking. He grabbed his head with them to make them stop, to try and make the thoughts of working on another wounded man stop. He bent over and looked at the ground with his head in his hands and leaned against the Hesco wall. The thought of a friend dying paralyzed him.

"Are you alright, man?" Nichols asked him.

"I can't do it man, I can't do it." Ryan had kept his focus on the ground, not turning to look at Nichols when he answered. SSG Loredo walked over to him.

"Where is Winston!" SGT Brown said.

Winston walked out of the wood structure, just in his camouflage uniform. His plate carrier, rig, and helmet were still in his room. He didn't even make eye contact with the men, didn't even approach them. "I can't."

The men of Third Squad looked in shock. "Get your shit and let's go! Guys are in contact!" SSG Loredo said as he chased Winston back into the wood structure. He turned back to Ryan, "Ryan, let's go!" Ryan had slid down the Hesco wall he was leaning on and was sitting on the ground, his eyes still staring at the gravel, but his mind was elsewhere.

SSG Loredo went to the TOC to see if the request for a QRF had been made yet. "Not yet. They haven't taken any casualties. I'll let you know if they do call though," SGT Maher said.

SSG Loredo left the TOC to find SGT Bragg. "Bragg! I need to borrow Nguyen. I need him to fill in for Ryan."

"Nguyen!" SGT Bragg yelled as he ran to his room to grab his gear. If Nguyen was going then so was he.

Nguyen shot out of his room as SGT Bragg ran by, his gear slung over his shoulders. "I heard, I'm going, I'm going," he said as the two ran out to join the other men of Third Squad.

SSG Loredo shook his head and cursed under his breath. "I can't believe this shit." He joined the men outside to wait for the call.

"Flannery, they're trying to flank you!" SSG DeMeo said over the radio. The fighters had shifted their position along the wall to try and get an angle on Flannery and Figueroa. "We are going to start picking up fire and you guys are going to run back to us."

"What?!" SGT Flannery replied.

"Yeah. We will open up with the 240. When you hear that, get your ass over here," SSG DeMeo said. As soon as he said it, McDaniel stood up from behind the wall with the 240 machine gun, the carrying handle in one hand and the pistol grip in the other, and began firing at the enemy to the south.

SGT Flannery turned towards Figueroa. "Alright, Fig, we got to go!" he shouted and waved to Muhammad Duis to follow. The two men sprinted across the field as fast as they could in an "every man for himself" fashion and dove over the wall into the grape field on the other side.

Once the squad was whole again, and the enemy lost their opportunity to single out men in the open, they broke contact and disappeared into the orchards south of the canal. The men moved up to do a quick BDA but didn't stick around long enough to let the enemy regroup and hit them again. Second Squad fell back and made their way back to COP Tynes.

Upon the return of Second Squad that evening, both Ryan and Winston were taken to the back corner of the outpost, away from the guard towers or anywhere else someone could listen in, a place where they could be talked to in private. SSG Loredo, SGT Brown, and SGT Knollinger listened to the men. They listened to their fears, to their concerns. They heard them out, they tried to reason with them.

"Look, this shit sucks, I get it. But you don't think that every guy out here doesn't feel the same way?" SGT Knollinger tried to reason with them. "We've all been on the same patrols."

"You don't think that we are scared too?" SGT Brown sympathized. The two men's gaze didn't leave the ground.

It was a dangerous thing, fear, and it spread like fire. All the men of Two Charlie were scared, and every single one of them didn't want to go out on patrol. To risk seeing another buddy get hurt or die was all the men thought about. However, none of them even considered just straight giving up and refusing to go out on patrol. That was unheard of; no one knew that was even an option. You weren't just giving up on yourself, you were giving up on the guys. Nobody was going to do that. Nobody except for Ryan and Winston. The two men let that fear control them, let it overcome that decision. They refused to go out anymore. There was no talking them out of it, they had made up their minds.

This put SSG Loredo in a hard position. He couldn't just let them have their way. If the other men saw there were no consequences to this decision, then there would be a risk of a domino effect and possible others that would follow suit. But the two had been good soldiers up to that point, and he didn't want to destroy their careers over it. He cared about his men and didn't want that for them.

"Alright," Loredo finally said. "We'll give you a break, but you'll be pulling extra tower guard in the meantime." He thought for a moment, he couldn't let them fill the other Joes' heads with any more fear or give them any ideas. The platoon was a castle of glass as it stood, and they didn't need anyone throwing rocks. "You aren't to talk with any of the other men. You only respond to team leaders and above if they address you, is that understood?"

Ryan and Winston's gaze left the ground and looked up at SSG Loredo. He had made up his mind, and there would be no convincing him otherwise. The two men's eyes dropped back to the ground. "Roger, Sergeant," they both mumbled with shame in their voices.

"Good. You can start now. Ryan, you relieve whoever is in Tower Two. Winston, you take Tower Three." The two men left to grab their gear and head to the towers. Loredo looked at Knollinger and Brown. They all shook their heads and then followed the two back into the wood structure.

## CHAPTER 14

# One Shot, One Kill

Ryan and Winston's refusal to go out on patrols led to more guys having to fill more spots. Not only did the platoon need to fill in spots for First Squad on patrols, but now there were two spots in Third that needed to be filled as well. The platoon numbers were dwindling, and they barely had enough men to patrol, provide a QRF, and conduct tower watch at the COP. Two Charlie was running on fumes alone.

But they made it work as there was no real relief of reinforcements on the horizon. Third Squad guys would fill the slots for First Squad, and First Squad guys would fill in the slots for Third. The entire structure of the platoon kind of broke down and a "Thirty First Squad" was formed, as the guys started referring to it. It basically consisted of whoever was ready for the battle that day, sometimes with an entire fireteam of team leaders going out together. And the fighting didn't let up.

The men experienced firefights daily at this point, and the enemy was constantly adapting. The fighters in the area made it clear they didn't want the Two Charlie men south of the second canal. They had drawn a line in the sand and let them have it every time they tried to cross it. The men had hung a whiteboard in the TOC with a three-day schedule that would be constantly updated. It would say things like "Wednesday: First Squad–Babur to conduct a meeting with village elders, Third Squad–QRF" or "Thursday: Third Squad–Khosrows, First Squad–QRF, Second Squad–Night patrol of Druia." But now, all that it read was "Go to the second canal," and that is how it remained.

The murder holes in the mud walls became a constant threat to the men of Two Charlie, as they would constantly be ambushed and pinned down from them. The enemy would wait behind the walls in view of their IEDs they had set for the Two Charlie men to walk by and wait for the boom. If the boom did not come, they would open up on the men, causing havoc among the ranks in hopes to get them to set it off, much like they had attempted the day Lovelace got shot. The men of Two Charlie tried their best not to play that game and, when possible, SGT Lachance would call in the Kiowa helicopters to do gun runs and run them off into the orchards. This was effective, but not ideal as the enemy would get away to fight another day. The men of Two Charlie weren't completely helpless on the ground though. They had a secret weapon—Moon.

Moon and SGT Rush had spent a lot of time at COP Tynes. They arrived in late February after assisting Bravo Company in their AO for the earlier months in the valley. They were pushed out to Charlie Company after the call came that they needed a sniper team.

SGT Rush and Moon jumped on the call to join the men of Two Charlie. They liked it better at COP Tynes anyway. Going to COP Tynes was like going to Neverland, with guys in mismatched uniforms and wrestling around within the protection of the outpost walls. It also didn't hurt that both had come from Three Charlie before being moved to the battalion's scout platoon. They had friends within the ranks and knew the guys were solid fighters, despite their relaxed uniform standards.

SGT Rush and Moon went through sniper school together and became a pretty close duo, being inseparable since they were paired as a sniper team. SGT Rush, already having a deployment under his belt, liked being the go-to guy for a soldier like Moon. Moon had become like a little brother to him. Rush loved learning about Moon's interesting experiences, and he had a lot of them. As an adolescent, Moon was a nationally ranked BMX rider. At one of his competitions, he saw a baseball diamond and asked his dad what it was. That was the day he decided to pick up baseball. He got good at that too, so good the Atlanta Braves drafted him out of high school in late rounds. He declined the offer and decided to go to the University of Arizona, but after only about a semester he decided to serve his country instead. He told his parents he needed to do this first. That decision ultimately led him to being a sniper in the Arghandab with SGT Rush as his spotter. Moon was an excellent sniper and showed off his skills in sniper training. He often moved while standing on his sniper school lanes and was typically the first man done. On one of his practice lanes he even fired one of his shots while standing, which impressed many of the cadre and men that knew about it. Now he was implementing those skills on the battlefield. The men of Two Charlie were happy to have SGT Rush and Moon, especially when things started to really hit the fan.

"We bait 'em," Loredo said to SGT Rush, standing among the men in the pre-patrol brief. "Have you guys halt just south of the first canal with good eyes on the walls along the second. We move up to the second canal and get them to shoot at us, have Dru rain 203s over the wall to keep them from running, and you guys shoot 'em through the murder holes."

Rush liked this plan. It wouldn't be putting Moon and himself in the direct line of fire but would give them a chance to level the playing field. "Alright," he said looking at Moon. "You think you can make that shot?"

"Worth a shot," Moon replied, cradling his tan M110 rifle against his chest.

The men pushed out and headed south, skirting the first canal, looking for a good spot for the sniper team to set their trap. There was a large perimeter wall around one of the grape orchards with a small hut built perfectly in one of the corners. The roof of the hut was slightly shorter than the perimeter wall, giving the two men just enough cover if they lied in the prone. The spot was close enough to COP Tynes that Tower One could cover their six. It was the perfect spot.

"Alright, you guys wait here. It's time to set the bait." SSG Loredo said, leaving them in the field once they got a good overwatch set up.

The squad pushed to the south, staying just to the west of Route Highlife in the grape fields. They reached the grape fields on the north side of the second canal, within view of the intersection where Neenan died. They began moving west, heading away from it. That intersection had haunted the men since that day. It was the gateway to the Devil's playground.

"They see us," the interpreter said to SSG Loredo. "They are getting ready to shoot, they are just waiting for us to go a little bit further." The men all ducked behind cover in the grape furrows as they heard the news, waiting for the imminent volley.

"Viper Four, do you guys have eyes on anything yet?" Loredo whispered over the radio.

"Not yet," SGT Rush replied.

It was all too quiet, as the men listened to the wind blow through the leaves of the fields, awaiting the impending attack. The tension in the air could have been cut with a knife, but was lightened by the idea that, this time, they were the cat. Then, as the gust of wind faded along with the sound of the leaves, the quiet stopped.

Ratatatatatatatat!

The enemy opened fire on the men in the grapes with their machine guns. Rounds snapped and zipped by the men as they answered with their own volley of gunfire and grenade launchers launching grenades over the wall.

"Viper Four!" Loredo yelled over the radio but wasn't answered with a reply. Instead, the reply came in the form of 7.62mm rounds snapping over the men's heads, zipping through the holes in the mud walls.

Crack! Crack! Crack!

Moon let out a volley of rounds from his rifle into the murder holes, and the enemy fire began to diminish. "Fuck yeah! I got one," he shouted.

"Keep it up! Right hole! PKM barrel!" SGT Rush called out and Moon adjusted accordingly, sending more rounds down range.

"Pick up the fire!" SSG Loredo yelled at the men of Thirty First Squad. The men pushed further south, closer to the holes so they too could get a good shot on them, Moon covering them the whole way. They threw grenades over the wall when they got within reach, it felt good to be winning for once.

The enemy must have tucked tail and ran as the men advanced because they were nowhere to be seen after the men pushed past the wall. All that remained behind the holes in the wall were fresh pools of blood in the dirt and signs of the wounded being dragged away.

"Two Three, Viper Four, did we get any?" SGT Rush asked anxiously over the radio as the men conducted a BDA on the other side of the wall.

"You definitely tagged a couple," SGT Maher responded over the radio. "There is blood everywhere. No bodies though." It was a small victory but didn't truly feel like one without the confirmation of a dead enemy combatant lying in a pool of their own blood. The men of Two Charlie were thirsty for more.

"Moon! Phone!" SGT Maher shouted from the TOC. Moon had been lounging in the kitchen area, snacking on things while he waited for his turn to use the platoon's satellite phone. The men only got a 30-minute phone call each, so he needed to make it quick. He snagged the phone from Maher and made his way to the roof of the Quonset mud huts where the phone had the best signal.

Night was the best time to call because nighttime in Afghanistan was daytime back home in the States. That and you didn't have to risk getting shot at during the night, standing on the roof holding the antenna of the phone in the air, exposing yourself to get a good signal. Every now and then a call would drop, but for the most part it was the best spot.

Moon waited as the phone rang. "Hello?" His mother's voice finally came across the other end.

"Hey, Mom, how are you?!" Moon said, happy to hear her voice.

"Hey, Chris! How are you doing, son?" she replied with glee in her voice. Moon didn't get many chances to call home, so she was always happy when he did.

"Good, Mom. I'm good. How are things back home?" Moon replied.

His mother started carrying on the conversation, talking about all his friends and family back home and what they all had been up to since his last call. She filled him in on all the changes to the neighborhood and his hometown. It felt good to escape the valley, if only for a little while. Moon smiled as he listened to his mom talking. When she ran out of things to share, she turned the conversation back to Moon. "How are things with you? Where are you now?" she asked.

"I'm back with Charlie Company, Mom," he replied.

"Oh good! You always like being with those boys, don't you? Have you had any time to pick up and throw a ball around with any of them lately?" she said.

"Nah, we don't have a baseball to throw, but one of the guys did get some lacrosse sticks in the mail. Been trying to get better at that. Can't let Rush beat me." Moon replied.

His mother laughed at the last comment. "No, we can't have that. Is everything else going well?"

Moon paused for a moment. "Yeah, everything is good, Mom."

"You know I pray for you every day, son?" she replied, a little shaking in her voice.

Moon swallowed, "I'm okay, Mom. Don't pray for me, pray for the guys." He looked at his watch, his 30 minutes were almost up. "Hey, Mom, I got to go, it was great hearing your voice. I love you."

"I love you too, son. Be safe," she said as Moon clicked the button to end the call and made his way off the roof to hand off the phone to the next guy.

Moon and Rush continued to be a vital asset to the men of Two Charlie as they attempted to take back the valley from the enemy, or at least they did what they could with what they had. They continued to push into Lower Babur, always getting shot at before successfully making it into the village. They continued to press the second canal, only to suffer the same results. The line was drawn, and the men could do little to push it back with the numbers they had. They didn't even have enough guys to make up a full QRF, even by leaving only a skeleton crew back at COP Tynes. But they didn't give up either. They showed up each day for the fight.

Moon made his next impact in a firefight near Lower Babur. The men had gotten into a scramble and sent the enemy fleeing deeper into the orchards, out of the reach of the Kiowas, but not out of the reach of Moon.

"They're getting away on that motorcycle!" SGT Knollinger yelled, pointing at the motorized trike toting a small cart on its rear. There were at least three men speeding away down the road a few hundred meters from the Two Charlie men. The road was straight enough that Moon was able to keep them in his crosshairs just long enough.

Crack!

The round went sailing down the road, through the branches of the trees, and impacting one of the passengers in the cart. The man was ripped from the vehicle and flew into the ditch. The loss of weight caused the rest of the vehicle to sway to one side and flip over as it rounded the corner, throwing the remaining passengers just out of sight, not allowing for a follow up shot.

"Got him," was all Moon said, as the other men cheered at the sight. They didn't press on as they didn't want to push their luck. They had gotten another small victory that day. Best not to let the valley take that from them.

The small victories didn't go unnoticed, and it wasn't hard to figure out the root cause behind them. The enemy became wary of the man carrying the tan rifle and referred back to their original tactics of baiting the men into IEDs. It felt good to know that Moon had reinstalled some fear back into the enemy. That is exactly what a good sniper is supposed to do, psychologically affect the battlefield.

The men of Thirty First Squad tried a different approach to the second canal one day. SGT Knollinger led the men west through the town of Jelawur in an attempt to make it look as though they were just conducting another shura or buying flatbread from the local market as the men had usually done in the past. Instead of heading back down Route Red Dog to return to COP Tynes, they changed course and headed south as soon as they reached the west end of the village, disappearing into the grape fields. They continued to push until they made it to a clearing between two grape fields along the second canal.

"You getting anything on the ICOM?" SGT Knollinger asked the interpreter.

"They are watching us. They know we are down here," the interpreter replied.

"Set up an overwatch? Have Brown and his team, the 240, and snipers set in while we cross?" Maher suggested to Knollinger.

"Sounds good to me," Knollinger said as he relayed the plan to Loredo and the rest of the squad over his radio.

Knollinger moved his team into the open field, the clods of tilled dirt made it more difficult to get good footing and move quickly without risking rolling an ankle on the uneven terrain. Moon and Rush watched through their scopes next to the 240 gun team hidden among the grapes. As soon as Knollinger's team cleared the field, they set in their security and Brown's team moved up next. One by one, they filed through the open field.

"Alright, Bowman, let's move," SSG Rosa said to Bowman and Stegic as they picked up the 240 machine gun and began to move into the field. "Last man," Rosa said to Rush as he followed his gun team into the field.

"You ready?" SGT Rush asked Moon, still peering through the scope of his rifle at the mud walls to the south. "Let's go." The two men got up and entered the field right as Rosa and the gun team were about to hop the wall into the grape field on the other side, joining the rest of Thirty First Squad.

"Everyone in the grape furrow!" SGT Knollinger yelled to Rosa and Rush; he and the interpreter had just picked up chatter that the enemy was going to shoot.

Pop! Pop! Pop! Ratatatatat! Pop!

The enemy erupted as they all began to fire at the men in the open field. SSG Rosa grabbed Bowman and Stegic and the three men hurdled the wall into the grapes. "Cyclic!" Rosa yelled, instructing Bowman to open up with the 240, and he did without hesitation, firing his hundred-round starter belt into the trees to the south. He glanced at the open field as he loaded the next belt of ammo to see SGT Rush and Moon sprinting towards them. Dirt kicked up all around the two men as rounds impacted the ground and snapped by them.

"What?" Moon stopped and turned towards SGT Rush, thinking he had said something to him.

"Keep fucking moving!" Rush ordered as he turned Moon and pushed him forward. They raced their way across the field, diving headfirst over the wall next to Rosa and his gun team.

The enemy continued to unload, pinning the snipers and the machine-gun team in the field. The rest of Thirty First Squad picked up the fire, for they weren't the ones getting shot.

Nichols and Jackson unloaded with their SAWs, and Dru began launching 203 grenades. SGT Bragg took his 203 grenade launcher and fired a grenade at the wall to the south. He watched as it impacted against the wall next to one of the murder holes. He quickly reloaded the tube and went to try again.

"Bragg! Aim Higher!" SGT Brown yelled his way, almost laughing at his miss.

"No shit," Bragg thought to himself as he let the second grenade fly, perfectly clearing the mud wall and impacting the foliage just behind it. Brown gave him the thumbs up and continued to fire. It had been a minute since Bragg had shot a 203, and he definitely wasn't as effective as Dru was. The two continued lobbing grenades over the wall.

Knollinger moved his team down the canal, trying to get an angle on the men behind the wall and cut off their exfil. Brown's team followed as the men bounded together down the wall.

"Bowman, stay on my ass," SSG Rosa yelled as the gun team moved through the grapes. Rosa would pause occasionally to check to make sure Bowman and Stegic were still with him, and to return fire to cover their movement.

Eventually, the men found they had chased the enemy all the way down to the second canal intersection, the one in which they had lost Neenan. The fire died down as the enemy began to flee south.

"They ran into that abandoned structure!" Knollinger yelled.

"Rosa, do you still have that LAW?!" Loredo shouted back at the gun team.

Rosa had been carrying the M72 LAW rocket launcher with him that day. He unslung it from his back and held it into the air so that Loredo could see. "Right here."

"Let me have it," Loredo replied with a grin on his face.

"Fuck you! I'm shooting it. I carried it this whole time." Rosa replied as he moved up to the front of the grape rows, past the rest of the men. Maher followed him to provide cover and they got into a position where they could fire the rocket directly through the front door of the abandoned building. "Backblast area clear!" he shouted as he sent the rocket soaring into the old mud structure. The men cheered as a cloud of dirt spurted out of every opening. If any of the enemy had been taking shelter in there, they wouldn't be anymore.

The men returned to COP Tynes all with smiles on their faces, all but two.

"What's wrong man? That was fun," Knollinger said to Rush.

"Yeah, you weren't the ones getting shot at," Rush replied.

"Whatchu mean?" Knollinger asked.

"They waited for US to get into the open," Rush said. He was right. The enemy waited, letting the whole patrol walk through the clearing, making them think it was safe. They waited until they had a clear shot on the man with the tan rifle before they opened fire. They waited for Moon.

The men of Two Charlie soon received a new squad leader to help reinforce them in the valley from their loss on 7 June. SSG Middlebrook was sent from Alpha company to become First Squad's new squad leader. He was a seasoned leader, having deployed with the unit on their previous fifteen-month deployment. He had been a part of Alpha company up to this point and had only heard the stories of what Charlie Company had been up to in the valley. He was eager to see if the stories were true. However, he knew better than to step into his new role high and mighty, demanding a firefight from his new men. He knew he would get that experience in time.

Middlebrook linked up with his new team leaders Bragg and Maher to give them the run down for how he was going to handle his new position of squad leader. "This is your squad," he explained to the two men, "I'm just here if you need me." Bragg and Maher nodded in content. It put them at ease knowing there wouldn't be some unnecessary power struggle with a new leader at hand and they took him to meet the rest of the guys. It was clear to Middlebrook that Maher and Bragg were very protective of their men.

Young and Nguyen were chilling in Young's room watching a movie. Bragg opened the plywood door and walked in. "Sup, bitches, come meet your new squad leader." Middlebrook was a little taken back by the fact that the two didn't get up from their bed when he entered, but he didn't want to make a fuss about it. "Sergeant Middlebrook, this is my SAW gunner Young, and this is Johnny Nguyen. Nguyen is our squad EMT."

Middlebrook looked the men over as the two finally stood to shake his hand. "Whatcha watching?" he asked.

"*Marley and Me*," Young replied.

"Oh, I've seen that movie! Kinda sad, the dog dies in the end," Middlebrook responded.

The two men looked at him blankly. Apparently, this was the first time they were watching that particular movie. He hadn't picked up on that, and just spoiled the ending for them.

"Yeah, well, I saw the Arghandab movie. You die at the end," Nguyen replied.

Middlebrook didn't know what to think of that response. He must have been kidding, but it was hard to tell with Nguyen. He just stood there baffled. Bragg took notice and interrupted the silence. "That's just Johnny Nguyen for you. He grows on you."

CHAPTER 15

# 24 Jun 2010

The men of Two Charlie were riding on the high of their micro victories. It felt good to be winning for a change, but there was still one thing they hadn't done. They needed to take back the second canal from the fighters in the valley. They needed to send them a message, that they weren't going to let them walk all over them and control the Devil's Playground, not without a fight. It would raise the morale amongst the men, reassuring them they were still in the fight.

"We should go back to the second canal intersection. Set up another TCP. Show the fighters that's our spot," Lt. Farrington said to SSG Loredo and SGT Knollinger as the three men brainstormed in the TOC with the rest of the leadership.

"That didn't turn out very well for us last time," Knollinger replied, thinking of the IED blast that devastated First Squad.

"Well, how can we do it and be successful?" Farrington asked. The men thought for a moment.

"We could bring the trucks," Loredo suggested. "Have them for extra protection from IEDs and have the trucks' heavy weapons system and communication platform to support us."

The men had been reluctant to bring the trucks south of the first canal. "I don't know. The roads become quite narrow and don't allow for much freedom of movement. Would we even be able to get them down there? And what about the big IEDs?"

"We haven't been down there with vehicles this whole time, so why would there be one big enough to blow the trucks up? We could use the trucks to set off the IEDs. Roll over them," Loredo continued. "All that thing will do is blow off the tire and then we can be like 'Haha, we have a .50-cal, now fuck off.'"

The two men looked at each other and smiled. It was a feasible plan. Something different. "We're taking this shit back," Lt. Farrington said.

Loredo nodded. "Let's do it!"

It was decided they would only take three trucks, two MATVs and the MAXPRO. They didn't want to bring all the trucks, as there was barely enough room for the three at the intersection. However, the limited number of seats meant only a certain number of guys could go. The load plan needed to be made.

"Brown, you're staying here," SSG Loredo said to SGT Brown. "Headquarters element is coming to pick up you and DeMeo tomorrow. You're going home." SGT Brown and SSG DeMeo had deployed to Afghanistan earlier than the rest of the unit as a part of ADVON (Advanced Echelon). Subsequently, this meant the men had to leave earlier too. That or the Army would have to pay them extra money for the extra months they stayed, and the Army wasn't going to do that. Rae would also be leaving with them, as he was to go through armorer training to become the company's new armorer.

"Maher will take your seat," Loredo said as Knollinger wrote down Maher in one of the trucks. SGT Brown smiled. It was surreal to be going home, to be getting out of the valley. At the same time, it didn't feel right to be leaving his men now, with over a month and a half still left in the deployment. He tried to focus on the fact he was leaving his guys in good hands, they had Loredo and Knollinger to look after them. SSG DeMeo was just happy knowing his time in the valley was coming to a close—he was ready to be heading back home.

"Knolly, put Ryan and Winston on the load plan," Loredo continued. "Let's get them back in the saddle." The two men had had enough of a break from patrolling, and it was time for them to get back at it and lighten the load of the other men that had been picking up theirs. Knollinger nodded as he wrote down Winston and Ryan's names as drivers in Truck Two and Three, then assigned Doc Taylor to the trail vehicle. He figured it would be good to have the two as drivers, that way they were required to stay put in the vehicle in case the gunner needed the vehicle to move. He didn't quite trust them to be dismounts yet; he thought they might freeze in a fight.

"No, we don't need Doc, we have Ryan. Take Ryan and Winston off as drivers and make them dismounts," Loredo explained.

Knollinger hesitated. "I don't know," he said as he put the marker to the whiteboard but didn't make the switch.

"What do you mean you don't know? Do it. I'll speak with them tonight. It will be a perfect opportunity to get them back out there and prove to the guys that they are still with us," Loredo said.

Knollinger continued to hesitate to make the change. "I don't trust them."

"Well, I do! And that's what I told you to do," Loredo fought back. Knollinger made the change. "Now who is going to be in Truck One?"

Knollinger wrote his name in the truck commander's slot for Truck One. He knew this was the truck that would be "searching" for the IEDs, and he wasn't going to put anyone else in that position. He sat there for a moment and thought about who he could count on to be in that position with him, who was willing to roll, and who he knew would step up to the plate knowing they were probably going to get blown up. He raised the marker back up to the board and wrote "Bowman" as the gunner and "McDaniel" as his driver. He knew Bowman would do anything for him and McDaniel was just always ready to roll. "I'll talk with these guys, but I want them as my driver and gunner."

"Okay," Loredo agreed. "Sir, you'll be in Truck Three and I'll take Truck Two. I'll take Dru as my driver with Chancy and Jackson. Put Ryan and Winston in the back seats with you, Knolly. Maher, Farnsworth, and Nichols can pile in with the lieutenant in the MAXPRO."

"Any room for the rest of the scouts?" SSG Farnsworth asked.

"I don't think so. Looks like Moon and Rush will have to sit this one out," Lt. Farrington replied.

"How about getting Hale in on this one? Get him his CIB," Farnsworth asked. Hale was another member of the scout platoon. He had been sent down to Charlie Company to earn his Combat Infantryman Badge (CIB). This was a badge that every infantryman gets after receiving contact and engaging the enemy. It's a badge of honor and kind of a big deal in the infantry community. Hale hadn't seen any action yet during this deployment, and it had become common for the scouts to send guys to Charlie Company to get into a fight and earn their badges since the fighting in the area was so kinetic.

"Yeah, I forgot about Hale. Take Farnsworth out and put Hale in with the LT. We will get him his CIB for sure," Loredo said with a smile. The rest of the men laughed under their breath.

The men recessed their meeting and went to let the guys know the plan for the following day and enjoy the rest of the night, leaving SGT Knollinger in the TOC to finish up writing the names of the load plan on the board. He stared at Ryan and Winston's names as dismounts on the board. "Nah," he said as he took his sleeve and erased their names, rewriting them as the drivers of the trail vehicles. He understood what Loredo was trying to do, but he just didn't trust them. He added Doc Taylor back to the last truck, set the marker on the board, and left the TOC to go to talk with Bowman and McDaniel.

"McDaniel," Knollinger said as he knocked on the plywood door to McDaniel's room.

"What?" McDaniel replied. He had just gotten off of tower guard and was getting ready to pass out for the night.

Knollinger entered McDaniel's dark room. "We are going to do something really fucking stupid," he said as he sat down next to him.

McDaniel, a little nervous and confused, replied, "Well, if you're bringing me in on it, then I know it's stupid."

Knollinger continued. "We are going to take a truck and deliberately run over an IED."

"… And?" McDaniel replied.

"Will you drive the truck?" Knollinger asked.

"Haha. Oh, no. No, no, no," McDaniel laughed, but then saw that Knollinger was being serious. He stopped laughing and then went on. "Okay."

Knollinger smiled. "You're my boy, Blue. I'll see you in the morning."

The next day the men went over the patrol brief with the rest of the guys. SGT Brown joined them to say his last goodbyes to his men, as he didn't know if he would be there when they got back later that evening. He dragged his bags out into the gravel clearing to stage them for when Headquarters would come to pick him, Rae, and DeMeo up.

"Alright, we are going to conduct a mounted TCP at the second canal intersection. We will have three trucks. Knollinger, do you want to go over the load plan?" Lt. Farrington asked.

"Roger, the load plan is as follows," Knollinger said as he started to list off the names of the guys and what trucks they were in. He caught a glimpse of the fire in Loredo's eyes as he read Ryan and Winston as drivers. He knew he was going to hear about it for that one.

"Alright. So, we are going to use Truck One to clear the route to the canal. Guys in Truck One, get with Knollinger, he has more detail on what that entails," Lt. Farrington continued.

"If you get out of the vehicle, stay in the tire tracks," Loredo said. "I don't care if you're getting shot at, you do not leave the tire tracks. Is that understood?"

The men all nodded. They were all worried because they knew that intersection was probably lined with explosives, but their fears were lessened by the fact they had the barrier of the trucks and wouldn't be just walking out there, exposing themselves to another blast.

"If we come in contact, we have the support of the trucks' 240 machine guns and the .50-cal machine gun. As Loredo said, if we dismount, stay in the area the trucks have already cleared. Lachance, do we have any Birds on station?" Lt. Farrington asked.

"No Air Assets as of now. They have been assigned to assist elsewhere. I'll monitor the net and let you know if that changes throughout the day. No mortar support either," Lachance replied. The First Sergeant had sent the mortar guys on a mounted patrol.

"Alright. We got Doc Taylor as the medic, and since we have the trucks, we can CASEVAC any wounded to Terra Nova. They have a PA there who can work on any casualties, and we can get a MedEvac Bird from there." Lt. Farrington continued. "Any other questions?"

The men had none. They knew what was about to happen and they were getting themselves ready for a fight.

"Alright, let's load up," Loredo said. "Knolly! Come here for a second."

Knollinger made his way over to take his lashings for changing up the load plan behind Loredo's back. "What's up, Sergeant?" he said upon getting close enough for the two men to talk.

"You know what's up," Loredo responded. "You disobeyed me."

"I know, I just don't trust them yet," Knollinger replied.

Loredo gave him a stern look. He wasn't mad at him because he understood his distrust, just at the principle of disobeying him. "We'll talk about it when we get back."

Knollinger went over to his truck and began putting on his gear, The other men of his truck were there waiting for him. "Alright. So, like I said, we are going to use the truck to clear the route. We are going to straight up *Austin Powers* this bitch until we run over every square inch of ground. If there is a bomb out there, we are going to find it."

"Alright, sounds good." McDaniel said.

"Bowman, I don't want you standing in the turret. I want you sitting on the turret strap, feet off the ground. We can't have you breaking your ankles on us," Knollinger said.

"Yep," Bowman replied.

"Alright. Let's load up and go," Knollinger said as he and the rest of the men headed to the truck.

The convoy rolled out of COP Tynes and slowly rolled down Route Highlife, heading towards the second canal. The armor plating of the MATV turrets caught the low hanging branches of the trees along the first canal as they passed under them, ripping the skinnier twigs from their limbs. The truck's antennas bent and whipped back to their original upright position as they pushed through them, one truck at a time. It was obvious a vehicle of this size hadn't gone down that road in some time and it was like the trees were urging them to go back, grabbing at their vehicles with every opportunity.

They inched their way down the hard-packed dirt road, maneuvering through the tight grape rows on each side. Sometimes the truck would scrape the mud walls as they drove past, causing chunks of dried mud to crumble from the short walls.

"Keep doing that," Knollinger said to McDaniel.

"What, running into the grape walls?" McDaniel replied.

"Yeah." Knollinger answered.

McDaniel continued scraping the truck's front right tire along the rows of grapes, knocking off pieces as they continued down the road. Knollinger examined each row as it crumbled through his small bulletproof window, inspecting the exposed dirt for wires or jugs or any other signs of explosives.

The first truck approached the second canal intersection and began driving back and forth to run over more ground. When Knollinger was satisfied, he got out to guide the truck into a security position. He wasn't even sure if the width of the vehicle's wheels would clear the bridge, so he had to get out to see.

SSG Loredo watched as the door opened and Knollinger climbed out of his truck. Loredo adjusted his position in his seat, moving his arms to different positions to look out his side window. The trucks were always cramped when the men had their full gear on, and it was hard to find a good position to sit in the limited amount of space that was comfortable. It made Loredo antsy.

"What do you think, Chancy?" Loredo asked Lachance who was sitting in the back seat of his truck.

"I don't know. Looks kinda quiet." Lachance replied. The farmers in the fields were completely gone. There wasn't a single person in sight. An eerie feeling filled the air, making the hairs on Lachance's arm stand up. He quickly brushed them down.

"Stop here," Loredo said to Winston, instructing his driver to stop moving. "Let me get out and guide you." Winston did as he was told, and Loredo opened his door to escape the confinement of the truck. "Let's go, Chancy," he said after plopping to the ground and turning to close his door. Lachance followed, getting out of the vehicle next to him. Jackson popped out too and started heading up the road toward Knollinger. The men walked in front of the truck in the tire tracks. Loredo motioned for Winston to keep moving the truck forward.

Lachance, walking in the opposite tire track along Loredo, noticed out of the corner of his eye Loredo's head snap to look at something within the leaves of the grapes. Loredo grabbed his radio hand mic and pulled it to his mouth to say something.

BOOM!

Ryan and Lt. Farrington watched from inside the trail vehicle as a small cloud erupted from the ditch next to Loredo, instantly throwing dirt and grape leaves everywhere into the sky. They stared as Loredo cartwheeled through the air as he and Lachance were swallowed by the dust. They could hear small pieces of debris contacting the truck as it peppered the outside.

"IED, IED, IED," Farrington called over the radio.

Lachance opened his eyes, finding himself on his hands and knees as he slid across the solid dirt road. A thick dust cloud filled the air, blurring his vision of everything around him. All he could hear was a loud ringing in his ears. He turned to where Loredo had been standing in front of him. He wasn't there. He was lying on his side on the opposite side of the road about a foot away from him. The radio on his back was on fire, and his left leg was severed at his hip. It was still attached, hanging by a small strip of skin and muscle, and it laid on top of him with his foot resting next to his head.

Lachance crawled towards him, swatting the burning radio with his hands to try to put out the flames. Loredo moaned as the smell of burnt flesh and plastic filled the air around the men. Lachance's vision began to clear up and the dust started to settle around them. He began looking for either his or Loredo's tourniquet.

"Lachance! Lachance!" Doc Taylor screamed as he ran up through the dust from the rear of the vehicles. He took a knee beside Lachance to start rendering aid to Loredo.

"I, I can't find his tourniquet," Lachance said in an unstable confused voice; he had been rattled from the blast.

Ratatatatat! Pop! Pop! Pop! Ratatatat!

Gunfire exploded from the canal. The two men got down, covering Loredo like a human shield as rounds zipped and snapped all around them.

"Fifty meters! Ten o'clock!" Knollinger yelled from the front vehicle, calling out an enemy's position south of him as he and his dismounts returned fire. Bowman began to fire the truck's mounted 240 machine gun from the turret, unloading in the directions the men were calling out, not once letting up on the trigger.

"Forty meters! Two o'clock," Jackson said as he raised his SAW and opened up on the enemy he had just identified.

"Fifty meters! Four o'clock!" Dru shouted, launching a few grenades that way. The enemy almost had the men surrounded.

Loredo's gaze left Lachance and Doc as he looked to the second canal. He raised his hand and pointed towards a wall to the east of the intersection. A fighter was standing, trying to get a better shot at the convoy. Even after being blown up, Loredo was still calling out targets for his men. Maher made quick work of the fighter, unloading his rifle into him and he and Knollinger began to run over to assist with Loredo.

"Get him in the crater!" Doc Taylor yelled.

Lachance stood up and grabbed Loredo by the shoulder strap of his plate carrier. He lifted him completely off the ground and carried him to the crater left by the explosion in the ditch of the grape rows. Bullets continued to snap and zip over their heads as the men hunkered over Loredo in the hole. The .50-caliber machine gun from Truck Two began shooting over them at the fighters to the west. Doc Taylor began administering morphine and Knollinger put on a tourniquet.

"Eddie? Can you hear me?" Lachance yelled at Loredo as he stabilized his head and neck between his knees.

"What happened?" Loredo asked, in a faint whisper as his eyes rolled back and forth.

"Stay with me, buddy! Look at me Eddie, look at me!" Lachance said to him.

"Loredo, *mira*!" Knollinger told him, speaking to him in Spanish.

"It hurts. It hurts. Get it off. I can't breathe, get it off!" Loredo said as he pulled at his body armor. Lachance pulled the quick release cord in the front of the armor that made it fall into separate pieces. Doc Taylor took his trauma shears and cut the remaining clothes off the top of his body. Loredo's lower stomach was peppered with ball bearings and shrapnel, a rib protruded from his left side.

Doc Taylor pulled the collapsible litter from his aid bag and laid it next to Loredo. "You're going to need to help us out on this, Eddie," Doc said. Loredo took his arms and wrapped them around Lachance's neck, using his own strength to lift himself up. The other men slid the litter underneath him. Doc and Knollinger grabbed the litter and quickly carried him to the last truck in the convoy.

"Fuck!" Knollinger yelled out as the litter caught the ramp of the MAXPRO. It was sagging in the middle due to Loredo's weight. The thing was flimsy, like a blanket with handles, not providing much support for Loredo but making it easier for the two men to carry him. "Someone lift up his ass!" Knollinger called out, trying to free the litter from the steps.

Loredo must have heard him, because he bridged his ass off the litter using his remaining leg, freeing it from whatever it was caught on. "Let's go!" Doc yelled to Ryan and Farrington as they sat down Loredo in the back of the vehicle. Rounds pinged off the inside as they started to close the hydraulic door and get the vehicle turned around.

Lachance stood in the center of the road between the last two trucks as the men on the ground engaged the enemy all around them. "Charlie Nine Five, this is Charlie Nine Two, over!" He said over his radio.

"Charlie Nine Two, we have your location and situation update, go for Nine Five," the radio replied. Lachance could barely hear it over the commotion of the fight.

"Nine Five, Nine Two, copy. Requesting Close Combat Aviation and/or Close Air Support at this time, over." Lachance said aggressively into his hand mic. He had to cup it with his hands to try and mask all the gunfire in the background so they could hear him.

"Negative Nine Two. Air assets are assisting in other locations at the moment," the voice over the radio returned.

"God dammit," Lachance said to himself then held the hand mic back to his face. "Can you push them to us?"

"Working on it," the voice replied.

He turned and noticed a piece of Loredo's flesh hanging from the front bumper of the truck. He picked it up with his hands and threw it to the ground so the men wouldn't see it. He watched as ants immediately swarmed the piece of meat, tearing it into smaller pieces to carry it off to their nest. "Even the fucking ants are savages," he thought to himself.

Dru and Jackson pushed along the second canal to try to get an angle on the enemy shooting at them from the southwest. The enemy shifted their position, heading into the grape fields to the west. Knollinger fired as they popped in and out of the grape rows, walking backwards with each of his shots to try to retreat to cover. He bumped into Maher, who was shooting at the enemy to the east. The two looked at each other and had the same expression on their faces. "Are we really back-to-back right now?" Knollinger said as he continued firing. The enemy was all around them.

An enemy fighter kept poking around the corner of one of the walls on the second canal. Knollinger grabbed a grenade from his rig and pulled the pin, then chucked it at the wall. He slipped mid throw, causing it to land way short, plopping into the water of the canal. Knollinger looked at Maher as the two men waited for the explosion.

A large spout of water shot straight into the air and, oddly enough, both sides stopped shooting to witness the spectacle. The water droplets spread as they began to rain down all around them. As soon as the last drop of water hit the dry dirt, the shooting continued.

"Maher, what do you think we should do?" Knollinger said over the new eruption of gunfire.

Maher looked around at the guys. Hale and Dru were launching 203s, Jackson and Nichols were rocking their SAWs, talking their fire with each other and Bowman on the 240. The .50-cal had malfunctioned and Danziger was working to get it back up, shooting random bursts as he did. He finally leaned over to Knollinger and said, "We need to break contact!"

Knollinger agreed. "Get to the trucks!" he yelled to the dismounts as the men all scurried to the closest vehicle. Bowman continued to fire as the trucks got turned around, crashing into the grape field walls as they made their 500-point turns to face north. There was no time to figure out who needed to go to what vehicle, just that everyone was back and accounted for. They all piled in a vehicle, and Hale and the interpreter climbed in the bed of the MATV since the third truck was well on its way getting Loredo to Terra Nova. Lachance climbed on to the side of the vehicle and clung to the side-view mirror. Like a bat out of hell, they began to break contact.

The men at COP Tynes didn't need to hear the call over the radio, they could hear the extreme volley of gunfire coming from the second canal. It was like Battle of the Bulge was going on, as heavy weapons and explosives from both sides rang out. Everyone and anyone who wasn't on guard duties threw on their gear and just began running out the front gate.

"Bragg! I'm coming with you guys!" SGT Brown yelled as he fell in behind SGT Bragg's team. He only had a single mag for his rifle, as he had given the rest to his guys since he was leaving. He didn't care, he needed to get down there, to be with his men.

They sprinted through the wire and didn't even make it to the first canal before the MAXPRO blew past them on Route Highlife. It almost tipped over as it made the turn onto Red Dog and headed toward Terra Nova.

The other two trucks came by a few moments later. The last truck had Lachance holding onto the side and Hale in the bed. Bowman was still firing the 240 at the canal as the truck bounced around the dirt road. Hale launched one last 203 that direction as well as they passed the men from the COP and followed the first truck down Route Red Dog.

Crack! Crack!

Moon was on top of Tower One firing at fighters with his rifle. He was wearing PTs but had on his helmet and armor. You could see his bright pink Crocs from the first canal where the men stood.

SSG DeMeo climbed up to the tower as well. He kicked the Joe pulling tower guard out of the tower, got behind the 240 machine gun and began firing it wildly to the south. The men near the first canal took cover, as he was shooting right over them. They moved back to the outpost to get out of the way.

"What the fuck!?" Bragg yelled up to him in the tower as he approached.

"I just got two kills at the second canal. Confirmed! You guys need to go do a BDA," SSG DeMeo yelled down as he exited the tower. Bragg looked at Moon to see if he could confirm, Moon just rolled his eyes and shook his head.

"Doc, that fucking hurts!" Loredo said to Doc Taylor. Doc's kit was bouncing and hitting Loredo's leg on every bump.

"Stop fucking bouncing us around!" Doc Taylor yelled to Ryan as they bounced their way over every culvert on Route Red Dog. Doc removed his kit so it wouldn't hit Loredo and began to administer more morphine.

"I'm sorry," Ryan replied. There wasn't much he could do about it. The roads were rough, and the faster they went the rougher it got.

"Doc, don't let me fucking die," Loredo said.

"Dude, you're fucking good, bro, it's just one leg," Doc replied as he rechecked the tightness of the tourniquet.

The men rolled up to Terra Nova and Doc and Farrington unloaded Loredo into the aid station. The PA began to provide advanced medical aid while they waited for the MedEvac Bird to arrive. They wrapped an occlusive dressing around the injuries sustained to his chest and abdomen and bandaged up his leg. The entire time Loredo was conscious and talking to them.

The other two trucks from Two Charlie rolled in through the gate as the MedEvac Bird landed on the HLZ. The men climbed out of their vehicles and watched as Loredo was carried on a litter from the aid station to the helicopter. The men at each corner of the litter sprinted as fast as they could to get him out of there. The Bird took off and disappeared into the sky as the outpost was filled with a plume of dust.

When the dust cleared, Knollinger thought to conduct his post-patrol inspections of his guys, checking them for their gear and making sure they had all their sensitive items. Things got pretty hectic, and he didn't need any of his guys losing anything out there. Once he ensured they had everything, they would start to head back to COP Tynes.

"Where are your gloves?" the First Sergeant asked Lachance, noticing he wasn't wearing any.

Lachance glared into the First Sergeant's eyes. "Is he really doing this now?" he thought to himself. "I need new ones," he replied. "Mine have blood all over them." He turned to walk toward the trucks, away from First Sergeant.

Knollinger's guys had all their gear, but that's when it came to him. Oh, shit. In the chaos of getting Loredo out of there, they had forgotten Loredo's gear and rifle in the grape field. He sighed and turned his gaze to the ground as the realization crept over him.

"What's wrong, Sergeant Knollinger? You did good out there," CPT Christmas said as he approached the men of Two Charlie who were trying to come down from the adrenaline high they were on. They were lounging around their vehicles, waiting to load back up and return to COP Tynes.

"I got to go back," Knollinger replied softly.

"What?" CPT Christmas asked.

"Yeah, what!?" Lt. Farrington echoed.

"We don't have his weapon," Knollinger replied.

CPT Christmas was expressionless. He paused for a moment, then said, "Alright, see you later."

The men loaded back up and returned to Route Highlife, and back to the grape field they had been treating Loredo in. The sun was starting to set and the air began to cool. They had the overwatch of the F-15 fighter jets this time, which must have scared off the fighters as it was all too quiet along the canal.

"Where was it at?" Knollinger asked Lachance as they walked along the grape walls.

"Here," Lachance replied pointing toward the hole in the ground. Luckily, Loredo's rifle and rig were still there. His radio and NODs were still accounted for as well.

In the quietness of the field, Knollinger heard a rustling of leaves among the grapes. He stood on one of the walls to discover a small boy, no more than twelve years old, pulling up lamp cord from under the dirt and wrapping it around his arm like an extension cord. Knollinger was pissed. He didn't say a word, just sprinted toward the child, tackling the boy to the ground. If this kid was responsible for injuring Loredo, he was going to kill him. The small boy cried out, terrified as Knollinger held him in the air over his head by the collar. He was about to swing on the kid, beat him to a bloody pulp when the fighter jets flew overhead.

"Charlie Nine Two, this is Sabre Nine One. We have eyes on your location and have a clear view with our visuals, over." The call came over Lachance's radio from the fighter pilot above.

"Hey man, the Birds can see you," Lachance relayed the message to Knollinger, urging him not to go forward with harming the child.

"Have them pull off for a minute," Knollinger replied. His eyes turned red as his gaze didn't leave the little boy in his grasp who was struggling to get free.

Lachance called for the Birds to pull their eyes off of them. "Roger, Sabre Nine One. Requesting you move your visuals to our outer perimeter and recon for enemy movement."

"Roger, Charlie Nine Two. Just know that the site will still be monitored," the pilots replied.

Lachance knew this was a courtesy from the pilots. They saw the boy. "They're not pulling off man," Lachance replied, putting his hand on Knollinger's shoulder, calming his rage as he slowly lowered the kid to the ground. The boy took off as soon as his feet made contact with the dirt and disappeared into the grapes. Knollinger looked at the ground, and Lachance reassured him that was the right thing to do. "Come on man, let's go home."

The convoy returned to COP Tynes just in time to say their goodbyes to the guys leaving on ADVON. Brown, Rae, and DeMeo all grabbed their things and loaded them onto the Headquarters trucks that had come to pick them up and take them to Terra Nova.

"See you guys later!" SSG DeMeo said with the biggest shit-eating grin on his face, waving to the men as he loaded his things into the vehicle. He made sure to rub it in that he was leaving, and he acted as though what the other men had just gone through hadn't even happened. He was going home and that's all that mattered. His time was up in the Arghandab River Valley.

DeMeo saw Knollinger saying his goodbyes to Brown, and he felt the need to interrupt. "Hey man! Come here," he said as he walked up and hugged Knollinger. "I'm proud of you."

Knollinger was instantly filled with rage. "This motherfucker better get off of me or I'm going to shoot him in the face," he thought to himself.

The convoy loaded up to depart from COP Tynes. DeMeo blew the men kisses and waved as he climbed into the vehicles like he was on a parade. When they arrived at Terra Nova, Brown immediately hopped out of his truck and found the First Sergeant.

He tried to plead with him. "First Sergeant, I can't leave. Not now. Our platoon is already short as it is and now Loredo is gone. You gotta let me stay."

The First Sergeant just looked at Brown. "It's not my call. You're slated to leave. You must leave."

Brown's stomach sank. There was nothing he could do. His time was up in the Arghandab River Valley.

The men of Two Charlie were left in limbo the rest of that evening, waiting on any word of SSG Loredo's status. Was he going to pull through? It was unknown. As the evening carried on and the sun left the valley, so too did the tension of the unknown. If he had made it this long then surely he was out of the woods, he was going to pull through.

It was business as usual at COP Tynes. The men continued to rotate guard shifts in the towers, they ate a warm meal, and Knollinger and Rosa even got a workout in under the light of their headlamps. The men were convinced Loredo was going to be okay, that he was going to live. They even joked around about how he wouldn't have to worry about doing calf raises anymore.

As Knollinger was finishing his last set, he noticed another headlamp approach them from the darkness. It was SFC Cartwright. He came up to Knollinger and Rosa with an all too familiar look on his face. "Gather your boys," he said.

Maher came out of the wood structure with another soldier to relieve Jackson in one of the guard towers. Jackson was a little confused as his guard shift had just begun. It hadn't hit him until Maher had told him to go inside, drop his gear, and link up with the rest of Third Squad.

"No," Jackson said in denial as he came to the realization of the situation at hand. "We aren't doing this again."

"Yeah," Maher said as he walked inside to join the others. "We're doing this again."

## CHAPTER 16

# For Good Men to Do Nothing

The IED that killed Loredo was not a pressure plate, but a command wire set off by a trigger man much like the one that killed SFC Santos. The bomb was a homemade Claymore, which sent ball bearings flying through the air. Aside from the blast taking off his leg, the bearings ripped their way through Loredo's torso, causing severe internal bleeding that went undetected by the men treating him until he was able to receive higher care in the hospital at KAF. The hemorrhaging was not caught in time and Loredo died later that evening. Two Charlie yet again lost another good man.

Doc Taylor couldn't believe the news. He had been talking to Loredo the entire time. Loredo even moved himself on his own power when they MedEvaced him. They were quick to slap a tourniquet on and control his bleeding. He thought he was going to be good. He thought he was one of the guys he saved. Doc Taylor had forgotten the rule of the valley—in the end, the valley always wins.

Lachance couldn't help but think he should have been dead that day as well. That or at least maimed or severely injured, not walking around unscathed like he was. He was standing right next to Loredo when it went off. Loredo took the brunt of the blast, protecting him from the bearings and everything else that flew in their direction. Doc Taylor checked out Lachance after getting back to COP Tynes that day. He had a piece of shrapnel that had ripped and gouged his plates in his plate carrier along with a few rocks in his shins. Other than that, he still had all his fingers and toes. If it wasn't for Loredo, he too would have been hurt much worse or killed. He tried not to dwell on the thought of losing his friend. Not now.

Knollinger was left with the weight of leading the men of Third Squad now. His squad leader, Loredo, was gone. His Alpha team leader, Brown, was gone. The only one Third Squad had to turn to now was him. Everything was on him.

Rosa approached Knollinger. "Hey man, you want to take care of clearing out his room?"

Knollinger nodded and hesitantly walked to the mud room Loredo had called his own. He looked among his belongings that still lay on his cot or on his little plywood table. His computer was still open and turned on, a slideshow of photos streamed across the screen. A bag of one of Loredo's favorite snacks, flamin' hot Cheetos, lay beside the computer. It was still open with some of the Cheetos spilling out. At any moment Knollinger expected Loredo to barge in through the door, but that moment never came. Knollinger just stood there, staring at his shit.

It hadn't hit Knollinger until Loredo was gone, but the two men were similar in a lot of ways. He saw so much of himself in Loredo: his aggressiveness, his type of leadership, and the way they cared for their men. Knollinger began to break thinking about it.

He left the room and returned to Rosa in the TOC. "I can't do it," he said to him softly. "You gotta do it."

Rosa could see Knollinger was hurting. It was never an easy thing, inventorying the belongings of a dead friend. "I got you, Knolly," he said as he put an arm around Knollinger and led him out of the TOC.

Nichols and Jackson had to step up as team leaders and Knollinger filled in as Third Squad's squad leader. Knollinger didn't want that for his men, to be thrown into a position like that. He didn't want them to have to take point like they would now have to do. He just wanted them to keep rocking their SAWs in a fight and let him die, not them; they were still his guys. It wasn't that they weren't ready to take that role, it was that he wasn't ready. The team leaders of the platoon loved their Joes and would do anything for them to keep them from the gates of hell. Knollinger had a lot of weight to carry after that day. He had to keep his squad together, to keep them going. It was all on him now.

Two Charlie was pretty much combat ineffective at this point. They only had two squad leaders among the whole platoon, SSG Rosa and SSG Middlebrook, and didn't have a single full squad. First Squad was missing two guys, Second Squad was missing a guy, and Third Squad was now missing four guys since Ryan and Winston pretty much finalized their decision after that day. They were given Article 15s and would be punished under the Army's Uniform Code of Military Justice (UCMJ).

However, the platoon would get some relief. With the loss of men like Rae, Brown, and DeMeo to ADVON, the battalion had made plans to bring in a set of new soldiers from rear detachment. The platoon would gain a new set of "Cherries" just like they had received right before Santos died.

The new Two Charlie Cherries were dropped off at COP Tynes by the company Headquarters element the next day. Tubbs, St. Pierre, and Luke were all fresh out of basic training and airborne school. They had spent the last month at Fort Bragg on rear detachment, waiting on any word if they were going to get sent to Afghanistan with the rest of the unit or wait for their return. The battalion only had a little over a month left in the country.

Each day at Fort Bragg, the young men would fall into formations, and the rear detachment officer would read them the casualty reports from the battalion. The men were reminded daily of what they were about to walk into if they got sent over as the officer read them the names off the casualty reports. Guys from Bravo Company, Alpha Company, and Charlie Company were constantly stepping on IEDs, so the list was quite extensive. The injury reports were usually amputations, not just scratches. The wounded soldiers that had made their way back to Fort Bragg after being treated at Walter Reed also filled the new guys' heads with the horror that had been going on in the valley. It messed with the Cherries mentally as they awaited the word each day.

They finally got orders from command that they would be shipped to Afghanistan to help the battalion pack Conex boxes and aid in the battalion's withdrawal. This was a relief to the men, as they didn't feel they were ready for anything that was going on in the valley. The only training they received was in Basic, so they could shoot a rifle and that was about it. They hadn't spent months learning to maneuver and fight effectively like the other guys had.

They flew into Afghanistan and spent a week in KAF, awaiting their Conex-packing detail. To their surprise, they were flown to the battalion headquarters outpost in the Arghandab, OCCD. It was on the opposite side of the river from Charlie Company and slightly on the mountain range that overlooked the valley. The Cherries gawked at the vast greenness of the valley from this elevated outpost, and they began to realize they weren't just going to be packing Conex boxes.

Displayed in the battalion's TOC was an American soldier's helmet with a gunshot hole through the center of it. A guy from Alpha Company had just gotten shot in the head by a sniper and the battalion kept his helmet as part of an investigation. The new guys examined the hole and the ripped Kevlar fiber. They began to wonder if they were even ready for what they were about to face.

Two days later, they were dropped off at Terra Nova, then taken to COP Tynes. The Cherries stood at parade rest next to their bags in the gravel clearing of COP Tynes as the other men of Two Charlie swarmed around them. They were all in mismatched uniforms, some wearing PT shorts and tan shirts, some in their ACU uniform but without their top. It was difficult for the new guys to distinguish rank among the men due to the mismatched uniforms and the fact that none of the men addressed the other by rank. They were all a hardened group of guys at this point and looked decades older than the Cherries, who looked like children. Pink Crocs tended to be a common trend among the men of Two Charlie, which the new guys found quite odd.

"Dammit, Tubbs, you're a short fat White guy," McDaniel said to the young new private. "I had a fifty-dollar bet that you were gonna be a fat Black guy. You owe me fifty bucks, Tubbs."

"Roger that," Tubbs responded, unsure of how to address McDaniel.

"You were half right," Nichols said as he walked past the men to McDaniel to collect his money. Nichols didn't look at the Cherries. He could sense the timidness coming from them, and the valley was no place to be timid. He worried and wondered what kind of a chance they stood in the valley.

The men barked at the new soldiers, ordering them to grab all their bags and gear and carry it to the room where they would be living. They yelled at them and hazed them as they ran through the living quarters. They dropped their gear in a cave-like mud room of the old school building and were corralled into the common area to be divvied up into their new squads.

"St. Pierre," Maher called out to the new soldiers. "You're with us in First Squad. Rostran, introduce him to the rest of the squad."

Rostran approached St. Pierre with a smile and led him away from the other Cherries. "Don't get too close to me when we are in a firefight, okay?" he said.

"Why?" St. Pierre asked.

"Because I have the SAW. If you get too close to me, you're gonna go deaf," Rostran smiled.

Luke and Tubbs were assigned to Third Squad under Nichols and Jackson. The two men were brought to meet their new squad leader, Knollinger. Knollinger was working out in the platoon gym, benching between a rickety rack built out of two by fours.

"Hey, Knolly," Jackson said as the Cherries followed him into the gym. "New guys are here."

Knollinger re-racked the bench and sat up to look at them. He had a slight look of disappointment in his eyes. He didn't say a word, just walked over and removed two of the plates from the bar and handed one to each of the Cherries. "Do wall squats and hold this out in front of you."

The two men did as instructed, and Knollinger laid back down on the bench to complete another set of his workout. They struggled to keep the 45-pound plate extended out in front of them. Luke and Tubbs winced as the plate slowly lowered until it finally rested on their thighs. They had conducted physical training back at Fort Bragg before leaving to come to Afghanistan, but that was pretty easy and it showed. They were not physically hardened like the men of Two Charlie, climbing over wall after wall to get into a fight day after day.

Knollinger looked at them with disappointment. "You're probably gonna die," was all he said to them. "Jackson, Nichols, get these guys' gear squared away. We are walking to Terra Nova tomorrow for Loredo's boots and rifle, and battalion is sending us a new squad leader."

It was decided that Loredo's boots and rifle ceremony would be held at Terra Nova instead of COP Tynes. Some men loaded up in the trucks, and the rest walked to attend the ceremony. The Cherries got to witness the hard, battle-torn men they had just met break down and let out all their pain during the event. It was surreal, and made all the stories of what they had heard back at Bragg really sink in and become real. Then, like flipping a switch on, they watched as they turned back into the war-hardened men they were introduced to.

Two Charlie was assigned a new staff sergeant, SSG Gerhart, to join them as Third Squad's new squad leader. Gerhart, like Middlebrook, also came from Alpha Company so he was no stranger to the valley and just how intense the fighting had become on the Charlie Company side. He was freshly promoted; the SSG patch was literally put on his uniform the day he arrived to Charlie Company. Gerhart was kind of a hothead, as he had done multiple deployments in Ranger Battalion. He gathered his bags, loaded them on the trucks, and joined his new squad to dismount back to COP Tynes.

"Look, I'm not trying to change anything up around here. It's pretty obvious that you run the show," Gerhart said to Knollinger as they walked through the village of Jelawur down Route Red Dog to COP Tynes. Gerhart examined his new men. He watched how they moved as a squad. He could tell by how organically they moved with one another they had formed a bond, and he knew he shouldn't mess with what they had. It was pretty evident they trusted Knollinger and not himself, as whenever he would ask something of the men they would hesitate, looking to Knollinger for confirmation. The men returned to COP Tynes and got Gerhart established in his new home and readied themselves for another patrol in the valley.

"Bragg, Sergeant Middlebrook," Maher called from the TOC. "PL says that he wants us to go over the plan for the patrol tomorrow. We are trying to go to Babur. Show Middlebrook what we have been dealing with."

Bragg and Middlebrook made their way into the TOC. "So, what's the plan?" Middlebrook asked his new team leaders.

"Well, we are going to push into Babur," Lt. Farrington said as he pointed out the village on the map to Middlebrook.

"Okay. That's not that far of a movement," Middlebrook said, looking at the village on the map just over two kilometers away from the outpost.

"No, it's not. Problem is we get ambushed every time. We never make it there," Maher said. "The fighters in the area don't want us anywhere near that place."

"Sounds like a movement to contact to me," Middlebrook said. He could sense the uneasiness in his two team leaders. They had basically been doing movement-to-contact patrols every day for the past couple months. Each time it was like a roll of the dice on whether someone was going to get hurt or be killed. They needed to be precise on their planning—every step counted.

"What if we go way north?" Bragg suggested.

"What do you mean?" Lt. Farrington asked.

"We can leave early, well before the sun is up. We shoot way north, through the desert, and drop down into the buildings of upper Babur," Bragg said as he dragged his finger across the map, demonstrating his suggested route.

Maher nodded. "If we get there before sunrise, that might work."

"Have you guys taken that route before?" Middlebrook asked.

"Not without the trucks," Bragg replied. "It'll be pretty open up there until we get into the village, but we will have the cover of darkness on our side."

"That sounds good to me. I think once we make it into the village we will be fine. What is our exfil plan?" Lt. Farrington asked.

"Well, if we don't get shot at, Route Red Dog?" Bragg suggested. Maher shrugged in agreement. It sounded just as good as any other exfil route, and it wasn't near the canal.

"Alright. Brief the guys and get them ready. We leave early tomorrow morning," Middlebrook said.

The men of First Squad headed out as planned, early that morning well before the sun rose in the valley. They didn't see its warm glow until they were just reaching the first khalats of upper Babur, and the people were emerging from their houses to start their day.

They pushed south through the village, making their way through the maze of mud buildings. The villagers that noticed their presence panicked, immediately returning to their homes if they were close or running the other way down the alleys if they weren't. By the time the sun crested the horizon, it was very evident the Americans were occupying the town.

"We need to find and talk to the village elder," Lt. Farrington said. They chased down the locals and asked for the elder's whereabouts. None were cooperative, either stating they didn't know or not saying anything at all.

"I got him right here!" Maher said from around the corner of an alley. He had cornered the old man and wasn't letting him escape.

Farrington and Middlebrook both approached the old man with the interpreter. "What's going on? Why is everyone afraid?" they had the interpreter ask.

The old man didn't look at them. Just behind them, over their shoulders. He turned to look behind himself, over his shoulders. He was terrified of who might be watching the conversation at hand.

Maher pinned the man against the wall. "Answer him!"

The old man finally came to words, his hand pointed south towards the orchards as he spoke. The fear in his eyes echoed in his voice, and Maher removed him from the wall.

"What did he say?" Middlebrook asked.

"He said that the Taliban are down there. They have a bomb on every path and every bridge. They have their ambushes ready. He said you can go down there and fight them, or not. He doesn't care, he just wants you to get out of his village," The interpreter relayed, the same look of fear now overtaking his face.

The men were caught off guard. It was the first time a villager was honest with them. Usually, they laughed, lied, and would say they didn't know anything, only for the Two Charlie men to get ambushed as they left the area. This time something was different. This time the poor local man was afraid.

Bragg looked at Middlebrook. "We, uh, we aren't going down there, right?"

Middlebrook looked at Farrington and the two men came to a nonverbal agreement. "Fuck no, you heard them. They are waiting for us. Doesn't sound like we have the tactical advantage to me. Sir, are you satisfied here? Can we RTB to COP Tynes?"

Lt. Farrington nodded. "Yeah. We aren't going to be able to talk to anyone here anyways. Take us back, Bragg."

Bragg pushed further south into the village until they arrived on Route Red Dog, where he followed it until they met the large clearing between Babur and Druia. It was about a two-hundred-meter flat clearing with a small grape field in the middle to break up the openness. As soon as Bragg broke the cover of the village and stepped into the open, the interpreter's radio began to chatter.

"Bragg! Get back!" Middlebrook shouted. "They see us and are getting ready to shoot!"

Bragg sprinted back to the waist-high wall along the road to rejoin Nguyen and Young. Maher and his team along with the gun team were along the same wall about fifty meters behind them. Middlebrook, Farrington, Lachance, and the interpreter were between them. Rostran readied his SAW. Vasquez noticed two small children playing in the road next to them. "They wouldn't shoot at us with the kids around," he thought to himself, putting himself at ease as he watched them play. He began messing with St. Pierre. "Man, I hope you called your mom last night."

The men waited behind the wall, scanning the trees of the orchards to their south. It was quiet. Too quiet.

"Lachance, do we have Kiowas on station?" Farrington asked.

"Roger. Longknife is on the net. I have them in a holding pattern out of earshot," Lachance replied. "I can bring them in if you want."

"No, have them hold off. But be ready," Maher interrupted.

The Kiowas would not engage the enemy unless they were actively engaging troops on the ground. The men of Two Charlie had literally received radio transmission from them in the past calling out enemy ambushes waiting for them. Men hiding behind walls with PKM machine guns and RPGs wasn't enough for them to engage, so the men of Two Charlie needed to get them to shoot at them before receiving any help from the helicopters.

"Hey Bragg," Maher said with an all-too-friendly tone over the radio.

"What?" Bragg replied, wondering what he was about to pitch.

"You see that grape field in the clearing?" Maher continued.

"Yeah," Bragg replied.

"You think you can make it there if they start shooting at you?" Maher asked.

"You want to use Alpha team as bait?" Bragg asked. He examined the clearing. There was no low ground they could use to conceal themselves, and no cover. Just flat, open land until the grapes, then more flat, open land until the mud walls around the khalats of Druia. The only advantage was the tree line along the canal, the one where they most likely would receive fire from, about a hundred meters away, so it wouldn't be a close ambush.

"Draw their fire, you'll have my team with the gun team to cover you along with the Kiowas once they open up. We just need to get them to shoot at us first," Maher said.

Bragg stared into the darkness of the shadows of the tree line to the south of him. He could feel the enemy staring back, waiting for them, but he couldn't see them. He stood up and looked at Nguyen and Young. "You see that grape field?" he asked, pointing to the clearing. The two men nodded. "As soon as they start shooting, we are going to book it there. Understood?" The two men nodded again, ready to follow Bragg into the upcoming fight.

They walked out, exiting the cover of the village and entered the opening. Even with all their gear—their armor, their helmets, the support by fire, and the Kiowas ready to rock a ways away—the men of Alpha team couldn't feel more naked.

Ratatatatatat! Pop! Pop! Pop! Ratatatatat!

The enemy started unloading on the men, as expected. The rounds whizzed and snapped by the men in the opening. Bragg turned towards Young and Nguyen to yell at them to run but the two of them were way ahead of him. The three men "Scooby Dooed" their way across the clearing, hectically shooting at the trees to the south as they begged their legs to carry them faster.

Rostran opened up with his SAW along with the gun team, and St. Pierre started firing next to him. Vasquez fired off a few 203s and then noticed the children playing in the road were screaming in terror. He ran over to grab them both and threw them down behind the wall next to him. The enemy shifted fire towards the support-by-fire team, and rounds whipped past the men along the wall. Dirt kicked up all around them as bullets smacked the wall in front of and behind them.

"Get a smoke on 'em! Mark them!" Lachance said. He was on the radio calling the Kiowas, giving them directions on how to approach their upcoming gun-run strike.

Vasquez grabbed one of his purple 203 smoke grenades and sent it flying towards the enemy. The round hit and purple smoke started to plume directly between two of the enemy fighters. "Damn. That was a good shot," Lachance said, impressed, then continued to talk on the radio. "Target is marked with purple smoke. Take a west-to-east approach and light them up."

The Kiowas came in and flew overhead, immediately shutting up the enemy fire. The Two Charlie men drew down their fire as well.

Bragg let out a sigh of relief. "Alpha team is up. Now what?" he asked over the radio as they pulled security from the cover of the grapes.

"Hold tight there, Two One Alpha, we are picking up to join you." Middlebrook replied. The rest of the men picked it up and began to push north back up into the village before pushing west to join Alpha team in the grapes.

"St. Pierre, make sure you pull rear security," Vasquez said.

"What?!" St. Pierre yelled.

"Rear security!" Vasquez repeated himself pointing two fingers to his eyes then pointing them toward the rear of the movement.

"He can't hear you," Rostran said with a smile. "He is deaf."

The men set in their overwatch in the grapes, and just as Alpha team was going to pick it up and push to Druia, more chatter came over the interpreter's radio.

"They say they are bringing in their sniper team!" the interpreter yelled. Every man got down behind the short mud walls of the grapes when they heard that. They hadn't encountered a sniper team yet, at least not one they knew of.

"Are the Kiowas still on station?" Middlebrook asked.

"Yep, I have them out of earshot, they're ready to reengage if needed," Lachance responded, holding the radio hand mic to his ear waiting to call them back in.

Middlebrook looked at Bragg with a smile. "Want to try your luck again?"

He knew he didn't really have much of a choice. "Alpha team, let's go."

The men moved into the clearing once more, this time a little more pep in their step. They didn't really know how to avoid getting sniped, so they just tried things like randomly changing their pace, jogging for a little before walking then back to jogging. Unpredictability was their ally here. They were about fifty feet from the first mud wall of Druia when a single shot rang out.

Crack! … Zeeew!

The bullet had to have passed right between Bragg's legs—he felt it. It stopped him dead in his tracks. It took his breath away, but it missed him.

Crack!

Another round rang out and zipped right between Lachance and Farrington in the grapes, exploding the dirt between them. Lachance took a knee and raised the mic to his face. "Troops in contact! Engage the previous marked target location. I'm also marking targets with my tracer fire." He said as he fired his rifle at the enemy in the tree line.

The men reengaged with a volley of gunfire as the Kiowas flew in over them, releasing a volley of rockets and .50-caliber machine gun bursts into the trees. The explosions rang through the valley and silenced the gunfire. That was the last time the enemy fired at the men that day as they made their way back to Tynes.

The next day Intelligence, Surveillance, and Reconnaissance got word through ICOM radio chatter that the men had taken out a few fighters along with a Taliban commander in the valley that day. Drones picked up footage of a large motorcycle gathering outside of the Shuyens where the fighters were having a funeral for their fallen commander and the other men that died that day.

"Let's fucking go!" Rush said, wanting to set up an ambush and smoke the rest of them as they left the funeral.

"We can't," Cartwright said.

"Why the fuck not?!" Rush countered. "We got them all in one spot. Let's drop a bomb on 'em. Let me and Moon pick them off. Do something."

"It's a funeral," Cartwright continued. "We can't go shooting up a funeral."

"Why not? They shot at us after ours!" Rush countered, but deep down knew nothing was going to happen. The men of Two Charlie just had to be satisfied with the fact they had "unalived" a top dog that day; they had to be content with the realization they couldn't do anything to take out the rest of the pack.

CHAPTER 17

# The Cavalry Has Arrived

July began and the men of Two Charlie were coming to the end of their time in the valley. They received word they were going to get their replacements in the next day or two, and they could begin the process of leaving the valley, their Left Seat Right Seats. The light at the end of the tunnel was dim, but in view.

"Who's taking over for us?" Lt. Farrington asked SFC Cartwright in the TOC.

"101st," Cartwright replied.

"Screaming Eagles," Farrington replied.

"They'll be here tomorrow," Cartwright explained. "We need to set up a tent for them to stay. We still got that green one in the storage hut?"

"Probably," Farrington said.

"Get some of the guys to start setting that thing up," Cartwright ordered.

The next day, the 101st leadership arrived at COP Tynes. It was only about eight men, but it was enough for the Two Charlie guys to gather their first impression. They watched as eight larger bald men plopped out of their vehicles. The 101st guys were strong for sure, some even made Lachance and Knollinger look small, but definitely didn't look like they could keep up in the valley. To fight here, you needed to be mobile.

The 101st guys were escorted to the TOC where they got their first glimpse of their new home and were introduced to Lt. Farrington and SFC Cartwright. "Welcome to COP Tynes." Cartwright said to the men, holding out his hand to shake the 101st's first sergeant's.

"First Sergeant Banister, I'm the battery's first sergeant," he spoke as he met Cartwright's hand for a shake.

"Battery?" Farrington asked.

"Bravo Battery. 1st of the 320th Field Artillery Regiment," he replied.

A look of horror sunk in across the faces of the Two Charlie men. When they heard they were being replaced by the 101st, they assumed they were going to be replaced by an infantry unit, not field artillery. These men were trained to load large cannons and fire them from miles away in support of the infantry, not be them. Their larger appearance was starting to make more sense.

"Is there a problem?" First Sergeant Banister asked. He could see the look of shock on the men's faces.

"We … Just … Uh," Farrington tried to gather his words. The new unit already had the disadvantage of arriving during the height of the fighting season, but it felt like a double whammy that they weren't even an infantry unit. "These guys are so fucked," he thought to himself.

"I assure you, we went through your infantry JRTC before we deployed. We are more than capable of conducting infantry operations," the 101st captain said to the men, but his words landed on deaf ears.

"You said your battery is coming?" Cartwright asked. An artillery battery is about the equivalent in size to an infantry company.

"Correct," First Sergeant Banister replied.

"Well, what you might lack in fighting skills you will make up for in numbers, that's for sure. The way that this fight needs to be conducted is by taking ground and holding it, saturating the area, and preventing them from placing their bombs everywhere. We haven't been able to do that with our numbers dwindling less than a platoon. We can show you around the area, patrol with you, but the advice we are going to give you is saturation. Not sure where you all are going to stay though, we only have enough rooms for a platoon-size element. You'll have to expand on what we have here," Lt. Farrington said.

"We can talk more about that later, let's show you around," Cartwright said, directing the men out of the TOC to begin their tour of the outpost.

Once the 101st men were out of earshot, Maher looked at Knollinger. "These guys are so fucking dead," he said.

Knollinger kind of chuckled. "Yeah." The two couldn't believe the Army had sent a non-infantry unit to one of the deadliest regions in the entire country.

The 101st men might have been doomed with their new AO they were inheriting, but they were fortunate to be inheriting COP Tynes. The men of Two Charlie had turned that place into a home. They went from pissing in piss tubes and sleeping in the mud rooms or under a parachute at night to each man having his own room, a functioning pump to take showers, electricity, a gym, actual fighting-position towers, porta johns, and they even had gotten air conditioning and internet within the past couple weeks. Living at Tynes was good, leaving the wire was not.

The next day the 101st shuttled more of their men to COP Tynes. They unloaded their bags and gear into the green tent and began to get ready for the day.

The men of Two Charlie decided to take them out on a patrol and show them the immediate area in the town of Druia, and to see how they maneuvered and conducted themselves on their first Left Seat Right Seat. The 101st guys got their gear and linked up along the inner Hesco wall for a pre-patrol brief and inspection, something the Two Charlie men had done day in and day out.

"What the fuck?!" Jackson said as he checked the 101st guys' SAW gunner. He had a single two-hundred-round drum of ammo in a Molle pouch attached to the center of his plate carrier, and another hundred rounds loaded in his SAW. He had no Camelbak or water of any kind.

"What's wrong?" the soldier asked.

"You're going to need at least three times that much ammo, and all the water," Jackson said, shaking his head at him. He had the soldier look at Nichols and his SAW rig set up. Nichols let the man look at his gear but said nothing to him. He didn't want to know another dead man.

"That's a lot of weight," the soldier said, questioning if Nichols would even be able to move around with all that on. "Is carrying all that ammo really necessary?"

Nichols and Jackson just looked at each other. They had the same look of "these guys are so dead" on their faces.

The men did their patrol brief and went out into the surrounding village of Druia. It was easy to distinguish the 101st men from the Two Charlie ones just from the way they moved. The Two Charlie men would take a knee and pull security on instinct when taking a short halt, the 101st men would just stand there. Even the Two Charlie Cherries conducted themselves better tactically on patrol than the 101st leadership did.

"What are you doing?" Jackson barked at one of them who was just standing beside him while he was pulling security.

"What do you want me to do?" the soldier replied.

"Get the fuck down and pull security," Jackson replied.

The patrol went on like that and the Two Charlie men led them to a place where they could look out at the maze of grape fields and orchards. It was the same place they had gotten their first glimpse of the valley when they first showed up. The look across the 101st men was one of serenity. They had no concept of the severity of what they were walking into. They were treating the whole thing like it was just some training exercise they were on back at Fort Campbell, and they were way too cocky. The men continued back to Tynes and retired for the evening.

The Two Charlie men spent the remainder of that night telling the 101st stories of their experiences, and the dos and don'ts of the valley. They described how to avoid bombs and how the enemy fighters would try to bait them into them. They spoke of the murder holes. Then they spoke of the men they had lost to all the

IEDs in the valley, and the hard reality of it not mattering how many bombs they dodged, eventually there would be one they didn't. They told them the hard truth and rule of the valley—in the end, the valley always wins.

"I don't think they actually get the severity of the situation at hand," Knollinger said to the Two Charlie leadership in the TOC. "We need to show them what a fight in the valley is like."

"Agreed," Lt. Farrington said. "Where do you want to take them?"

"Easy, we go to Babur," Knollinger explained. "That or we take them to the second canal. Same shit we have been doing every day."

"Do you think they are ready for that?" Farrington asked.

"Doesn't matter. They are going to have to be," Maher said. The men all knew the reality of the situation. The Two Charlie men would do their best to get them ready for the valley, to show them what they could, but in less than a week's time the men of Two Charlie would be gone. COP Tynes would be the 101st's, and the grapes and pomegranate fields that went along with it. It sucked, handing them over something they weren't ready for, destining them to a fate of getting fucked up. But the only thing they could do was try to best prepare them for it. The only thing they could do was show them what the valley really was. Show them the Devil's Playground.

"Let's go to Babur," Gerhart said.

"Alright, Third Squad is going to take them to Babur. What are we going to do about QRF? We know that we are going to get into a fight," Farrington spoke.

"First Squad will QRF in the trucks. We can take them right down Route Red Dog. We have never done that in the past. When you come in contact, we will be on our way with the heavy guns of the trucks to support you." Maher said.

"So, we take the 101st leadership, who else?" Gerhart said.

"Take their medic, give Doc Taylor a break. He can be on the load plan for the QRF," Cartwright said.

"What about the scouts?" Farnsworth asked. He didn't want his guys to go and risk getting hurt or killed, not this close to the end, but he knew how important it was to have a sniper with the men.

"Your call, we don't need you but would love to have you," Cartwright said.

"I'll go. I'll let Rush and Moon know that they can stay," Farnsworth replied.

"Let's have Flannery come too, he can take Alpha Team, that way Jackson doesn't have to be both team leader and SAW gunner," Knollinger said.

"How many guys will we have going?" Farrington asked.

"Third Squad, at least a squad from them with their leadership, their medic, Farnsworth, Chancy, we can get Bowman to be RTO," Knollinger said as he counted a finger for each element. "A lot. It will be one of the biggest-size elements we have patrolled with for a long time now. Probably since the clearing operations."

"A lot of moving parts. Could be a good thing though. Might deter them from a fight, having that many guys in the area," Lachance suggested.

"I doubt it, but I guess we will see," Farrington said.

"Alright, looks like we are going to Babur," Gerhart exclaimed.

Farnsworth walked out of the TOC to inform Rush and Moon they weren't going out while the rest of the men plotted the route. He emerged out of the darkness of the night and approached the mud room the two were staying in. Rush was just outside, smoking a cigarette in the dark.

"Hey, tomorrow I'm going out, but you and Moon are staying," Farnsworth explained.

Rush took a drag from his cigarette, "You're going out?" he asked, exhaling a cloud of smoke in the night sky.

"Yeah, they don't need all three of us." Farnsworth replied.

"Fuck you, if you're going out, then I'm going out," Rush said. He put his cigarette out and walked into the room where Moon was watching a movie on his laptop. Moon paused the movie and looked up at him. "You're staying back tomorrow, me and Farns are going to go out," he said.

"I'm fucking going if you guys are going," Moon replied.

Rush looked at Moon sitting on his cot. He wanted to tell him no, but he didn't want to cause any guilt for his soldier if anything happened to him or Farnsworth while Moon wasn't there. He felt like Moon's big brother, that he needed to protect him. But as young as Moon was, they were all men in the valley. "Alright," Rush said.

"I'll let the guys know we are all going," Farnsworth said and disappeared back into the darkness.

"Hey, Mom," Moon said as he sat down in the dark with the satellite phone.

"Chris! It's so good to hear your voice. How are you?" His mother replied.

Moon thought about telling her about everything going on. He thought about telling her about Loredo, about the intensity of the fighting they had been experiencing every day. He wanted to, but he knew better than to worry his mother. "I'm okay, Mom. How is everyone back home."

Moon's mother carried on talking about her trip to the grocery store, and the neighbor's son graduating high school. She could tell that something was off about her son. He seemed more distant and less lively than his usual self. "Is everything alright, Chris? Are you still with your Charlie Company boys?"

"Yeah. I'm still with the Two Charlie guys," he said, still unsure if he should speak his thoughts.

"I pray for them every day, son, just like you asked," his mother replied.

Moon held his head in his hand. "Thanks, Mom," was all he was able to get out without choking on his words.

"Well, is there anything else I can send you? What do you need?" she continued, trying to cheer up her son. It was hard because Moon seemed so distant on this call.

"Mom," Moon said, then stopped himself.

"Yes, son." she replied.

"Will you pray for me?" he asked.

"Of course, dear! I always do," she replied.

"Thanks, Mom." Moon replied. He looked at the time and noticed that his 30 minutes were almost up. "Hey, Mom, I gotta go. I love you."

"I love you too, son. Be safe." She replied.

## CHAPTER 18

# 06 Jul 2010

The men prepared to step out on the patrol to Babur the next day. Knollinger approached the leadership of the 101st men to fill them in on what was going to happen. "Give me your best guys for this one," he said to First Sergeant Banister, then went on to prepare his own men.

The day pushed on, and the men ate their lunch, waiting to step off into the fray once more. They gathered around the internal Hesco wall for the patrol brief like they had done time and time again. The 101st guys joined them, putting their gear down among Two Charlie's.

Knollinger inspected the 101st men and went up to First Sergeant Banister. "I said give me your best guys," he said so the rest of the men couldn't hear.

"These are my best men," First Sergeant Banister responded.

Knollinger sighed and walked back to the front of the group of men. "Alright. Today's patrol we are going to go to the village of Babur." He looked around at the men listening to him. There was a night and day difference between the Two Charlie men's response and the 101st's. The Two Charlie guys all had the same look on their faces, as they knew what they were walking into. The 101st's was that of excitement, eagerness, and almost joy. They had no idea what they were walking into and figured Knollinger was just trying to scare them. "We aren't going to make it there," Knollinger continued to explain the plan he had come up with the night before. "We receive contact every time we push that direction, so expect nothing different today. There are way too many dudes on this movement, so we are going to break up the element. On the east side of Druia, there is a clearing right after some ruins. The formation will split there into two different elements and provide a bounding overwatch. Gerhart will take Alpha Team down into the orchards along the canal and set up a support-by-fire position with the gun team. Once they are set, Bravo Team and myself will push into the open and try to draw some of the enemy's fire. Hopefully Gerhart's element will already be in a good position to engage that enemy from the flank."

"Where do you want us?" First Sergeant Banister asked.

"Split up your men among the two elements. Stay with whatever one you leave with," Gerhart replied. The first sergeant nodded.

They went on, going over the common things that are addressed in a pre-patrol briefing. "Alright, any other questions?" Knollinger asked.

The Two Charlie men stood silent, all awaiting the word to don their armor and head out on patrol. The 101st guys just stood there, not knowing what to say. "Alright, let's get it on," Knollinger said, and the men executed.

Moon picked up his rifle and saw Winston sitting in the corner of the outpost watching them. He walked over to talk to his friend before following the men out the front gate. "Hey, man, I'll see ya when I get back."

Winston looked at him. "Yeah, I'll see ya."

The patrol pushed out the front gate of COP Tynes and conducted their radio checks. "I got you Lima Charlie," Farrington replied to each check as he monitored the radio in the TOC with the remaining 101st leadership and Cartwright. They moved through the southern outskirts of the village of Druia until they reached the ruins on the eastern end.

They entered the crumbling remains of one of the buildings and conducted a short halt for the rest of the patrol to catch up. "See anything, Flan?" Knollinger asked as he stepped over one of the decayed walls.

"Nothing yet," Flannery said as he peaked his head over the wall.

The interpreter listened to the ICOM radio as it began to chatter. "They see you," he replied as Flannery ducked his head back behind the wall.

The men all took cover among the old debris and waited for Knollinger's team to get set in so Gerhart could move up with Flannery and his team.

Farnsworth turned to Rush, "What do you want to do? I think I'm going to go with Knollinger," enquiring whether Rush wanted to go left and provide overwatch with Knollinger then move into the open field or move up right with Gerhart's element and be the support by fire.

Rush thought for a moment. He figured Moon and himself should probably go with the gun team to help engage the enemy once Knollinger's team moved into the open. They were better suited there than running through gun fire in the open. They had done enough of that in the past. That wasn't where they belonged.

"Well, we should probably go with the 240s, so we'll go right," he replied to Farnsworth. Farnsworth nodded and took his place among Knollinger's guys.

The men moved up and along the canal until they came to a footbridge. They took a knee and conducted a short halt as Gerhart cleared the bridge of any bombs. Once cleared, the men pushed up along the path. Each man had a very uneasy feeling as they walked down the dirt path along the canal, they could feel it in their bones that something wasn't right. Each step was getting harder and harder to take as the eeriness crept in.

Rush turned toward Moon to check their spacing. He was too close, within ten meters of where Moon was standing. The whole movement was too close with the 101st guys gunking it up. He paused for a moment to give him some space and then continued when Moon was about ten meters in front of him. Moon turned to look at him over his left shoulder, cradling his rifle high against his chest like he always did. His focus turned north, trying to spot the other element when the bomb went off.

BOOM!

Rush watched as earth came up all around Moon, engulfing him out of view. The concussion of the blast rang out through the men, shaking the ground they stood on, and it threw anyone that was too close through the air. Rush was thrown against the mud wall that lined the path. The blast peppered him with small debris as the cloud consumed him. Nichols felt the blast against his back and he fell to the ground, Tubbs somersaulted behind him.

"IED, IED, IED," Knollinger called over the radio as he watched the dust shoot through the tops of the trees along the canal from his position. He began to sprint towards the cloud, the rest of his team behind him.

Flannery took a knee and called out to his men. "Nichols! Nichols! Are you okay!"

Nichols did not reply. He didn't hear Flannery's initial calls. His bell was rung, and he was just starting to come back to the reality of everything happening around him.

"Nichols!" Flannery continued to call.

"I'm good! I'm good!" Nichols finally replied. "Get the fucking medic, it's Tubbs!"

The dust around the men began to settle, and from it Tubbs emerged. He made his way to Nichols along the wall and sat down beside him. He was alright, a little concussed, but had all his fingers and toes.

"I'm good," Tubbs exclaimed.

That's when the scream bellowed from the remaining dust cloud. "AAAAAAAAAAAH!" The men could feel the pain in the call.

"Flan, is your team up?" Knollinger called over the radio.

"Roger, we're up," Flannery replied.

"Viper Four, are you up?" Knollinger called out. There was no reply. "Viper Four, are you okay?!"

"No … I'm not okay!" Rush finally called back over the radio. "Medic! Medic! Medic!" The dust still fogged the air, and he couldn't see Moon, so he started to crawl towards the sound of Moon's screams.

"AAAAAAAAAAAH!" Moon wailed as Rush finally got to him. Rush could see the aftermath of what the blast had done to his friend as Moon lay in the deep crater. Moon's left leg from the knee down was stripped to the bone until about the ankle where it was broken off. The bone was pure white, like ivory, as it protruded from the bright red flesh of his leg. His right leg was gone just above the knee, ending in a hunk of muscle and flesh. His hip was peppered with shrapnel wounds. Rush grabbed Moon's arm, which was the closest thing to him. It was missing a thumb and was filleted open. Rush began to apply a tourniquet to Moon's arm when he felt Gerhart, Farnsworth, Flannery, and Knollinger join him at his side.

The men grabbed Moon from the crater and began putting tourniquets on what was left of his legs. "AAAAAH! It hurts so bad!" Moon yelled as the tourniquets were wrenched down.

"You're going to be okay, buddy," Gerhart reassured him, trying to hide the trembling in his voice.

Bowman arrived on scene with the radio. Knollinger tightened his tourniquet a little more then turned to Bowman. "Call up the Nine Line!" he said.

Bowman stared in horror at what was left of his friend. His eyes didn't leave the carnage. Knollinger grabbed the hand mic from off his rig and began the first few lines of the Nine Line MedEvac. He handed the mic back to Bowman, and Bowman continued to relay the information of the Nine Line across the radio.

The boom shook the plywood walls of the TOC back at COP Tynes. Bragg and Farrington turned towards each other. Their jaws dropped in horror as doom crept across their faces. "Go!" Farrington said to Bragg, instructing him to get the other guys to load the trucks for the QRF, but Bragg was already well on his way out of the TOC, and the other men were already running to the vehicles.

Farrington turned towards Cartwright in the TOC who was listening to the Nine Line. The men didn't know if it was a Two Charlie guy who was injured, or if it was one of the 101st guys. "I'm going on the QRF," Farrington explained as he went to grab his gear.

"No, you aren't," Cartwright replied.

"I'm going!" Farrington protested.

"No, I'm going. You need to stay here," Cartwright said as the battle roster number of the wounded man came over the radio. It was Moon.

Cartwright grabbed his things and left the TOC to join the guys gearing up and starting the vehicles. "Let's go. It's Moon. It's Moon," he called out as he made his way through the wood structure.

Rosa heard his calls. The fact it was one of the Two Charlie guys filled him with anger. "Not again," he thought to himself as he threw his gear on and sprinted to the lead truck. He had just gotten stitches in his finger that day and was not supposed to go out on patrol for two days, but that didn't matter. He climbed up into the turret and readied the 240.

Bragg climbed into the truck commander's seat of the lead vehicle and put on his helmet. He looked over to his driver to see if they were ready to roll. To his surprise, Winston was geared up behind the wheel. Winston had heard the calls, he knew Moon was hurt, and it was enough for him that he couldn't just sit there and do nothing. Bragg looked at Winston for a moment, deciding on what to do. There was no time to waste, so he just got his attention and yelled over the roar of the vehicle engine, "You good?!"

Winston nodded. "I'm good."

"Rosa, you good?!" Bragg yelled up to him.

"Yup!" Rosa replied, rewrapping his finger in the turret.

Bragg threw on his headset. "Alright, let's fucking go!"

"Get him on a litter!" Knollinger barked at the 101st medic. The man fumbled through his assault pack and pulled out a poleless litter. Knollinger snatched it from the man and began to unravel it. The men lifted Moon onto the litter, each grabbing a corner, and began to move him back to the north side of the canal towards the ruins. They sprinted back over the small footbridge; with all the jarring of the litter, Moon's bone would get caught on Rush's pant leg. He winced each time, but there was nothing the men could do. They needed to get him out of there, they needed to get him off the X.

They stopped short in the field, exhausted from all the energy they had just exerted. Moon was so heavy despite missing almost half of his body. They took cover in a ditch and Gerhart rechecked the tightness of the tourniquets.

The 101st medic began to render aid. He pulled out an IV bag and began to try and establish an IV. He couldn't figure out what he was doing wrong, as the IV would not take.

"What's wrong?" Farnsworth yelled at him.

"It's not working," the medic explained.

Farnsworth looked at the IV. It was being administered to an arm with a tourniquet applied to it. "There's your fucking problem!" Farnsworth yelled as he pointed out the mistake to the fool. The Two Charlie men grabbed the equipment from the medic, pushed him out of the way, and began administering aid themselves.

Farnsworth took his hands and examined his pelvis. It was clearly broken, and when he moved it Moon yelled out in pain. Farnsworth had never heard a man scream that loud.

"Where is the MedEvac Bird?!" Moon called out. The MedEvac was delayed out of KAF and had not yet left.

"You're going to be okay," Gerhart tried to reassure him. That was all they could do at this point. They had stopped the bleeding, and the 101st medic was useless and didn't even have morphine to give him.

"I'm gonna fucking die!" Moon said, now realizing the extent of the damage that had been dealt to his body. "I don't have any legs."

The trucks rolled up along Route Red Dog and turned into the open field. They encircled the men, giving them some cover from the surrounding area. Doc Taylor hopped out of his truck and ran over to the men providing aid to Moon.

"I did everything I could. I did everything I could," the 101st medic said over and over again as Doc ran by. Doc didn't care to listen to him, he needed to get to Moon.

"Water," Moon said faintly. "Water, please."

Gerhart stepped away and said quietly to Knollinger, "He's going to fucking die man," his voice quivering.

The sound of rotary wings started to be audible in the distance. Hope filled the men as they reassured Moon. "Stay with us, Moon. The Birds are coming. Can you hear them? The Birds are coming," they all said.

"They want the medic to ride with him," Bowman relayed the info from the radio.

"No. I want Sergeant Rush to go," Moon replied.

Rush looked at Knollinger. "I'm getting on that fucking Bird with him. I don't give a fuck what anybody says."

"Sergeant Rush," Moon said faintly, calling for Rush. "Tell my mom, I love her."

"You're going to tell her yourself, man. Come on! Stay with us," Farnsworth urged him.

The MedEvac Bird roared as it landed in the field next to the trucks, kicking up dust everywhere. The heavy weapons systems on the trucks began to fire into the surrounding area, deterring any fighters that might have been waiting for their chance to shoot down the helicopter.

"Sergeant Rush," Moon said as he turned his head toward Rush. "I love you."

The men carried Moon to the Bird and loaded the two men in. It lifted off, kicking up more dust into the orange sky of the evening sun. The men of Two Charlie watched as it got smaller and smaller on the horizon.

"Charlie Two Six Romeo, Charlie Six wants to know if you have his rifle, over," the voice came over the radio headset. Bowman didn't have to relay it to the rest of the men, they heard it as well. The commander was referring to Moon's M110 sniper rifle, and the men had no idea where it could be. It was lost in the blast.

"Negative, Charlie Six, we do not have the location of his rifle," Bowman replied over the hand mic.

"Roger, Two Six Romeo. Charlie Six says that you need to locate that rifle before you can RTB. How copy?" The voice responded.

Bowman looked at the other men. Was the commander serious? He wanted them to search the area, an area that probably had more IEDs, to find a rifle? There was no use arguing about it though. They were going to have to do it regardless of whether they wanted to or not. "Roger," Bowman said over the radio.

The men pushed out carefully along the canal, looking for any signs of Moon's rifle. They combed the earth, at least as best they could without exposing themselves to hitting another IED or getting ambushed.

The men found little of his rifle. The buffer spring was laying here, the laser mount there, and the lens cover was hanging from a branch of a tree. What they did find plenty of, however, was pieces of Moon. His kneecap lay along the canal, his heel, and random other chunks of bright-red charred flesh lay all around the surrounding area. It was still warm to the touch as the men picked up the chunks and gathered them in a body bag from one of the trucks to try to keep the ants off.

"Charlie Two Six Romeo, can you give us a SITREP?" the company would continually call over the net, irritating the men on the ground. They couldn't just wait for them to send a SITREP (situation report), they had to call in for one every ten fucking minutes.

"We have his buffer spring, his laser mount, and his scope cover, over," Bowman responded each time, and each time they were met with the same response. Keep looking.

The sun started to go down in the valley, and visibility was getting worse as the light got dimmer and dimmer. Were they expected to look for something they couldn't find during the day at night under night vision? They finally got the call from Command. "Charlie Two Six Romeo, Charlie Six says what you have found is sufficient in rendering the weapon inoperable. You can go ahead and RTB."

"Roger," Bowman replied over the radio. "Two Charlie en route to COP Tynes, time now." The men stepped into the darkness as they began to head back to COP Tynes.

The men returned to COP Tynes and gathered in Loredo's Kitchen. It was the only lighted area in the outpost that could house all the men, including the 101st. They all stood by, patiently waiting for word on whether Moon made it or not. Dinner was ready for them and warm in the mermites, but the men didn't touch it. They didn't have an appetite.

SFC Cartwright and Gerhart walked out of the TOC. They didn't say a word until everyone was there to hear. "Moon's alive," Gerhart said with relief. "He's conscious, and they said he is doing well after his first surgery. They will fly him to Germany in a day or two."

The men felt a little relieved to hear the news, but they had learned the hard way with Loredo not to completely let their guard down. He still wasn't out of the woods, but he wasn't dead.

They couldn't even call it a win. Even though Moon was alive, what kind of life would he have after that? He would never be able to pick up a baseball again, that was for certain. But the valley hadn't won either, not that day.

"It's good to get this experience now, with the people who have been through it still around," one of the 101st soldiers said. "It's good to see you do it before we have to do it by ourselves."

This infuriated the men. They couldn't believe he actually said that. Was he fucking kidding? They all leered in the poor bastard's direction.

Knollinger interrupted the hate-filled silence. "Look, it sucks. It's scary. This is going to happen to y'all. But we can't let that deter us. We have to keep going out. Y'all are going to have to keep pushing. Y'all are going to have to keep fighting. But some of y'all just aren't going to make it."

The Two Charlie men left the 101st with that thought and retired for the night.

CHAPTER 19

# Vengeance in the Valley

It was determined during the BDA that the IED that injured Moon was a radio-controlled IED (RCIED). The trigger man watched from afar as each man walked over the explosive device that day. He waited for one particular man to set off his bomb. He waited for the man with the tan rifle, he waited for Moon.

The men called in a MedEvac Bird that night to pick up the pieces of Moon they collected in the body bag. It was an "at the convenience of the pilot" call so, of course, the pilots didn't get there until midnight. They spent an hour trying to get the pilot to land at COP Tynes, as the Bird hovered over the clearing the men used to park the vehicles in. The dust kicked up engulfed everything in the area, blinding the pilot's view of the HLZ. After several unsuccessful attempts, they decided to land at Terra Nova instead, and the men had to meet them there. So, after a devastating patrol, the men were awoken from their sleep to head to Terra Nova to drop off what was left of their friend. All because a MedEvac pilot couldn't land on an HLZ. The cherry on top was that they had an early wake up to go out again the next morning. That patrol came across another small RCIED that was detonated prematurely; luckily, no one was injured. Just another close call for the men of Two Charlie, and another wakeup call for the 101st.

Farnsworth grew angry about the loss of one of his best sniper teams, Moon and Rush. He decided it was time to bust out his secret weapon, his bolt gun, the M24 sniper rifle. The only problem was he didn't have any data collected for it, so he was unsure of how much he needed to adjust the sights to hit targets at varying ranges.

He took his rifle to Moon's perch on top of Tower One and began scanning the second canal for any possible targets. He figured the second canal was about a good eight hundred meters away, so he would have that data point. The first canal was about two hundred, so there was another data point. Every now and then he would catch glimpses of the fighters sneaking around the fields or along the canal. He would call it up over the radio to get confirmation to shoot; and when that confirmation came, he would send it.

"COP Tynes, this is Longknife Two Four," the Kiowa pilots came over the radio. "We have spotted a guy on the roof of a building in Jelawur with an AK. He might have taken a few shots at us, not quite sure, over."

Farnworth sprinted to the tower with his rifle in one hand, a radio in the other, and his pink Crocs on his feet. One of the 101st guys followed him to watch. "Longknife Two Four, this is Viper Five, I'm scanning for the target. Can you confirm that you are taking fire, over."

"Roger, Viper Five, he took a couple shots at us," the helicopter pilot came back over the radio.

Farnsworth scanned the rooftops of the village through his scope until he was able to identify the man they were speaking about. He wore a black turban and had an AK-47 in his hands. He didn't know if the data he had collected for his rifle was on or not, but he gave it a go anyway. He put the crosshairs over the man and pulled the trigger. The scope bounced with the recoil of the rifle, but when it came back down the man was gone.

"Holy fuck, you just hit that dude!" the 101st soldier said.

Farnsworth doubted the man. "There's no way," he thought to himself.

"Longknife Two Four, this is COP Tynes, we just had our sniper engage the man, can you conduct a flyover again to confirm the target is down?"

"Roger, COP Tynes. Stand by," the pilot replied. Farnsworth continued to scan and listen to his radio. He didn't think he hit the man and wanted to be ready for a follow-up shot if it presented itself. "Roger, COP Tynes. The target is laying on the roof with his head split open. Good kill." Farnsworth smiled.

"Holy shit!" The 101st soldier said in disbelief. "You shot that guy in the head from this far?"

Farnsworth picked up his rifle and radio. "God damn right I did," he said as he climbed down and walked off with a grin.

Moon's condition continued to be stable, and they began the process of getting him prepared to move to Germany. The fact he was stable enough to move relieved a little of the worry from the men of Two Charlie, but they still had plenty to worry about. They still had to finish readying their replacements for the fight in the valley they were about to inherit.

The leadership of Two Charlie held a meeting in the TOC a day later. They were to discuss going out on one more patrol. They needed to show the 101st the terrain south of the second canal, they needed to walk them into the Devil's Playground.

The Two Charlie men were battle fatigued. They had fought day in and day out in the valley for so long. They had taken so many casualties they were unsure if risking going out on another patrol was worth it. It was so close to them leaving, they didn't know if it would be worth the risk. They gathered in the TOC so the team leaders and squad leaders could voice their opinions and openly share how they felt about conducting one last patrol.

They passed around an empty water bottle as a "speaking stick" so each man could voice their thoughts uninterrupted.

"If we get south of the second canal, which we won't, we probably aren't all going to come back. I just want to throw that out there," Maher said. He passed the bottle to Bragg.

"I don't want my guys going," Bragg said. "I'll go for them," he said and passed the bottle to Knollinger.

"I want revenge," Knollinger said. He was on whatever side would let him put as many rounds into the valley as he could after Moon got injured. "It's not worth another casualty, but I personally want to go."

He handed the bottle to Lachance. "I don't mind going to bang it out, but don't want to see anyone get blown up. That shit sucks," he said. "I don't think that this entire war is worth losing people for like that, but if one of you is going, then I'm going."

The bottle was passed around the room as they discussed the topic further. Did they want to have to explain to another soldier's family why their loved one died, and why it happened so close to coming home? No. Could they live with themselves after the fact, knowing the 101st guys were going to die and they didn't do everything they could to try to prevent that? Also no. The bottle made its way through each man's hands before it finally came to Rosa.

"This is a tough one for me. This is my third deployment with this platoon, and this is the first time we've gone through all this bullshit with casualties. My guys have been going out every day. We lost a lot. But at the same time, we can't lose ground. Especially with the unit coming in. They need a good handoff. They could get slaughtered out there." Rosa paused, then continued. "If I gotta go out, and I'm going out with this group here, that's fine with me." He looked at the water bottle for a moment. "When we cross that second canal, I think there is going to be so much shit set in there, we're going to have a catastrophic IED that's going to take out a bunch of people."

The bottle was put on the table and the men left the TOC. Ultimately, everything the men said didn't matter. The decision to push down south of the second canal was going to be made by someone who wasn't sitting in that room, and that decision was already made. The men would push south of the canal and enter the Devil's Playground one more time.

After the leadership meeting, Knollinger gathered the guys of Third Squad. He wanted to run it by all of them to hear their thoughts and see if they would follow him for one more fight. He stood in front of the guys of Third Squad in their gathering. He took a second to look over each one of his men as they looked at him. He thought for a moment and pictured them as the Joes they once were, before they left Fort Bragg. He thought of their clean uniforms, their innocent smiles, and their young faces. He thought about how he had to show and teach them everything. It made him tear up. Now, the men that stood before him were no longer Joes, these men were men. Their uniforms were tattered and stained with dirt, they had lost their smiles, and their faces had aged years. He no longer had to teach them anything, as they were very knowledgeable of their craft, masters none the least. He didn't know if he could ask this of them. He didn't know if he could ask them to go out one more time. They looked at him in silence, waiting for what he had to say.

"We have to push south of the second canal, right into the Devil's Playground. You know some crazy shit is probably going to happen. There is no way that we are getting out of this one unscathed. If you don't want to go, you don't have to. We can get someone else to replace you for this one. I don't care who's going out, but I'm going with them," Knollinger said to the men.

The men all sat in silence as they truly considered Knollinger's words and the weight of the decision they were about to make. After a moment, the silence was broken.

"I'm in. If you're going, then I'm going." Nichols replied. Knollinger's eyes began to water.

"I'm in." Dru replied.

"If you guys go, I'm gonna go, but I think none of us should go," Jackson said.

"I'm out." McDaniel said with a grin. "Just kidding. You know I'm in if you're in."

The planning began for the final Left Seat Right Seat with the 101st. This would be the last patrol the men would conduct together and the 101st would technically be in the Left Seat, the driver's seat. Farrington and Knollinger made the route plan, after carefully looking at all the overlays of all the routes the platoon had ever documented taking. They ran it by the 101st leadership, ensuring they understood the route and how important it was to stay on it. This time the Two Charlie men would not be there to lead. They would only be present to observe and make sure the 101st men didn't do anything stupid. They were in the Right Seat now, just along for the ride.

The plan was for the patrol to push south of the second canal and take over an abandoned compound to create a warm base to try to occupy the area and conduct patrols from. Twenty-three 101st soldiers would lead out the next day, early in the morning under the cover of darkness, with twelve Two Charlie men. The command was kind enough to grace them with the presence of a Navy dog team for this operation to help alleviate the risk of hitting an IED.

They were to conduct this warm base for thirty-six hours before returning to COP Tynes. It would be the Two Charlie men's last chance to get back at the valley. It would become known to them as The Last Patrol.

CHAPTER 20

# The Last Patrol

The men were delayed in their departure the next morning due to the 101st RTO. He had loaded the incorrect frequencies and fill in all the radios and needed to go through and reprogram them. The Two Charlie guys waited along the inner Hesco wall at COP Tynes for what seemed like forever until they finally stepped off just as the sun was rising in the valley.

The 101st took point and led the men through the grape orchards south of the first canal, the bomb dog Dix in front of them. They climbed over wall after wall, avoiding the urge to take any path they came across as advised by the Two Charlie men. They had to lift Dix over multiple walls the dog could not jump himself, then one by one climbed over themselves. It was a slow-moving patrol, and the Two Charlie men watched and critiqued their successors.

"Your guys need to pull security when we are in a short halt," Jackson barked quietly towards one of the 101st leadership. "They can't just be standing there doing nothing." The 101st guys looked like they were on a walk in the park, not patrolling through a heavily IEDed and Taliban-infested battlefield. They stood there and watched and waited for Dix to clear the southern path along the second canal, then they continued to stand and watch each man cross the canal. It was like they were waiting in line for the slide at their local pool.

The RTO's foot got caught on a tree root in the water, causing him to lose his balance with all the additional weight in his pack. He tumbled and fell under the water, submerging his radio. The Two Charlie men were quick on the scene to get him back on his feet and out of the canal while the rest of the 101st just watched.

"You got to keep that out of the water," Farrington said, pointing to the radio. "Check to make sure it still works."

One of the 101st SAW gunners rolled an ankle climbing out of the water onto the bank of the canal and was sitting on the ground along a mud wall. He was rubbing his ankle and didn't get up as the men ahead of him began to push forward.

"What are you doing?" Knollinger said, annoyed with the poor bastard.

"I rolled my ankle," the soldier replied. "My pack is too heavy."

Knollinger looked at the man with disgust. "Oh, yeah. No problem. I'll call the Greyhound bus and they will come and pick you up," he said, sarcastically reassuring the man. The soldier was initially relieved by the upbeat tone of his voice, but then realized the ridiculousness of Knollinger's statement. "Stand the fuck up and start walking!" Knollinger said to the man as loud and as sternly as he could without giving away their position.

Farrington noticed another man's pack was fairly bulky. He prodded at it to investigate its contents. "What do you got in here?" he asked. The soldier took off his bag and opened it to reveal what was inside. To Farrington's surprise, the man had an ammo can full of 240 ammo. It was still in the metal can with the seal unbroken. Infantrymen always bring spare belts of ammo for the machine gun with them on patrols, but they take the ammo out of the can before they load it in their bags. This gets rid of the extra weight and bulkiness the can may impose and makes the ammo more readily available. He thought that was common sense; apparently not. Farrington dug deeper and found a bandolier of 5.56 ammo, the rounds still on the clips and not loaded into magazines. Farnsworth joined Farrington and continued to pull things out of the pack. The men looked at each other as they pulled cans of Rip Its out of the bottom of the bag. Rip Its were an energy drink the Army sent out to the soldiers for a morale boost and to keep them awake on guard, not to drink while on patrol. "What the fuck?" they thought to themselves. It was too late and not the place to fix it now, they would address it once they had made it behind the walls of the compound.

The patrol pushed further and further south of the second canal, further into the Devil's Playground. The 101st men continued to fall, trip, and suck their way through the orchards. They were not used to carrying all the extra weight with them, especially in the humidity and heat of the valley. The Two Charlie men continued to be on high alert as they made their way to the abandoned compound. They could feel the evil in the air, as it had been some time since they had set foot on ground south of the canal, and it made the hair on the back of their necks stand on end. There was no way they were not being watched at this point.

Tubbs, being as short as he was, had difficulty climbing over one of the higher walls around one of the orchards. Much like the 101st, he was new to the terrain and wasn't quite as fit as necessary to successfully maneuver around the valley, especially with all the extra weight he was carrying for this patrol. He struggled to mantle over the wall, trying as hard as he could to get his rig over the top.

"Tubbs, get over that wall," Gerhart said as he gave him a boost. The boost was a little too much and caused Tubbs's bag to slide over his shoulder and pull him the rest of the way over the wall. Unable to control his descent, Tubbs tumbled to the ground on the other side, rolling his ankle. He carried on, pushing through the pain, but it definitely slowed him down. His ankle was pretty shot, and he hoped they would reach the compound soon.

The sun was beginning to crest the horizon in the valley, and the heat and humidity started to creep in as the men approached the outer walls of the abandoned compound. The men had Dix enter first to clear it of any possible bombs, and then the Two Charlie men flowed in after. The courtyard of the compound was lush with six-foot-tall sunflowers among a garden of marijuana plants. There were Quonset hut khalats that lined two of the walls, each with their own door to a room, much like the school structure at COP Tynes. The men cleared all the rooms, and different corners of the compound, and the 101st flowed in after them.

"We need to get security positions established on the roofs of those buildings," Gerhart said. The Two Charlie men helped the 101st climb up on the khalat roofs overlooking the northwest and northeast of the compound. They handed up a 240 to one of the men and they set the gun team in. They placed a couple claymores near the entrances of the compound. The enemy had to see the men move into their positions, as their plan of moving in under the cover of darkness was blown.

"I just saw a guy running to the north with a machine gun!" one of the 101st soldiers said.

"Well, don't tell me about it, shoot him!" Jackson said to the man.

"But he wasn't shooting at me," the soldier responded.

"Okay, but he was maneuvering on your position," Jackson replied. "Was he getting closer or farther away?"

"He was getting closer," the worried soldier replied.

"Okay, I get rules of engagement, but if someone with a gun is actively maneuvering on you, that's the same as shooting at you," Jackson explained.

The soldier paused for a second. "I need to ask my squad leader."

Jackson shook his head. "This is going to be bad," he thought to himself.

The platoon's interpreter began to pick up conversations among the fighters now waking up in the valley. They knew the men were in the area and were trying to pinpoint their exact location. "They know we are in their village," the interpreter said.

The men continued to scan the trees of the orchards from their positions on the roof, waiting for the inevitable attack. It got quiet, as the men waited in the morning sun.

The ICOM radio continued to go off with the enemy's chatter. The interpreter's face grew more and more worried as the conversation went on, until he finally shouted to the Two Charlie men, "They are moving in to attack us. They know where we are." The men on the roofs readied themselves for the barrage they expected to soon follow.

Crack!

A single shot rang out. The soldiers on the roof returned fire with their machine guns. They unloaded into the orchards, but there was no more enemy fire. "Bro, stop!" Knollinger yelled over the machine guns. "They're just harassing us, trying to figure out where we are and what we got. They aren't even really shooting at you yet, and when they do start shooting at you for real you won't have anything left to shoot back with."

The single-shot harassment fire continued, as the enemy maneuvered to the east of the compound. There was a plowed open field and then a wall on the opposite side where they were moving behind and trying to get a better angle on the men. Farnsworth climbed to the roof of the Quonset huts and hid in between the dirt humps. He scanned the area, trying to get the location where the fire was coming from.

Crack!

The round whipped next to his head and impacted the hump of the roof he was hiding behind. It exploded with dirt and peppered his face. He fell back behind the cover and wiped the pieces of dirt from his eyes. It was a close call, had the round been a few inches higher it would have hit him directly in his face.

"God damn, Sergeant. You almost got shot in the face," Luke said in amazement as he got down next to him behind the cover.

"Luke," Farnsworth said, sighing with relief and happy to still be alive, "Shut the fuck up and fire your weapon."

The fire continued, and Lachance called in the Kiowa helicopters to conduct gun runs on the surrounding enemy. "They are trying to draw us out of cover," he said down to the rest of the Two Charlie guys from the roof.

"Yeah, but we can't just sit here and let them probe us like they are," Gerhart said. The compound only had two exits, and if the enemy could zero in on them, they would be stuck and surrounded. Movement is key to infantry tactics, and being stagnant for too long could turn out to be a death trap. "We are letting them set the conditions. We got to do something."

Farrington, Gerhart, Knollinger, and Lachance all gathered with the 101st leadership to formulate a plan as the men pulling security on the roof continued to receive fire. They huddled in one of the rooms and discussed what to do as sporadic gunfire rang out over them.

"Let's hit them with One Alpha." Knollinger said, referring to a common battle drill among infantry men. The plan was simple, to get a squad of guys out in the fields, so that when the enemy engaged the compound, they could maneuver and engage them from the flank. They were going to go out, push straight north through the grapes, and then move to the east to flank the men shooting at them.

"Can we get the dog team out there?" Farrington asked.

The men turned to look at the dog handler who was tending to his panting dog. "Dix is done. He's too hot. When he gets overheated, he becomes less effective at finding shit. I'm afraid we can't be of use to you guys anymore until it cools down out there." It wasn't even noon and the temperatures had already almost reached one hundred degrees.

The men nodded. "So, no dog team. Who all is going out on this?" Farrington asked.

"Take a squad of my guys with you," one of the 101st lieutenants said.

"I'll go with them. Chancy, will you come with me so we have the Birds to cover us if it gets hairy out there?" Gerhart asked.

"Yeah," Lachance said.

"Alright. Sir, you and Knolly stay here with the rest of the guys and set up a QRF if we need it," Gerhart said.

"They already zeroed in on the two doors of the compound, you can hear rounds pinging off the metal doors. You think I could set off a claymore as a distraction? Keep their heads down so you guys can get out?" Knollinger suggested.

"Might be a good idea," Farrington said and Knollinger smiled.

"I need your guys to have their game faces on," Gerhart said, looking at the 101st lieutenant.

The lieutenant nodded. "We won't let you down."

The men left the room to begin prepping for the patrol. Gerhart snagged Knollinger as he was about to leave and pulled him close so that only he could hear. "If something happens, and I don't have any legs, don't let them save me." Knollinger paused, thinking about the possible reality of what Gerhart had just expressed to him. "I'm serious," Gerhart said, letting Knollinger go and went to join the other men to prepare for the movement.

BOOM!

The explosion from the Claymore mine rang out through the valley, and the 101st SAW gunner began shooting his machine gun, covering the other men as they began running out of the compound. They all fired their weapons to suppress any enemy fighters until they got to the closest cover outside the compound walls. Gerhart gave one last nod to Knollinger as he and Lachance followed the men out of the compound.

The ICOM radio exploded with chatter after the Claymore had gone off. "What are they saying?" Farrington asked.

The interpreter listened in for a few more moments. "Eh … Achmed, was that your bomb? … No … Abdule, was that your bomb? … No … Majid? … No." He translated as the calls came over the radio. The fighters in the area were trying to figure out if the Americans had triggered one of their bombs. The thought of how many bombs the enemy had all around them made the men's stomachs sink.

The patrol moved through the thick orchards and pushed north until they had reached a clearing. The men of the 101st started really sucking as the patrol tempo began to slow to a stagger. The humidity under the branches of the pomegranate trees was like a rainforest, and the heat had climbed to well over a hundred degrees even in the shade. They had brought a 240 gun team with them, and the men were not used to carrying all the extra weight required to operate the gun in the intense heat. It was starting to make Gerhart nervous.

"Come on. You guys got to keep up. We gotta push through this clearing and get into the grape furrows on the other side," Gerhart said to the men. He looked at them, unsure if they would be capable of even standing back up, then turned his worried gaze to Lachance. "Dude, I don't know if I've ever been so scared," he said.

Lachance, unbothered by the situation, just shrugged and replied, "Nah, this isn't too bad." He looked up as a Kiowa flew directly over, its pilot saluting the men on the ground. Lachance had the Birds on station. He knew they would keep the enemy at bay for the time being.

The men pushed across the open field and into the grape furrows. The sun, now high in the sky, was beating down on them. The 101st staggered to make it into the cover of the grapes, throwing themselves over the three-foot mud walls.

"We are right on top of them! We can't do anything because of the helicopters," one of the enemy fighters called over the radio.

"Longknife Two One, Charlie Nine Two. Can you guys pull off out of earshot? We are gonna see if we can't get these guys to start shooting at us," Lachance called to the Birds over his radio, signaling to them to move out of the area but be ready to spring their trap like they had done in the past. That's when the first 101st soldier went down.

"Hey, Sergeant! Johnson passed out!" one of the 101st soldiers called from among the grapes. Gerhart ran over to the man. It was the 240 gunner. He was clearly suffering from heat exhaustion, as his eyes had rolled into the back of his head and his skin was cold and clammy.

"Fuck!" Gerhart shouted. He grabbed the man's pack to get him some water. Rip Its spilled out of the bag. "Are you fucking kidding me?" Gerhart exclaimed looking at one of the other soldiers.

"Longknife Two One, this is Charlie Nine Two, can you cancel my last request? We are going to need you to return to overwatch. We have a slight problem on the ground here," Lachance said calmly over his radio, calling the Birds back from their distant positions.

Another cry was heard a few feet away in the grapes as another 101st soldier succumbed to the heat. The 101st medic began administering IVs to the men and tried to cool them by taking off their gear and clothes and sheltering them in the little shade the grape leaves provided. If their temperatures were to get too high, they could die.

Gerhart called up the heat casualties over the radio and instructed the remaining men to drink water. When they told him they didn't have any water, he instructed them to eat some of the grapes. They continued to help the medic treat the fallen men when a third soldier went down. Another soldier tended to him, as the medic was busy trying to get one of the men to start breathing. The man cried out as his muscles began to cramp uncontrollably. "Hey, bro! I've got friends who have been hit by IEDs and didn't bitch this much!" Gerhart told the man.

Gerhart looked at Lachance and they both had the same look of concern across their faces. Were they going to be the only ones left to fight back against the inevitable attack as these guys continued to drop one by one? The helicopters could only remain overhead for so long before they would have to go refuel. Gerhart picked up his radio. "Knolly, I need you."

"We got to go!" Knollinger said as he rallied up the Two Charlie men. Doc Taylor and Tubbs would stay back with the remaining 101st soldiers in the compound. Tubbs's ankle was pretty messed up, and they didn't need Doc because they had the 101st medic out there. The remaining Two Charlie men snuck out the back door of the compound and began heading north.

The enemy radio chatter continued as the fighters strategized their next move. "They are sitting still and are not moving. We have them pinned and surrounded. We need to attack! We need to attack!"

Knollinger looked around for the fastest route to get to Gerhart and Lachance. He saw a narrow road that would take them directly north to the grape fields the men were stuck in. It would get them there quickly, but they would risk stepping on a possible bomb. He thought for a moment about whether it was worth the risk. That's when Gerhart came over the radio reporting another 101st heat casualty. "Fuck it," Knollinger said and began sprinting down the path. "No IED! No IED! No IED!" He yelled out as he ran as lightly as he could, the rest of the men behind him.

"They have another group moving towards them. Let's wait for them to get together before we attack," the ICOM radio chatter called out.

The Two Charlie men reached the grape fields and Gerhart walked them into his position over the radio. They reestablished security around the men, as they had started to receive random sporadic fire. Gerhart and Lachance had never been happier in their lives to see them. "We thought we were going to die out here," Gerhart said as they greeted each one of the men.

"What do they got you pinned down with?" Jackson asked Gerhart.

"Dude, I'm not pinned down because of what they are shooting at us with, I'm pinned down because these fuckers can't move," Gerhart replied, pointing to the incapacitated 101st soldiers. "We need to establish security for the MedEvac to get these four fucks out of here. I'll go out there, but I want that 240 to come with me."

Knollinger grabbed the 240 from one of the unconscious soldiers and looked among the men to see who the best gunner would be. His eyes met McDaniel's and he smiled.

"I know," McDaniel replied. "Give me the fucking gun." They opened the men's remaining bags to loot them of their ammo and water before heading into the field. To their surprise, the 240 ammo was still in the ammo cans, and the ammo cans were still in the wooden crate they had been shipped in.

"No wonder these dudes were going down, they were literally carrying around crates of ammo," McDaniel said as he cracked open the crates, ripped the ammo out of the cans, and grabbed a few Rip Its. McDaniel and Gerhart made their way into the open field to establish security for the incoming MedEvac Birds.

"Rosa, we are literally right next to the second canal. I can see the intersection from here. I need you out here," Knollinger came over the radio in the TOC at COP Tynes. "I need you out here."

Rosa looked at the 101st leadership in the TOC that were trying to figure out how they were going to salvage the mission. "Look, put your guys up in the towers and take ours out. We got enough guys here to get a squad together to go down there and help them out."

"Negative, Sergeant," the 101st commander said. "We are in charge now. We are doing our thing. We are going to get them out of there one way or another. We're trying to figure out aircraft availability to get them out."

"Sir, you're going to lose a Bird to an RPG down there. Let us go and get our guys out," Rosa responded.

"Negative, Sergeant. This is our mission. We are going to get our guys out of this situation," the commander said.

"Situation? Your guys are the reason we are in this situation," Rosa replied.

Cartwright grabbed him to calm him down. "We got to keep our cool, and help the guys out there keep theirs," he said.

Rosa took a deep breath and apologized. He took the hand mic to the platoon radio and called back to Knollinger. "Hey, Knolly, just calm down a little bit. Take a deep breath and do your thing. We are working on it. We will be there as soon as we can. I know you'll be fine, just continue to fight the way you have been trained."

There was a silence over the radio for a moment until Knollinger finally replied. "Alright."

Back at the compound, Doc Taylor was tending to a 101st soldier who had been carried down from the roof. He was barely conscious, another heat casualty. The men moved him into one of the cooler mud rooms of the compound, out of the heat of the sun.

"You got to help me out here. Breathe!" Doc Taylor said as he began to administer an IV to the man. "Blink if you understand me." The soldier did not respond. "Blink!" Doc shouted at the man and his eyes began to flutter. "Good job. Keep breathing, that is your main concern now."

Doc Taylor worked to establish an IV as two more 101st soldiers were brought down to him in the room. They both were severely dehydrated and confused. "How many more guys do we have out there pulling guard?" Doc asked. The Two Charlie guys were gone on the QRF and there were three heat casualties along with the two men in the room with him. He wondered how many were left to pull security or fight off an attack on the compound.

A 101st staff sergeant, SSG Peltier, looked at him. "Not a lot," he said. Unsure of what to do, he looked toward his platoon leader, Lt. Pantaleo. "Sir. I'm actually starting to get fucking scared," he said as more shots rang out over the compound. "Our guys weren't ready for this."

"Get up on the roof," Lt. Pantaleo said, and Peltier left the room to get back into the fight.

McDaniel and Gerhard made their way across the open field to the far side of the smoke grenade that was marking the landing zone for the incoming MedEvac Birds. They dove into the two-foot-tall grass, concealing themselves from the enemy. The fighters began to shoot in their direction and continued to shoot at the men in the grape field taking cover and preparing to move the casualties. With rounds whipping by, they dared not expose their position, but they needed to shoot to provide covering fire for the approaching Bird.

McDaniel began shooting the 240 machine gun in the direction of the enemy fire. He couldn't see through the grass, so he wasn't really hitting anything. Gerhart got up on his knee and began to engage the enemy with his rifle while directing McDaniel's fire. "Left! Right! Left! There!" he shouted, directing McDaniel's fire into the murder holes in the mud wall. The enemy fire had not been too intense, as there were only random rounds zipping by them, until the helicopter arrived on scene.

When the helicopter flew in low overhead to make its landing in the field, it blew the grass the two men were hiding in flat to the ground. McDaniel and Gerhart lost their concealment from the enemy and were left exposed in the middle of the open field.

"Fuck!" the two men yelled, as they began to fire their weapons as fast as they could. Dirt began to kick up all around them, as the enemy fire intensified and more of them shifted their fire in their direction. McDaniel traversed from murder hole to murder hole with the machine gun, never letting go of the trigger.

Gerhart was going through magazine after magazine with his rifle, as he emptied them into the holes. He dropped a mag and threw in another. McDaniel saw out of the corner of his eye the magazine Gerhart had just put into his rifle. It hadn't fully seated in the magazine well, so he yelled up to him, "Your mag is not in! Your mag is not in! Slap it!"

Gerhart slapped the mag and continued to fire. "Thank you!" he shouted over the roar of the gunfire.

The rest of the Two Charlie guys in the grape field began to carry the unconscious half-naked soldier onto the MedEvac helicopter. They dragged his deadweight to the Bird and loaded him up, then returned to the grapes to help the others. Knollinger looked at one of the other 101st soldiers who was still conscious. Knollinger was exhausted and thought to himself that this guy was so fat, there was no way he was going to be able to carry him. "Bro, I'm not carrying you. You're either going to die here or you're going to get up and run," he said. The man got up and wobbled his way to the helicopter.

The first Bird took off and the enemy turned their fire on the second one that had come in for its landing in the field. Lachance had Luke shoot his 203 smoke grenade at one of the compounds the enemy was shooting from, and the Kiowas came in guns hot with their rockets. The last of the 101st heat casualties were loaded onto the second Bird and taken out of the valley.

"Let's go!" Gerhart yelled as he helped McDaniel to his feet; the two men sprinted their way through the enemy fire back to the grape field to take cover with the rest of the men. Dirt kicked up all around them as they both dove over the first mud wall of the field, piling in among those already there.

They were instantly relieved to be among the cover the grapes provided, and the enemy fire started trickling away to silence. The fighters had missed their window to get the men in the open, it was time to regroup and reorganize.

The Two Charlie men took advantage of the lull in the enemy fire to do the same. Knollinger, noticing how exhausted McDaniel was, grabbed the 240 from him and slung it around himself. The sling was so narrow, and his rig was so bulky with all his gear and his rifle, that it squeezed the gun tight against him. He wasn't going to be effective if he needed to shoot it. "Hey, I got to be in the middle of the group with this thing," he said.

"I'll take point," Jackson replied, and Nichols, McDaniel, and Luke fell in behind him.

They made their way through the grape fields, the two SAW gunners on point, until they came across another open field with a few mud huts on the other side of the clearing. Just past the mud huts, there was a break in a wall which opened to the road that led all the way back to the compound. They needed to get there.

Jackson pushed into the open field with Nichols, McDaniel, and Luke. They immediately started receiving fire. One of the mud huts had a murder hole dug out near the bottom of its wall, and an enemy fighter had begun shooting at them from it. The men hit the deck and began returning fire, Knollinger stepped up with the 240 and began to hip fire the hundred-round belt that dangled from the weapon. His rounds sprayed all around the hut; some smacking the dirt walls of the hut, some the ground in front of it, and some the wall behind. It looked like a scene from *Rambo*, and Farnsworth couldn't stop himself from laughing.

"Get to cover!" Knollinger yelled to the men. He was quickly running out of ammo. Dru came up beside him with his 203 and with a single shot launched a grenade into the small opening. The blast shot dust from the hole and shook the ground beneath them. There was no more shooting after that.

Jackson made his way to the break in the wall. As soon as he crossed the opening, a fighter from no more than fifteen feet down the road opened up on him with a PKM machine gun.

Ratatatatatat!

Jackson spun and fell back out of the way, rounds flying inches from his face, as he crashed into McDaniel and Nichols behind him. The three of them piled on the ground then scrambled to take cover against the wall. Luke sent a few rounds down the road, but he too was forced to take cover as the wall exploded in front of him from the intense fire.

"We're pinned!" Jackson called back to Knollinger.

"Frag it!" Knollinger yelled back.

Jackson looked at the other men. "Whose got a grenade?"

Nichols pulled a grenade out of his pouch and held it out to the men. Exhausted, McDaniel took it from him and began to unwrap the electrical tape securing the spoon. Once it was free, he grasped it firmly in one hand and began to pull the pin with the other. "Come on you, bitch. You can do it. Quit being a pussy," he said, talking to himself as he struggled to remove the pin in his state of exhaustion. The pin finally came free, and he reared back and sent the grenade flying through the air. The other men watched as it flew in almost slow motion. Their gazes quickly filled with horror, as it seemed the frag was not going to clear the wall.

"Short!" Farrington yelled from behind a small dirt berm.

"Oh, fuck, we just fragged ourselves," the four men along the wall thought. They winced and watched the grenade as it barely cleared the wall and disappeared to the other side. A sigh of relief overcame them and, a second later, so did a large boom that shook the wall.

The men picked up and reentered the road. The poor bastard had to have caught the grenade. His clothing was covered in dust and blood as it began pooling around him on the side of the road. His legs stuck out into the road, and one of his sandals was missing. They ran as fast as they could to the compound. McDaniel didn't even stop to throw up, he just ran and dry heaved into his hand. They called in their approach over the radio and without hesitation or delay, the large metal door cracked open and the men all filed in one by one behind the safety of the mud walls.

"Fuck those guys!" McDaniel yelled as he took his helmet off and threw it across the ground inside the compound. It skipped like a stone on a placid lake before colliding with one of the mud walls. His anger wasn't aimed towards the fighters, rather at the 101st men they had just almost died saving.

Gerhart gathered the Two Charlie men around him. They were all exhausted, dehydrated, and sick from running off pure adrenaline. They hugged and smiled as they gathered their breath in the cool dark mud room and drank some water.

"I have no idea how we aren't all dead," Jackson said with relief.

Gerhart grabbed him by the head and pulled him in close. "I'm proud of you guys. All of you. Every last one of you did the right thing out there, and we are never going out with these guys again. Ever, ever, ever again."

Their moment was ruined by the screams of a 101st SSG that was screaming bloody murder from one of the mud rooms. Gerhart ran in to see what had happened. Doc Taylor was tending to the man who appeared to be injured.

"My legs!" the SSG screamed.

"What's wrong with him? Where is he hit?" Gerhart asked.

"He's not. He's just cramping," Doc Taylor replied.

"You've got to be fucking kidding me," Gerhart exclaimed, as he turned his attention to the distressed man. "Shut the fuck up! They are going to hear you out there!" he yelled at him. He looked upon the other couple of 101st soldiers in the room. They were lying propped against the wall, IVs in their arms.

The ICOM radio began to increase with more radio chatter. The helicopters circling overhead reported seeing more fighting-age males entering the area. COP Tynes even came over the radio reporting movement approaching their location. The interpreter relayed the messages they were saying. "Kill everyone. Don't let any of them leave alive. If possible, try and capture one of them." The men began to fear for the worst.

They needed to work on getting the 101st casualties extracted out of the compound and a resupply of ammo, IVs, and water for the remainder of them. They were running low on supplies. It wouldn't be long before the rest of the 101st men would go down and need to be treated, and soon to follow would be the Two Charlie men. That, or they would run out of ammo and be overrun.

There was an empty, plowed field just east of the compound that they could land a MedEvac and resupply Bird in. They called for one over the radio and the men began getting into position to enter the open field to cover the Bird when it came.

Lachance climbed up on the roof to begin directing the Birds onto targets on the ground to cover the incoming resupply and to relay the position of the men on the ground. He had been non-stop communicating with the Birds overhead, using them to push the enemy back, to keep them away from the compound. Lachance keyed his hand mic to speak to the pilots. "I think we are going to push my guys out into this open field to my east ..."

Crack! Snap!

A round zipped by Lachance's face as he ducked behind some cover on the roof. "Yeah, I almost just got shot in the face," he said calmly to the CCA helicopter pilots over the radio as he continued to guide them into the areas they were receiving fire.

"Did that come from the east?" a soldier asked from the ground below.

"I think it came from the west," Lachance replied and got back on his radio.

"We need to hit that compound over there with an airstrike," Gerhart said, referring to the compound the men had received a majority of their fire from throughout the day.

"We can't, our rules of engagement won't let us. Too high of a risk of civilian casualties," Lt. Pantaleo replied. He was afraid of a bomb killing a noncombatant in the area, something that, if it happened, he would have to live with the consequences of.

Gerhart looked at the man with rage. "I got an element back at COP Tynes saying we have movement this way, alright? So check this out, I don't know if you know this or not, but everyone around here fucking hates us. The Birds say they are clear to engage. If you don't clear them, I will fucking take your radio and take the battery out so you can't talk anymore. You are not putting my fucking guys in danger anymore. I'm not going to beat around the bush and play these dumbass games. I don't give a fuck about your chain of command, I don't give a fuck about your guys out here, I care about my fucking Joes. You guys need to think about our guys who have been out here for eleven months." He paused, as he could see the 101st lieutenant's anger grow. "Are we good, sir?"

"Yea, we're good," Lt. Pantaleo said.

"So, if they see those dudes again, I need you to tell them you are clear to engage. Roger?" Gerhart said. The platoon leader looked at him, not giving him the answer he wanted. He wasn't going to lose his career and wind up in prison over Gerhart's heated tantrum, but the Two Charlie men were doing everything they could to help his men.

"Nobody is going to get in trouble, sir," Farnsworth tried to reassure the man.

"No one is going to get in trouble. They're fucking shooting at us. I'm not trying to be a dick. I'm not trying to be disrespectful. I mean this in the most respectful way I can, but your whole squad just went down out there, and MY guys had to go fucking save them. Now I'm going to have to go secure an LZ. This was supposed to be a partnered mission, where I advise you guys on what to do out here, and instead it's turning into a search and rescue for your platoon," Gerhart said. He looked the man over. He still didn't seem convinced on whether or not he should be approving targets for large air strikes outside of the gun runs the helicopters had already been providing. "We good?" Gerhart continued.

"We're good, Sergeant," Pantaleo replied.

"Then tell them to engage these fuckers that are trying to kill us right now," Gerhart smiled.

When the MedEvac/resupply Birds were a few minutes out, five Two Charlie men along with a few 101st ran out into the open field to the east, taking cover along the perimeter walls of the field to provide cover fire for the approaching Birds. Lachance had Apache attack helicopters in the air to support them.

The men began exchanging fire with the fighters as they tried to shoot the approaching aircraft. Shots rang out and the 101st aided their heat casualties to the helicopters to be taken away. A second helicopter landed in the field and kicked out two large black body bags, what the Two Charlie men referred to as a "speedball," full of water, medical supplies, and ammo. The aircraft took off into the air engulfing the surrounding men in its dust. The Two Charlie men waited along the perimeter walls for the 101st to return to the field and grab the speedballs. They returned fire at the random shots taken at them. They waited for a few minutes. The 101st never came to recover the bags, they stayed in the confinements of the compound.

"What the fuck?! You guys were supposed to go get those," Knollinger said as he ran out into the open field to recover the equipment. He dragged both the heavy black bags behind him through the open field to the compound. The rest of the Two Charlie men fell back from their positions behind him.

Knollinger was pissed. "We've gotten MedEvac Birds in here for them! We gave them IVs! We shoot for them! We carry their weapons and gear!" Knollinger said as he threw the bags against the compound wall. "What else can we do? We've done everything for them!" The tension between the two groups had reached its boiling point.

McDaniel climbed down from the roof as a 101st soldier relieved him from guard. He dropped down and landed funny on his knee. "Fuck," he called out. Gerhart and Jackson came to his aid after seeing him fall. He had hurt his knee before in the deployment and it had locked up pretty badly back then. "It feels just like it did back then," he said as Jackson and Gerhart helped him to the cool mud room. Gerhart looked at Knollinger; they needed to start figuring out a plan to get their men out of there.

"Get some more speedballs ready!" Rosa yelled to the Two Charlie men back at COP Tynes. They had been the only ones preparing all the equipment and resupplies for the guys out on the patrol. The 101st men there had done nothing.

Tensions were high back at the outpost as well, as only Rosa and Cartwright were allowed in the TOC with the 101st leadership. The rest of the men got too heated about the decision to not let them act on sending out a ground QRF when Knollinger asked for one. So, they were left outside to prepare gear and wait for any word of what was happening or what the men out there might need.

"We've got air assets approved to have them insert us in," one of the 101st captains said.

"Great, I'll get a squad of my guys ready," Rosa replied.

"We will handle this, Sergeant," the captain replied.

"Sir, it seems that things are pretty tense out there. I feel like it will ease some of the tension between the guys out there if our guys see some 82nd patches coming out of those Birds," Cartwright explained.

The 101st captain looked at him and thought for a moment. He looked at the load plan and the total seats they had available on the aircraft. "You can bring four of your guys," he finally replied.

"Roger that," Cartwright said. "Rosa, go get four of our guys ready for an air assault. Get the rest ready to convoy them over to Terra Nova to be picked up by the Birds."

The men in the compound went back out into the open field to cover another round of MedEvac/resupply Birds. Tubbs and McDaniel were to be extracted to Terra Nova on one of the helicopters, as they had both become immobile due to their injuries. Farnsworth switched out his bolt gun for McDaniel's rifle and ammo. He figured he wasn't doing much with his single-shot weapon out here and wanted an M4 for the rest of the fight. They waited in their fighting positions as the helicopters began to come in.

The first Bird landed and a handful of 101st men walked off into the open field, unsure of what direction to go. The Bird took off, leaving them in the open field. The second Bird came in and touched down fifty meters away. It had four of the Two Charlie men: McPherson, Flannery, Figueroa, and Barthel.

Flannery was the first to step off the Bird and he took a knee in the field. Figueroa and Barthel followed and dove into the prone beside him. McPherson was the final man out of the aircraft and didn't waste any time. He saw no reason to hang around in an open field and wait for the helicopter to take off, especially while they were getting shot at. He ran by the men towards the walls of the compound. Flannery followed suit, and Figueroa and Barthel were on his heels after him. The four men sprinted into the compound with their heavy assault packs full of ammo and water.

The helicopter took flight and left Tubbs and McDaniel on the ground. McDaniel watched as the gap between the aircraft tires and the ground grew. He hobbled into the open field, trying to wave the pilots down as he was engulfed in dust. "Waaaait! Waaaaait!" he screamed over the roar of the rotary engine to no avail. He was horrified as he thought his ride out of the Devil's Playground had left him.

"There's another Bird coming in man," Farnsworth said as he laughed at McDaniel's overreaction. "Get the fuck back to cover."

McDaniel, relieved and slightly embarrassed, got back on his feet and hobbled back over to Tubbs in the ditch. The third Bird landed, and the two men got aboard. It took off and carried the two away from the battlefield.

When it was clear, Farnsworth started directing the lost 101st guys towards the compound. "Over there. Go!" he said while pointing towards where Gerhart and Knollinger were trying to wave them in.

CRACK!

A single round zipped from behind Farnsworth and caught him in the arm. It spun him around like a top and he fell to the ground.

"You okay, Sergeant?!" a worried Luke asked as he returned fire in the direction the shot came from and came to his side to render aid.

Farnsworth looked up at the wall beside him. There was blood splattered along it. "God damn," he said, as he hesitated to inspect his injuries. Luckily, it had just barely grazed the side of his bicep. "I'm good. It's just a graze. Let's get out of here," he said, and the two men ran back into the compound.

The fighting slowed dramatically as the sun hung in the evening sky. The four Second Squad men made their rounds to give the guys in the compound water and ammo, and to replace the men pulling security on the roofs. Knollinger barked for the incoming 101st men to replace his guys on guard. The 101st captain that had just arrived in the air assault grabbed Knollinger by the shoulder.

"Get off me!" Knollinger said as he spun to face the man.

"You're out of control," the captain said to him.

"Your decision making is out of control," Knollinger replied, leaving the man before his temper got the best of him.

Farnsworth went to Doc Taylor to have him treat his "gunshot wound." Doc cleaned it thoroughly and placed a simple band aid over it. The 101st captain noticed the Ranger scroll on Farnsworth's right sleeve of his uniform. He too had been part of Ranger Battalion, so he decided to talk with Farnsworth to get an idea of what had really been happening on the ground.

"It doesn't seem that bad," the captain said to Farnsworth.

"Sir, you haven't been here all day. It's settling down now for the night, and it wouldn't have been as bad if your guys could move. You have to understand, it's a little frustrating carrying your fucking dudes all over the place back and forth across open fields all day."

The leadership entered the mud room to start discussing a plan of action to get them out.

"The surrounding IED threat has grown since we have been so stagnant for so long. They probably have been able to emplace a few IEDs around us to add to the ones that are probably already out there. Is there any way we can get airlifted out of here, so we don't have to walk through a minefield?" Farrington asked the captain. He knew it was asking a lot, to coordinate air assets for extraction, but he didn't think it was completely off the table. They had air assets delegated to them all day. It would take a lot to convince the guys to walk out of there.

"Not going to happen. The assets in the area are being delegated elsewhere. We will have to walk out. We still have the dog team," the captain said.

"We are going to hit a bomb, sir," Gerhart said.

The captain turned towards Gerhart and Knollinger. "You need to exhibit calmness."

"It's not that calm of a situation, sir. We've been out all day saving this platoon's ass," Knollinger said.

"The situation isn't as bad as you think," the captain scolded him.

"No, it's a whole lot worse than YOU think," Knollinger replied.

The captain looked at him, then continued. "We walk out. We will push out behind the dog team. An element from Terra Nova can clear up to the second canal and secure it for us until we link up with them and continue to COP Tynes."

"When are we pushing off, sir?" Farrington asked.

"We will have to wait for the Terra Nova element to clear the second canal, so probably not until under the cover of darkness," the captain replied.

"That would cut down the risk of getting ambushed," Farrington said. "There is still the risk of IEDs though."

"We need to establish a good route then to link up with the element out of Terra Nova at the second canal," the captain replied.

"Look, just push straight north," Knollinger said.

Farrington looked at Gerhart and Knollinger. The Two Charlie men were all exhausted from the long day. They wanted to give their men as much time as they could to rest before having to walk back to COP Tynes. "Can we wait till the early hours of tomorrow, right before sunrise, give our guys a chance to get some rest?" Farrington asked.

"Fine. We step off before sunrise." The captain replied.

## CHAPTER 21

# The Valley Always Wins

The evening sun left the horizon, and the valley filled with cool air as it turned to night. The Two Charlie men all hunkered down on the cool concrete floor of the mud room together and tried to get some sleep. The ICOM radio kept them awake, as it picked up the final chatter of the enemy before they bedded down for the night. The enemy commanders were conducting roll calls of their men. They all listened to the transmissions and were pleased when several fighters never answered when they were called to report in. It made the men smile, a minor victory in the valley.

The night went on, and multiple big explosions were heard in the near distance. It shook the walls of the compound, and the men could feel the concussive force from the blasts in their chests. "That's why I don't want to walk out of here," Knollinger said.

"It's the Devil's Playground, man." Lachance said. "This place is hairy."

"Maybe it's one of those fuckers putting in a bomb," Farnsworth said. "Maybe they got some of their wires crossed and blew themselves up." Lachance smiled as they both laughed at the thought, trying not to dwell on the reality the enemy could be putting out more bombs for them to step on when they finally moved out.

As the morning light just began to lighten the valley, the men prepared for their final walk back to COP Tynes. The cool morning air filled their lungs as they exited the compound and entered the orchards one more time. It was the valley's last chance to take them, and every step felt like it was going to be their last. They didn't know how many bombs had been set out that night, they just assumed they were going to find at least one of them.

Dix and his trainer led the element north, and every man filed in behind them. The dog did his work, sniffing every nook and cranny of every mud wall they came across. The men slowly climbed through the walls of the orchards, slowly climbed through the rows of grapes, inching their way to the second canal.

The 101st captain was right on Farrington's ass, almost in his pocket. "Sir, get the fuck away from me. You're going to kill us both," Farrington told him, trying to get some space from the man if he stepped on an IED.

Another 101st soldier who had come in on the air assault took the break in the silence to voice his opinion on the whole operation. "You know, it wasn't that bad."

"Shut the fuck up," Lachance hushed the man. He was furious they weren't practicing noise and light discipline after all they had just been through over the past twenty-four hours. None of the 101st seemed to be taking anything seriously.

"I'm just saying, I don't think it was that bad," the man replied.

Lachance couldn't take it anymore. He stopped, walked up to the man, and started bitching him out. "You want to fucking die out here?"

"No, but it's war. People die. Y'all act like you're the only ones that have ever lost anyone," the 101st soldier replied.

"You're going to fucking die! They are going to bury you here! As soon as we aren't here to save your ass, you're fucking dead!" He felt his voice carrying. The man wasn't worth his anger, and definitely wasn't worth giving away their position to any fighters that might just be waking. He turned away from the man and kept marching.

The men pushed on, arriving at the second canal, and linked up with the element from Terra Nova. They continued north of the second canal, through the grape fields, and walked in the first canal all the way to COP Tynes. The men of Two Charlie couldn't believe they had actually made it back. All of them. Whole.

They downed their gear and stripped out of their soaking wet uniforms, changing into their PTs. The rest of the men had breakfast waiting for them. They ate their food, and separated the Two Charlie men from the 101st for the remainder of the day. They needed to cool their tempers before they could productively conduct a post-patrol briefing.

It didn't matter to them. They were done. They had done the unthinkable and lived to tell the tale. They finally got a win in the valley.

The next day Gerhart, Lachance, Knollinger, Farnsworth, and Farrington all met with the 101st leadership to discuss the after-action review. Gerhart had prepared note cards of points to go over with the leadership. They consisted of simple things to the men of Two Charlie, but they must not have been simple to the 101st.

Gerhart laid it down as tactfully as he could. "Your men need to be better hydrated. No more fucking Rip Its," he said flipping through his cards. "You guys need your team leaders to inspect their guys and their equipment before every patrol. Check them for water, their SI, and make sure that ammo is out of the ammo cans." The more he went on, the more condescending the whole speech seemed. "You guys need to conduct classes on patrolling, like what guys should be doing on patrol. No standing there doing nothing. This isn't a hike in a park, you're in a combat zone."

"That's enough, Sergeant." First Sergeant Banister said.

"I have a question for you all. Why did it take six hours for you to send a QRF out to us after the first casualties were reported?" Gerhart retorted.

"The IED threat was too extreme, and we didn't want to risk more heat casualties trying to get out to you guys, so we waited for air assets to get us in," First Sergeant Banister answered.

Gerhart just looked at the ground and shook his head, unsatisfied with his answer. "I guess I'm just used to being out there with hard-charging guys."

His tone pissed off First Sergeant Banister. "Look. We appreciate all you guys have done, we really do. What I don't appreciate, what gives me the ass, is your holier-than-thou attitude that we are incompetent and unprepared for this mission. Roger. I got that. We're a field-artillery unit tasked with an infantry job. Are we going to take casualties? Hell yes, we are. We know that." He paused for a moment to reflect on that thought. "But don't count us out. We're a fighting force. We aren't going to leave you hanging. We evacuated our guys, but we brought you twenty more."

The Two Charlie men glared at him. They wanted to reply to his comment. They wanted to say "WE evacuated your guys. WE got you out," but it wasn't worth the fight. They were tired of blame and they were tired of being angry. The reality was the men of Two Charlie were done. There was no reason for them to continue to fight about it. The valley belonged to the 101st now.

The following day the men spent packing the rest of their things into Conex boxes to be shipped back to Fort Bragg. They signed all the equipment over to the 101st leadership, and the 101st took over guard in the towers. Every man had felt like a huge weight had been lifted off their shoulders. They were still in disbelief they had actually all come back from The Last Patrol, and they were all unscathed. They had finally gotten the best of the valley. They had finally achieved a victory.

They let the emotions hit and, for the first time, finally had a moment to actually feel. There isn't an emotion that any human has identified to capture that feeling, the feeling of some sort of alternating relief, happiness, and excitement, mixed with guilt, anger, and rage all in one. People aren't meant to feel that big of an emotion set. What they were feeling could not be put into words, but you could see it in their smiles, as they had returned to their faces.

"Farns, First Sergeant Gondick has a message for you on the SIPRNET," Cartwright said as he found Farnsworth packing among the rest of the men.

Farnsworth followed Cartwright into the TOC and opened the message on the computer. It was short and simple. "Hey, SSG Farnsworth, give me a call when you get this."

"Can I borrow the sat phone?" he asked one of the 101st soldiers in the TOC. The man behind one of the computers listening to the radio didn't look at him, just extended his arm out towards him with the phone in his hand. Farnsworth took it from the man. "Thanks," he said as he made his way out of the loud room to make a call.

His conversation on the phone was brief with First Sergeant Gondick. Cartwright could tell watching him from afar that something wasn't right from the way his posture changed during the call. His shoulders sank, and his head lowered as his hand raised to hold his head. "Roger, First Sergeant," Cartwright caught him say as he approached. "I'll pass it on," Farnsworth finished, as he hung up the phone.

"Everything good?" Cartwright asked.

Farnsworth didn't know what to say. After a moment of silence, he finally replied. "We need to gather up the guys."

The men of Two Charlie gathered in the gravel clearing outside of the wood structure and awaited the news Cartwright had for the men. They laughed and joked. A couple were even rough housing like they used to do. It was good to see them like that again. Farnsworth and Cartwright walked up to them; Farnsworth fell into the back of the group of men, while Cartwright remained in the front.

"Alright guys, settle down. Settle down," Cartwright said.

"Did they say what day we are getting out of here?" one of the men asked. A few other soldiers rallied behind that question with cheers.

"No, I'm sure they will have more of a timeline for us getting out of COP Tynes in the next day or two," Cartwright said. His tone didn't match that of the rest of the men's. It seemed down, sad even, and the men picked up on it immediately. Their excitement quickly died off as they stood there waiting in silence for what Cartwright had to say. He looked up at them. "This isn't easy to say, boys." He paused, working up the courage to tell the men what he was about to say. "Moon didn't make it. He died in the hospital today in Germany of septic shock. He developed an infection, and his body couldn't shake it." He paused again for a moment. A breeze picked up, and it whistled through the valley. It was so quiet among the men that the breeze was all that could be heard. Not a single man said a word, not even a sniffle as their eyes began to fill with tears. Cartwright finished, "Moon's gone."

Just like that, the men had their victory over the valley taken from them. Just like that, they were reminded of the only rule in the valley—in the end, the valley always wins.

# Epilogue

The men of Two Charlie left COP Tynes to their replacements and were taken to Terra Nova. They watched from behind the Hescos for the next week as the 101st men started to patrol the valley and attempt to tame the Devil's Playground. On one patrol out of COP Nolen, they watched and listened from the TOC as a patrol stepped on an IED, causing multiple casualties. The 101st QRF was sent out, and they too hit an IED. Once the casualties from both elements were evacuated, the patrol hit a third IED on their way back to COP Nolen. The 101st were finding out the hard way what life in the valley was going to be like without the men of Two Charlie.

But for the men of Two Charlie, their time was complete. The men that were on The Last Patrol were submitted to receive Bronze Stars and a handful of other awards by the platoon's leadership, only for them to be denied by command. "That didn't really happen" they were all told as their awards got downgraded or outright rejected. Don't worry though, the same brass that denied the men their awards made sure they got their own.

Two Charlie was moved across the river to the OCCD outpost where the battalion Headquarters element had been operating. They patrolled that side of the river for the remainder of July and into August, but nothing substantial ever became of it. Just an attack by a rabid dog and a single firefight that wasn't that much of a firefight.

It wasn't until they loaded into the Chinook helicopters at OCCD to head to KAF that it fully sank in. McDaniel sat next to Figueroa in the red light of the Bird, bags and gear piled on top of them. They were crammed so close their cheeks were touching, but they didn't care because they were leaving the valley. McDaniel and Figueroa shared a common port window that they looked out of as the cargo helicopter lifted off the ground into the night sky.

"Look at it," McDaniel said. If the valley was going to take them, now was its last chance. They watched as the orchards and vineyards got smaller and smaller in the window.

"We did it. We're fucking out of here, dude!" the men smiled and called out in joy. The cargo hold was filled with the triumphant shouts of the men. They had made it out of the Arghandab River Valley.

The fight in the valley continued without the men of Two Charlie as the 101st's 1st Battery, 320th Field Artillery Regiment, continued to take ground. They suffered many casualties, 70 percent of their entire force, and by October the commander, Lieutenant Colonel Flynn, gave the orders to level the villages of Tarok Kolache, Khosrow Sofla, and Lower Babur. Those villages were bombed to the ground after it was discovered they were being used as IED factories and the villagers could no longer enter them. But that is another story for someone else to tell.

The men of Two Charlie got back to Fort Bragg and had one final get together before scattering like dust into the wind. Kristen Santos, Santos's wife, threw a Hawaiian t-shirt barbecue for the men when they returned. It was something Santos had wanted to do for them and she was determined to keep his promise.

After that, like roaches to the light, the men of Two Charlie ran their separate ways. A lot of the team leaders were stop-lossed so, when they got back, they got out of the Army. Of the guys that still had time left in service, some joined selection and became Green Berets, while others were moved around to different companies or units within the Army. The Army doesn't believe in keeping men together, rather it capitalizes on moving the experienced men around to spread out their knowledge and skills. Charlie Company had become notorious for the knowledge and skills they had picked up in the Arghandab River Valley, especially Two Charlie. Only two of the Two Charlie men remained in Charlie Company for the next deployment—Rae and Young.

The years went by, but the valley still had a hold of the men that had escaped its clutches. They might have left the valley, but the valley never left them. Throughout the years, they had been reminded of the rule of the valley time and time again. There has been one suicide among the men, and another attempted during the writing of this book. Men have come down with cancer, and one with multiple sclerosis, most likely due to burning their own trash and shit daily in the valley. Even though they were out of the valley, its rule still held strong. In the end, the valley always wins.

One of the guys from the platoon ended up being in country during the withdrawal from Afghanistan. He watched over the ISR feed as the Taliban slowly took back the Arghandab River Valley from the Afghan forces. Babur, Jelawur, Terra Nova, all returned to the enemy.

Some men reached out to each other throughout the years and stayed in touch but, for the most part, the men of Two Charlie ran away from the valley, and anything associated with it. It took almost twelve years before the men started to reach out en masse, as they had all grown tired of facing their demons on their own. It was time to reconnect with the only men who truly knew what they did in the valley, the men that were right there by their side.

The valley will come for them all one day—that is something they cannot avoid—but, in the meantime, the men of Two Charlie are starting to come back together. They are rekindling friendships and beginning the healing process. A lot of the men all got together for a reunion in April 2023. SFC Santos's son was getting married and the men of Two Charlie wanted to be there for that. It was a powerful weekend and, oddly enough, it had seemed like it was just yesterday since they were shooting the shit at COP Tynes. They picked up right where they left off, joking and laughing and, at some times, sharing some tears. It felt good to be together, once more, as Two Charlie.

# Killed in Action (KIA)

SPC Marcus Tynes — 22 Nov 2009
SGT James Nolen — 22 Nov 2009
SFC Carlos Santos-Silva — 22 Mar 2010
SPC Brendan Neenan — 07 Jun 2010
SSG Edward Loredo — 24 Jun 2010
SPC Christopher Moon — 13 Jul 2010

**May their names live forever**

# Letter From the Author

Dear Reader,

I began this journey with the intent to best tell the story of what happened during my second deployment to Afghanistan. I had spent the past twelve years running from the memory of the Arghandab River Valley, even though it consumed every aspect of my life and who I was. I ran away from my family as I didn't want them to see the man I had become, the man the valley had chewed up and spit out.

It took me twelve years to finally reach out to the men of Two Charlie. I did not know if they would want to talk to me, let alone see me. I didn't even know if they remembered who I was. I had thought about them probably every day for the past twelve years. So, I gave it a shot. I came in guns hot, asking them for permission to write this book. I knew that this was not my story alone to tell. To tell this story right, I had to tell OUR story, not just mine.

So, I embarked on my journey, traveling the country and linking up with the men of Two Charlie. It was so powerful, to see the men they had become. To see their families, their wives, their children. It gave me hope that one day I too could become a version of the men they are, a version of the greatest men I have ever known. To my surprise, the men met me with open arms. It was like not a day had gone by since we had last seen each other. It felt so good to see them, to have them back in my life.

I asked of them a heavy burden, to relive the things that have haunted us in great detail. I asked them to tell their side of our story. This task was easier for some than others, as some men were very open about what we did in the valley. Others had kept it tucked away for all these years. It was a heavy task nonetheless, and I thank each of them for doing it for me.

There came times where I questioned what I was doing, if it was right. I asked these men to go into that dark place one more time, to fan the coals that might still be smoldering in the back of their minds. The constant reassurance from the men was what kept me going forward. They believed in me and what I was trying to do. So, I pressed on.

We used the wedding of our fallen platoon sergeant's son as an excuse to get together, to reunite after over a decade of being on our own, and to honor the son of a man we considered a father ourselves. It was another powerful experience and meant so much to all the men.

The honeymoon was over, and I had to start the task of writing the book. I listened to each interview before every chapter, taking notes as I did. I began to piece our story together. I verified things across multiple sources. Luckily, I never really came across much contradiction as I went. We all remembered all too well what had happened in that valley.

I relived those days in great detail, trying to tell our story. It was difficult at times, I had a lot of sleepless nights, and some chapters were easier to write than others. But I had something I didn't have the past twelve years. I had the men of Two Charlie.

I listened over and over to the recordings as the men told our story. I relived it all, but I had been reliving those days for the past twelve years of my life. What was one more time?

So, I wrote the book you hold in your hands. Why? Well, I did it for a couple reasons. Ernest Hemingway said, "Every man has two deaths, when he is buried in the ground and the last time someone says his name. In some ways men can be immortal." I'll be damned if the names of the men that sacrificed everything for me die when I do. I'll be damned if the names of the men of Two Charlie fade away when the valley starts to claim us all. I couldn't stand the thought the only thing in the history books at Fort Bragg (or Fort Liberty, whatever the fuck they are calling it now) would be "The 2-508th PIR deployed to Afghanistan August 2009–Sept 2010." Period. That is unacceptable to me. I wanted it to be known the sacrifices that were made, how hard we fought, and I want their names to live forever.

I also wanted to stop living in the past. The valley still had its claws sunk into my flesh and wouldn't let up on its grip. Everything I saw reminded me of something in the valley. Every choice I made somehow correlated back to the valley. Somehow, I would always end up talking about the valley. I was like the old high school quarterback at the bar, still wearing his letterman jacket nudging the man beside him asking, "Hey, you remember the championship game?" I wanted to finally be free of the valley, to finally let it go. I don't know if I'll ever be able to let it go, but this process has definitely loosened its grip on me. Plato said "Only the dead have seen the end of war," and I am starting to understand what he means. This book is not pro-war, as I wouldn't wish what we went through on anyone but my enemies. This book is not anti-war, as I understand its necessity. This book is the reality of war.

Lastly, I wanted to do it for the men of Two Charlie, to help them explain to their loved ones why we are the way we are. I ran away from my family, not letting them get close enough to know what really happened, not letting them see what I had become. I know I was not the only one. It can be hard to talk about, and I get that. If I could help the men of Two Charlie with this book, give them something they can show to their friends and family that might help lift the weight of having to explain it to them themselves, I wanted to do that. I hope it brings my family closer to me as well as their understanding of everything I went through grows in reading this. For all they know I left home with everyone calling me Andy; when I got back, I moved to Colorado and introduced myself to everyone there as Andrew. I hope this book helps explain to them why and brings them closer to me.

There has been major healing in the process of writing this book, not just for myself but for the men of Two Charlie. We got the band back together and intend to keep our reunions going in the future. We bonded in trauma, there's no doubt about that, but I hope moving forward it defines who we are less and less. I know we will always have the valley as our origin story, but I hope our conversations shift from talking about firefights, to inquiring about how the kids are doing or how the new job is going.

The valley will come for us all one day, but until that day I will always be here for the men of Two Charlie. I love you all and am so happy to have you back in my life. Thanks for reading our story.

Forever and Always,

SGT Bragg

# Glossary

| | |
|---|---|
| **ACU** | Army Combat Uniform |
| **ADVON** | Advanced Echelon |
| **ANA** | Afghan National Army |
| **ANP** | Afghan National Police |
| **AO** | Area of Operation |
| **ARV** | Arghandab River Valley |
| **BDA** | Battle Damage Assessment |
| **BDU** | Battle Dress Uniform |
| **BATS** | Biometrics Automated Toolset System |
| **BIP** | Blow in Place |
| **Break** | Used at the end of a radio transmission to let the listeners know that the full transmission has not been transmitted and to stand by for the remainder of the transmission |
| **Butter bar** | Nickname given to a Second Lieutenant |
| **CAS** | Close Air Support |
| **CCA** | Close Combat Attack |
| **CCP** | Casualty Collection Point |
| **Charlie Mike** | Continue Mission |
| **CIB** | Combat Infantryman Badge |
| **CO** | Commanding Officer/ Company Commander |
| **COIN** | Counterinsurgency |
| **Conex** | A large, steel-reinforced reusable container for shipping military cargo or, when modified, for use as temporary accommodations |
| **COP** | Combat Outpost |
| **CPT** | Captain |
| **ECP** | Entrance Control Point |
| **EOD** | Explosive Ordnance Disposal |
| **Exfil** | The process of removing personnel out of a hostile environment and relocating to one occupied or controlled by friendly forces |
| **FO** | Forward Observer |
| **FOB** | Forward Operation Base |
| **FOO** | Field Ordering Officer |

| | |
|---|---|
| **FRG** | Family Readiness Group |
| **FSC** | Forward Support Company |
| **GWOT** | Global War on Terror |
| **HA** | Humanitarian Aid |
| **Hescos** | A large, sandbag like, barricade used to create perimeter walls for FOBs and COPs |
| **HHC** | Headquarters and Headquarters Company |
| **HIIDE** | Handheld Interagency Identity Detection Equipment |
| **HLZ** | Helicopter Landing Zone |
| **HME** | Homemade Explosive |
| **HVT** | High Value Target |
| **ICOM** | Radios that scanned frequencies to pick up on enemy chatter |
| **IED** | Improvised Explosive Device |
| **ISR** | Intelligence, Surveillance, and Reconnaissance |
| **KAF** | Kandahar Air Field |
| **KIA** | Killed In Action |
| **LP/OP** | Listening Point Observation Point |
| **LRS** | Long Range Surveillance |
| **Lt.** | Lieutenant |
| **LZ** | Landing Zone |
| **MATV** | Military All-Terrain Vehicle |
| **MAXPRO** | A maximum protection vehicle with a V-shaped haul developed specifically to help protect troops from IEDs |
| **MRAP** | Mine Resistant Ambush Protected vehicles |
| **NCO** | Non-Commissioned Officer |
| **NOD** | Night Optic Device |
| **ODA** | Operational Detachment Alphas |
| **PA** | Physician Assistant |
| **PC** | Patrol Cap |
| **PCC** | Pre-Combat Checks |
| **PCI** | Pre-Combat Inspections |
| **PL** | Platoon Leader |
| **PMCS** | Preventative Maintenance Checks and Services |
| **Pointman** | The man in the front of the formation in charge of navigating and leading the movement |
| **PSD** | Personal Security Detachment |
| **PTs** | Refers to the uniform worn by men when conducting Physical Training |
| **QRF** | Quick Reaction Force |
| **Quonset** | A building having a semicircular cross section |
| **RCIED** | Radio Controlled Improvised Explosive Device |

| | |
|---|---|
| **ROE** | Rules of Engagement |
| **RPG** | Rocket Propelled Grenade |
| **RTB** | Return To Base |
| **RTO** | Radio Telephone Operator |
| **Rucking** | A form of physical exercise that involves walking or hiking with a loaded backpack or rucksack, typically over varying distances and terrains |
| **S4** | Department in the Army responsible for supply management |
| **SAW** | Squad Automatic Weapon |
| **Scunion** | To lay down devastation, annihilation, etc. |
| **SFC(E-7)** | Sergeant First Class |
| **SGM** | Sergeant Major |
| **SGT(E-5)** | Regular Sergeant |
| **SI** | Sensitive/Serialized Item |
| **SITREP** | Situation Report |
| **SOG** | Sergeant of the Guard |
| **SP** | Start Patrol |
| **SSG(E-6)** | Staff Sergeant |
| **Stop-lossed** | A term used when the Army involuntarily extends a soldier's active duty contract of enlistment in order to retain them past their end of terms of service date |
| **TC** | Truck Commander |
| **TCP** | Traffic Control Point |
| **TOC** | Tactical Operations Center |
| **TTP** | Tactics, Techniques, and Procedures |
| **UCMJ** | Uniform Code of Military Justice |
| **XO** | Executive Officer |

# Rank Charts

Enlisted (Company Level)
E-1
E-2
E-3
E-4
E-5
E-6
E-7
E-8
These are the Joes
Teamleaders
Squad Leaders
Platoon Sergeant
No insignia
Private (PV1)
Private (PV2)
Private First Class (PFC)
Specialist (SPC)
Sergeant (SGT)
Staff Sergeant (SSG)
Sergeant First Class (SFC)
Master Sergeant (MSG)
Corporal (CPL)
First Sergeant (1SG)

Officers (Company Level)
O-1
O-2
O-3
Platoon Leader
Company Commander
Second Lieutenant
First Lieutenant
Captain

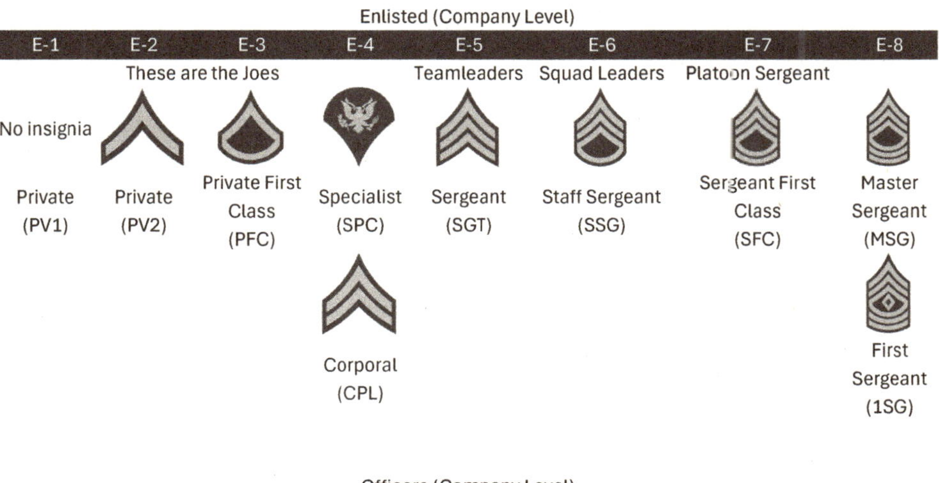

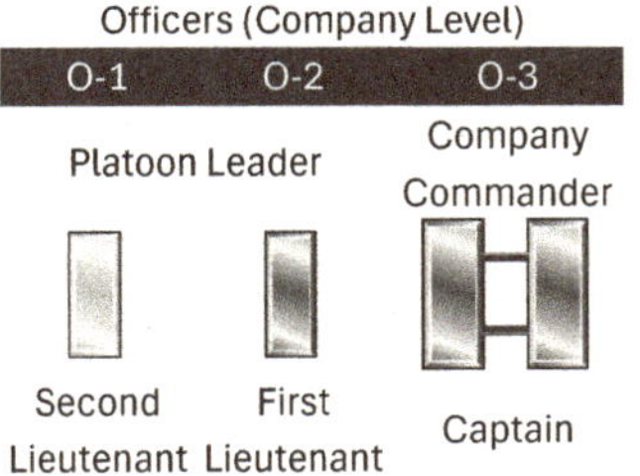

# Index

SPC Marcus Tynes
22 Nov 2009

SGT James Nolen
22 Nov 2009

SFC Carlos Santos-Silva
22 Mar 2010

**May their names**